THE REALITIES OF IMAGES:

Imperial Brazil and the Great Drought

Brazil and Drought Provinces

Transactions
of the
Americal Philosophical Society
Held at Philadelphia
For Promoting Useful Knowledge
Volume 91   Part 1

THE REALITIES OF IMAGES:

Imperial Brazil and the Great Drought

GERALD MICHAEL GREENFIELD

American Philosophical Society
Independence Square • Philadelphia
2001

ISBN: 0-87169-911-7
US ISSN: 0065-9746

Library of Congress Cataloging-in-Publication Data

Greenfield, Gerald Michael.
    The realities of images: imperial Brazil and the Great Drought / Gerald Greenfield.
      p. cm. -- (Transactions of the American Philosophical Society ; v. 91, pt. 1)
    Includes bibliographical references and index.
    ISBN 0-87169-911-7 (pbk.)
      1. Drought relief--Government policy--Brazil, Northeast---History--19th century. 2.
    Environmental refugees--Brazil, Northeast---History--19th century. 3. Droughts--Brazil,
    Northeast--Public opinion--History---19th century. 4. Elite (Social sciences)--Brazil,
    Northeast--Attitudes--History--19th century. 5. Droughts--Social aspects--Brazil,
    Northeast--History--19th century. 6. Seca--History--19th century. 7.
    Brazil--History--Empire, 1822-1889. I. Series.

    HV626.B6 G74 2001
    363.34'9298'09813--dc21

                                                                                2001022726

Design and Composition
Book Design Studio II

Acknowledgments

Throughout the research and writing of this book I have accumulated numerous debts, both professional and personal. Robert M. Levine, Sheldon L. Maram, Eul-Soo Pang, Eduardo Silva, Thomas E. Skidmore, and Steven Topik provided valuable critiques of earlier versions of this work. The two reviewers for the American Philosophical Society, Roderick J. Barman and Linda Lewin also provided extensive and insightful commentary. in addition, this book reflects insights gained through discussions with Francisco Luiz Teixeira Vinhosa of the Federal University of Minas Gerais, Enélio Lima Petrovich, Director of the Historical Institute of Rio Grande do Norte, and Geraldo da Silva Nobre, Director of the Ceara's Historical Institute. I am exceedingly grateful to live in this larger community of scholars.

While this book reflects my own intellectual journey, it also required physical journeys to Brazil. I consulted works in archives, libraries, and historical institutes in Fortaleza, Recife, Rio de Janeiro, and Natal. In each instance, I encountered cordial professional staff who facilitated my research. I also had the good fortune to find many individuals who offered me the precious gifts of hospitality and friendship. These included, in Rio de Janeiro, professors Francisco Vinhosa, Heloísa Toller Gomes, Eduardo Silva, and, especially, Maria Ana Quaglino; in Natal, Enélio Lima Petrovich, Dorian Gray Caldas, and Clyde Smith, Jr.; in Recife, professors Mark Jay Hoffnagel and Marco Antonio de Oliveira Pais; and in Fortaleza, Dr. Geraldo da Silva Nobre, Dr. Luis Santos, President of Ceará's Brazil-United States Institute (IBEU-CE), and professor André Frota Oliveira. With regard to Fortaleza, I must especially acknowledge what has become my "other" family: Dr. Eliane Maria Sousa Frota and her husband Dr. Marcos Antônio Freitas da Frota who invited me into their home and their lives, so that I eventually became the *tio americano* to their wonderful children, Elano, Elaine, Érico, and Marco Emílio. I cannot thank them enough.

Journeys also require financial support. My research has been aided by the generosity of UW-Parkside's History Department, Committee on Research and Creative Activity, and Faculty/Staff Professional Opportunities Development Fund, and the UW System's Sabbatical Program.

Howard Cohen, at the time Dean of the College of Liberal Arts and Sciences at UW-Parkside, merits special thanks for his help in structuring that sabbatical in a way that maximized my research time. The Center for Latin American Studies at the UW-Milwaukee also provided assistance, as did the American Philosophical Society.

Thinking of the many years during which this book remained a central aspect of my scholarly life, I want to express my deep gratitude to Robert M. Levine and to the late Sheldon L. Maram for their unwavering encouragement. My wife, Susan Smith Greenfield merits that same gratitude.

Contents

Contents

Abbreviations

In the interests of space, I use various abbreviations in the notes. In citing correspondence involving provincial presidents, I identify that office as "PP" then follow it with a hyphen and the abbreviation for his province.

AIHGB	Arquivo do Instituto Históricao e Geográfico Brasileiro
AL	Alagoas
AN	Arquivo Nacional
AN-JOP	Ministerio da Justiça, Oficio dos Presidentes
AN-P	Ministerio do Império, Presidentes, Correspondencia do Presidente da Provincia
APEC	Arquivo Público do Estado do Ceará
APEP	Arquivo Público do Estado de Pernambuco
BCN	Brazil, Congresso Nacional
CCS	Coleção Conselheiro Saraiva (at AIHGB)
CE	Ceará
CM	Camaras Municipaes
CSL	Coleção Sousa Leão (at AIHGB)
HAHR	Hispanic American Historical Review
ME	Minister/Ministry of the Empire
MJ	Minister/Ministry of Justice
PA	Pará
PB	Paraíba
PE	Pernambuco
PI	Piauí
PP	Provincial President
RC	Relief Commission
RN	Rio Grande do Norte
VP	Provincial Vice President

Map 1. Brazil and the Drought Provinces

Roraima

Amapá

Amazonas

Pará

Maranhão

Ceará

Rio Grande
Do Norte

Acre

Piauí

Paraíba

Pernambuco

Rondônia

Alagoas

Sergipe

Mato Grosso

Goias

Bahia

Mato Grosso
Do Sul

Minas Gerais

São Paulo

Paraná

Santa
Catarina

Rio Grande
Do Sul

Drought Provinces

Introduction

Toward the end of February in 1877, Caetano Estelita Cavalcanti Pessoa, scarcely a month in office as president of the province of Ceará, received a worrisome letter from the county council of Telha, a *municipio* of some six hundred inhabitants located in the Serra da Mattos. It reported that people were dying from starvation. The previous year's rainy season or "winter" had been sparse, and the harvest, poor. Now, this season's rains still had not appeared.[1] By the end of the following month Estelita had become sufficiently alarmed to pen a confidential letter to the minister of the empire, Antônio da Costa Pinto e Silva, warning that a general drought, or *grande sêca*, threatened the province.[2]

Estelita's expression of concern produced little immediate response. The Minister of the Empire seemed most concerned that provincial presidents not abuse those funds that by constitutional mandate were budgeted under public relief, while members of the Imperial Senate and Chamber of Deputies questioned whether an emergency situation truly existed. Indeed, a Conservative Deputy from Ceará, the famous novelist José de Alencar, cautioned that any declaration of drought was premature, given that rains could arrive as late as May or June, and still produce a "winter" in the backlands (*sertão*).[3] Back in Ceará, the Liberal press had a field day decrying Alencar's "betrayal" of his native province, while also chiding him for his ignorance of its climate and rainfall patterns.[4]

In Rio de Janeiro, Liberato de Castro Carreira, a Ceará Liberal, began writing a series of newspaper articles in the prestigious *Jornal do Comércio* under the heading *"Sêca do Ceará"*(Ceara's Drought), highlighting the precarious nature of conditions in his native province. Soon, that newspaper regularly included articles and letters related to the drought, lamenting its devastating impact, especially on the backlands masses or *sertanejos*, who already were fleeing the parched *sertão* in a desperate search for food and water.[5] As the absence of rain continued, these drought refugees, generally called *retirantes* (but also referred to as *os flagelados*, the "scourged" or "afflicted") crowded into the region's more favorably located settlements, especially those along the coast.[6] In January 1878, a new Liberal ministry headed by João Lins Veira Cansanção de Sinimbu took power and mounted a major program of public relief. Still, over the course of the ensuing few years, an immense drought-spawned diaspora saw *retirantes* traverse the vast expanse of the northern portion of the empire, journeying even to the distant Amazon. By foot and boat, they also left the region entirely, making their way to the plantations and cities of the south.

Whether within or outside of the official web of relief, *retirantes* encountered harsh conditions. Privation and disease, along with other hardships, took a massive toll. While available data do not permit an exact accounting, estimates for mortality range from 200,000 to 500,000. And even that high end figure does not begin to capture the full range of human suffering.

THE PROBLEM OF NORTHEASTERN DROUGHT

This was the Great Drought, three years of failed rains and misery enshrined in subsequent Brazilian historical memory as the worst drought ever to hit Brazil's northeast.[7] Drought had visited the region throughout its history, with the earliest recorded occurrences dating back to the sixteenth century.[8] Prior to the Great Drought, the last significant drought had taken place in 1844-45. That relatively long interval of good rains had reduced concerns with drought. That made the failure of rains in 1877 even more devastating, for it caught the provinces of the north totally unprepared.

Drought in one sense is a normal condition throughout much of the northeast, given the seasonal alternation of rains. Only coastal areas, and essentially only those south of the São Roque Cape, (located near Natal, the capital of Rio Grande do Norte) receive rainfall throughout the entire year. Even there, rainfall exhibits seasonal variations. Away from the coast, rains remain highly variable throughout the area, so that even when conditions are good in one portion of the region, another might be experiencing drought. Similarly, rain may fall for a time, but then cease, thereby effectively destroying food crops.[9]

With few exceptions, throughout the rest of the region, especially in the semi-arid interior, virtually no rains at all fall during the dry season. As the novelist Rachel de Queiroz has observed with regard to her native province: "Ceará is . . . a semi-desert region throughout almost its entire breadth with the exception of a very thin strip of shoreline. For six or seven months out of the year, its entire vegetation is bare of leaves, desiccated, apparently dead. (And that is in the good years.)"[10]

Fixing the precise calendar months for the rainy season becomes complicated in that it varies between coast and interior as well as within those areas. These patterns are discussed in some detail in Chapter 2. In general, however, rains fall during northeastern Brazil's summer and fall

(December-May), while the dry season coincides with winter and spring (June-October). Most of the rains concentrate in a few months, most typically March and April.[11] As previously noted, an additional complicating factor is the *sertanejo* custom of referring to the rainy season as "winter" even though in calendar terms winter coincides with the dry season.

On the heels of the Great Drought, other profound generalized dry spells occurred in 1888-89, 1900, and 1903-04. Drought became an officially recognized problem when, in 1906, the national government created the Superintendency of Studies and Works Against the Effects of Drought, the forerunner of multiple other national and state anti-drought agencies, departments, and study centers.[12]

Despite all this official concern, the numerous academic studies, ambitious plans, and publicly-funded projects, the specter of periodic droughts producing dislocation and death continues to haunt the region. As Nancy Schepper-Hughes affirms, "if there is one raw and vital nerve among *Nordestinos* [northeasterners] it is their horror of drought . . . and thirst."[13] Northeasterners see drought as both a cause and symbol of their region's relative underdevelopment, and claim that this reflects a long-standing pattern of government favoritism toward the south. In this view as well, the northeast has been exploited by southern business and financial interests, drained of both its people and capital. Outside the region, the derisive terms "drought industries" and "drought industrialists" express a widely-held belief that northeastern politicians have shamelessly exploited drought to provide patronage for their cronies, waxing rich off the misery of the ignorant masses.[14] This supposedly explains the long history of failed attempts to "solve" the drought problem.

The roots of this contemporary polemic, and indeed of the very definition of drought and relief as national issues, date back to the Great Drought. Questions of electoral manipulation, and the contrived or "artificial" nature of the drought in the sense that it served as a mechanism to siphon off public monies for corrupt purposes peppered elite discourse of that day. So, too, did critiques of the *retirantes*, including accusations that their own moral failings—especially a reluctance to engage in sustained labor—explained many of the problems associated with government-sponsored relief programs.

REPRESENTATION AND REALITY

In announcing drought's end to the national legislature in 1880, Sinimbu's successor José Antonio Saraiva declared: "No country has spent so much, in so short a time, to aid needy compatriots."[15] Emperor Dom Pedro II also celebrated those sacrifices and averred that the state had fulfilled a "sacred duty" and avoided the "depopulation of those provinces."[16] Those statements presented an official version of reality, a representation that emphasized the sacrifice of the nation and portrayed the government as caring, generous and effective in meeting the needs of the afflicted provinces.

Measured against the actuality of drought-spawned devastation and death and the ruthless exploitation of *retirantes*—much of which proceeded from the very nature of government policy—the words of Saraiva and Dom Pedro speak to the major theme of this book: the vast gulf between the discursive reality of imperial elites and the empirical reality experienced by the displaced *sertanejos* as they struggled to survive the ravages of the Great Drought.

In addition to documenting the existence of this disjuncture, I am interested in exploring its origins and impact. This search ultimately reveals how the conceptual world of imperial elites could interpret a cruelly exploitative relief system as a noble, self-sacrificing, charitable enterprise. At one level, exploitation was unself-conscious, a product of unquestioned assumptions and behaviors, many of which related to social class and political culture. At the same time, the exploitative nature of the drought and relief also reflected a conscious politicization of the crisis, both in local settings and at the national capital. And, finally, the nature of the backlands environment itself contributed to the failures of relief. These various realities, then, combined to magnify the suffering of *retirantes*.

Reference to discourse and representations of reality invokes questions of theory. Viewed broadly, the term "discourse" refers to "all forms of spoken interactions, formal and informal, and written texts of all kinds."[17] Conceptually, discourse analysis stresses the active, constructive nature of language. Texts, then, do not simply reflect societal values, assumptions, and power relationships; they actively "construct a version of reality."[18] If one such specific version or "representation of reality" gains sufficient authority, it in effect *becomes* reality. In this fashion, "language constructs the world of things."[19]

Recognition of the evocative and formative power of language, of course, is not a discovery of our immediate time. For example, writing about questions of power and authority, Thomas Hobbes ascribed great importance to definitions and names. He observed with regard to politics, "we ourselves make the principles . . . whereby it is known what justice and equity and their opposites, injustice and equity are."[20] And Rudyard Kipling affirmed that "words are of course, the most powerful drug used by mankind."[21]

Many scholars who work within a discursive framework view the world of texts as the only world for analysis. The discourse at once comprises the evidentiary base and the fundamental reality, and "the goals or motives of individual speakers become irrelevant."[22] Roger Chartier, however, warns us against "the dangerous reduction of the social world to a purely discursive construction and to pure language games."[23] He further suggests that "one must insist forcefully that history is commanded by an intention and a principle of truth, that the past . . . is a reality external to discourse, and that knowledge of it can be verified."[24]

If discourse analysis provides an entrée into the conceptual world of Brazilian elites—their "common mental universe"—the empirical contours of that "universe" must be sketched, for the construction of meaning occurs within specific contexts.[25] Clearly, as well, both the nature and power of ideas, concepts, and knowledge strongly reflect social processes and culture.[26] Moving beyond the "texts," therefore, I survey a wider variety of documentation to identify and evaluate the central conceptions and representations of reality embedded in elite discourse, and I explain both these conceptions and their peculiar rendering of reality by referencing them to their context—nineteenth-century Brazil.

Imperial elites approached the drought and relief in terms that proved congenial to their class interests. They also did so in terms of a specific set of knowledge. Discourse helps to identify that knowledge. The larger context, including an appraisal of empirical reality, allows us to understand something of its genesis and make judgments regarding its accuracy.

During the Great Drought, elites consistently held that the "worthy" poor merited charity. But, did all the displaced *sertanejos* deserve to be placed in that category? Elite discourse phrased that question and provided an answer. It did so by defining the categories of "worthy" and "unworthy" in terms of specific attributes or characteristics—ones that clearly reflected assumptions regarding the nature of Brazilian society, politics, and, as we will see, even of the nation's physical geography and climate. Clearly, then, then, it becomes impossible to understand and evaluate the discursive reality of the Great Drought in the absence of a broader consideration of imperial Brazil.

BRAZILIAN ELITES

A relatively small elite dominated imperial Brazil. The large-scale export agriculture that formed the bedrock of the nation's economy empowered the *fazendeiros* or planters, and those linked to them, and they provided the vast bulk of the empire's top leadership. In some respects, the term "elite" suggests a unity that masks significant distinctions and tensions. So, for example, the great titled landholders certainly stood apart from those who owned more modest parcels, and considerable social distance separated the heads of great merchant houses from those who led smaller corresponding firms. Clearly, as well, members of the national elite enjoyed higher status than those who could claim distinction only within the confines of their own locality or province. Furthermore, regional issues and party affiliation in some cases might divide elites.

Nonetheless, the Brazilian elite also had a unitary nature. To begin with, an elitist, hierarchical society reproduced social relations that emphasized status, power, and patronage. So, though rude and rustic by comparison with imperial leaders and holders of great estates, small-town politicos and local leading families behaved no differently in assuming the prerogatives of class and wielding power.

Even when economic change and accelerated urbanization seemingly altered the nation's socio-economic structure during the latter half of the nineteenth century, the conforming power of social class stunted significant change. In his classic study of São Paulo, Warren Dean wrote of the "merging of emerging elites," stressing the economic and family ties uniting plantation, finance, and industry.[27] Such tensions as those between agriculturalists and nascent industrialists, and between planters and commercial factors remained muted in Brazil. Rising middle groups in Brazil also cast their lot with the elites.[28] Furthermore, when the great planters themselves ceded positions throughout the bureaucracy in the latter portion of the century to the *bacharéis*, the liberally university educated, especially graduates of the nation's law schools, the social origins of a preponderance of this new generation of leaders lay within the landed aristocracy.

Shared social understandings, fostered through ties of education and family, characterized the *bacharéis*.[29] And this extended more broadly through the political elite who were united, according to José Murilo de Carvalho, by "ideological homogeneity," a shared view of the world "implanted by formal training, through common career experiences, through common political or life experiences, or through combinations of the above."[30]

I propose that discourse functioned as an additional causative factor of wide elite consensus. Elite discourse on the Great Drought clearly evidenced both shared language and shared understandings. This discourse had formative power; it created and disseminated particular constructions of the national reality. When Brazilian elites confronted their nation's problems, the causes and solutions proposed—indeed the very identification of these specific areas as cause for concern—showed little variation by party affiliation. Elites shared discursive repertoires, stylized ways of expressing reality; phrases commonly used at the court to conceptualize the Brazilian *problematique* also appeared in local settings. Discourse reflected and reinforced an elitist political culture that prized order and a cautious approach to change.[31] Whether ministers, senators, deputies, judges, or provincial presidents, Liberals or Conservatives, in heart and mind members of the Brazilian elite all spoke the same language.

GOVERNMENTAL STRUCTURE

Brazil had gained its independence in 1822 under Pedro I, son of the Portuguese monarch, João VI. He abdicated in 1831, returning to Portugal to take the throne. This ushered in a period known as the Regency, which ended in 1840 when João's son took over. He would rule until 1889 as Emperor Pedro II. Symbolically and institutionally the head of both the state and the government, the emperor exercised the *poder moderador*, or moderative power, which in theory served as a point of intersection for the legislative, executive, and judicial powers, each of which otherwise remained independent from one another.[32] In practice, the moderative power greatly strengthened the executive, which through it "had the means to make its own laws, to administer itself [and] to judge its own actions."[33]

The emperor called the national legislative assembly into session. This body had two *câmaras* or chambers, the *Senado* (Senate) and *Deputados* (Deputies or representatives). Senators served for life, while deputies were elected to four-year terms. The Emperor, however, could dissolve the legislature, which meant that new elections would be held. Between 1868 and 1889, only one legislature, the 15th—which sat from 1872 to1875—actually completed its full term. Since elections always delivered resounding victories to the party in power, the imperial political elite well understood that only the emperor's intervention could change the prevailing balance. Otherwise, the party out of power would remain so indefinitely, suspended in a sort of "Dante's Inferno."[34]

The espoused philosophical differences between Liberals and Conservatives veiled the fact that both were "basically conservative and anti-democratic."[35] The political parties of imperial Brazil never represented disciplined, homogeneous national institutions. Central Liberal or Conservative directorates might exist in the capital, and even anoint representatives in the provinces. But provincial politicos—keenly attuned to local power brokers and issues—typically followed their own instincts rather than any uniform, national party platform. Party identity in the provinces, then, responded more to the demands and needs of elite alliances and family networks than to political principles. In this setting, the parties served as mechanisms for expressing rivalry and contesting power among shifting elite coalitions.

As vehicles for patronage, political parties held significance for the staffing of key political positions at both the imperial and provincial levels. Even here, however, faction proved more decisive than party. Members of the same party might be bitter rivals, even heading separate factions, and seeking alliances and support within the ranks not only of their own party, but among the opposition as well. The parlance of the day drew significant distinctions between coreligionists, those who shared only the bond of party, and *amigos* or friends, people one really could count on.

The emperor also appointed the members of the Council of State. Acting as his advisory committee, it rendered formal opinions on a wide range of matters including appointment and dismissal of ministries (also referred to as cabinets), appointment of senators, and approval of legislation.[36] In selecting counselors, the emperor typically consulted with the president of the Council of Ministers. The president, (sometimes referred to in the literature as the prime minister) selected the the members of his cabinet. Those selected had strong ties to the national legislative assembly, for they had typically served (or were serving) as senators or deputies. And, from 1870 to 1889, every president of the Council of Ministers also was a member of the Senate.[37] Again, it is important to emphasize that the president of the Council did not gain his position not through election. Rather, he was selected by the emperor.

ELECTIONS

Because of the government's power over the nation's two-tiered electoral system, the President's party affiliation determined overwhelmingly the composition of the Chamber of Deputies. When Sinimbu took over as president of the Council of Ministers, new elections produced a unanimously Liberal Chamber of Deputies for the 1878-81 legislature.[38]

In the provinces, members of electoral boards acted as partisans, evincing little concern for constitutional legality. Since control over these boards translated into ability to control the results of elections, their composition reflected the results of struggles among competing factions of the locally powerful.[39] In this sense, electoral results not only reflected power, but affirmed it. One essential proof of power was the ability to produce the desired outcome.

The Duke of Caxias, whose Conservative ministry's final year coincided with the onset of the Great Drought, had attempted to deal with the vexing issue of electoral reform. Largely because of the efforts of Finance Minister Cotegipe, in 1875 his ministry secured passage of the *lei do terço*, or law of thirds, which sought to provide the opportunity for minority party representation in the Chamber of Deputies. The law had minimal impact, however, for "a little careful planning among electors responsive to the ruling party could still make sure that all its candidates won."[40] This system of rigged and managed elections was widely remarked. As one of Sinimbu's confidants pointed out, men who would be "incapable" of a dishonest or violent act in any other circumstance behaved in a totally different fashion when it came to elections.[41]

The more ardent proponents of electoral reform saw it as a means to transform Brazil into a modern, progressive democracy. In addition to calling for direct elections to replace the managed, two-tiered system's distinction between voters and electors, they also proposed an expanded franchise that would extend full political rights to non-Catholics. This, in turn, would make Brazil a more attractive destination for immigrants, while creating a government more responsive to the will of the people rather than one dominated by the executive. Caxias's inability to quiet the calls for electoral reform played a role in his ministry's downfall and provided the rationale for calling Sinimbu and the Liberals to power in 1878.[42]

THE PROVINCES OF THE NORTH

The provinces most affected by the Great Drought, Alagoas, Pernambuco, Paraíba, Rio Grande do Norte, Ceará and Piauí all form part of the present Brazilian northeast. Nineteenth-century Brazilians really recognized only two major regional divisions: the provinces of the north and those of the south.[43] To a great extent, the sugar industry and its associated planter elite defined the north, a function of the historic importance of sugar cane during the colonial period and the allied significance of sugar as a revenue-generating export product. By the time of the Great Drought, however, whether measured by profitability or world market share, sugar had fallen on hard times.[44] Ranching, another historically important activity, had contributed to exploration and settlement of the northern interior, and created a popular image of the backlands as a place of open ranges and leather-clad cowboys. Although cattle-ranching remained significant in several of the northern provinces, hides formed a distinctly minor component of the region's exports.[45]

A newer product, cotton, generally grown on smaller holdings away from the coast in the transitional zone known as the *agreste*, actually provided a greater share of Brazilian export receipts than did sugar.[46] Rubber, another new product, had not yet entered the boom that would create vast fortunes and a rush of activity in Pará and Amazonas, though it sufficed to create a demand there for *retirante* labor during the Great Drought.[47]

Despite the presence of these more dynamic economic activities, a miasma of decline hung over the provinces of the north. Rubber's area of production lay well outside the heartland of the traditional north, and its incipient surge brought no status benefits or financial rewards to the sugar planters.[48] That planter elite also had little direct involvement with cotton. When the *fazendeiros* conceptualized their region's status and problems, they emphasized the fortunes of sugar. So, for example, an 1878 agricultural congress organized in Recife by the Commercial Association of Pernambuco to consider problems afflicting the *grande lavoura*, or export agriculture, and attended by agriculturalists from several of the surrounding provinces, focused overwhelmingly on problems affecting sugar production.[49]

In the context of imperial politics, among these provinces only Pernambuco enjoyed significant status. To a large extent, it dominated several of its neighbors, transforming them into a "satellite block."[50] Control of a large bloc of votes brought greater success in the wheeling and dealing of pork barrel politics. Representation in the National Legislative Assembly was apportioned on the basis of population. A total of sixty senators represented the twenty provinces of Brazil in the Senate. Pernambuco ranked first among the drought provinces, with a population of about 842,000 and 6 senators. Ceará, with 722,000 held 4 Senate seats; Paraíba and Alagoas, with respective populations of 376,000 and 348,000, each had 2. At the bottom, Rio Grande do Norte with 234,000 inhabitants and Piauí with but 202,000 each had only a single senator.[51] A similar provincial pecking order held for the 122 deputies in the Chamber of Deputies that sat during the drought years. Pernambuco sent 13 deputies to that chamber. Ceará held 8 seats, Alagoas and Paraíba 5; Piauí came next with 3, followed by Rio Grande do Norte with 2.[52]

Combined, the six drought provinces had only 16 senators and 36 deputies, whereas the nation's most populous province, Minas Gerais, itself had ten senators and 20 deputies. Even cooperating, as they did at first to form a "drought lobby," those northern provinces on their own did not enjoy enough political clout to force favorable action from the national government. Support for an ongoing policy of drought relief rested on the degree to which it coincided with interests in other provinces, and a shared perception of a moral and constitutional obligation to succor the needy.

REGIONALISM

Northern distress in the 1870s reflected a comparative focus on other, more successful areas of Brazil. In the early 1870s, cotton, sugar, and coffee combined to yield nearly 80 percent of the nation's export receipts. But coffee, whose cultivation concentrated overwhelmingly in the south, by itself accounted for 50 percent of those revenues.[53] This economic disparity between the Brazilian north and south suggests the existence of regionalism as a significant factor in imperial Brazil. On a variety of specific issues, then, regional identity became a critical variable.[54]

Southerners, who saw themselves as forward-thinking and productive, often ascribed sugar's problems to northerners' tradition-bound approach to agriculture. Increasingly, after mid-century, they expressed resentment over the excessive political clout of northern sugar planters.[55] Northerners, however, saw the imperial government as the cause of many of their region's problems. They pointed especially to government policies related to banking, immigration, and railroad development as clearly favoring coffee planters. Northerners had little regard for immigration, whether state-sponsored or spontaneous. To that point, none of the national government's efforts had resulted in the formation of so-called *colônias* or agricultural colonies in the north. Responding to southern commentary regarding the high cost of relief, one northerner sarcastically observed: "for more than 30 years, official colonization has been a permanent drought for our finances."[56]

Railroad construction also had largely centered in the south. At the time of the Great Drought, the nation's most extensive line was the Dom Pedro II, whose trajectory was planned to run from the city of Rio de Janeiro to Minas Gerais and São Paulo. Begun in 1855 under private control, the state bought out the Dom Pedro II in 1865 when the line had only 133 kilometers of trackage. Over the next twelve years, state-sponsored construction raised that total to over 550 kilometers. By contrast, in 1877 Pernambuco's railroad trackage stood at about 160 kilometers, and Ceará's at about 40.[57] A northern planter noted that southern agriculturalists "awake to the whistle of the locomotive, which announces their proximity to the Court," and declared, "the South denies us everything."[58] The Pernambucan Agricultural Aid Society, pointing to the differentials in imperial funding, declared that southerners lived in "Asiatic luxury," while "we, the planters of the North . . . are obliged to restrict ourselves to the most limited subsistence."[59] Some of the policies implemented under the rubric of drought relief represented a long standing northern agenda that sought to redress perceived inequities in the distribution of imperial resources in support of material improvements.

POLITICAL CULTURE

As those regional issues suggest, the needs of *retirantes* did not drive the development of relief policy in terms of its specific contours and application. At both the national and provincial levels, relief entered into the ongoing calculus of factionalized partisan rivalry engaged in by Liberals and Conservatives, the nation's two major parties. Throughout the early months of the drought, for example, Liberals sought to undercut the sitting Conservative ministry. In Ceará, the Liberal Fortaleza newspaper, *O Cearense*, scathingly attacked Finance Minister Cotegipe for asserting that the drought's impact had been "exaggerated."[60] But in the National Legislative Assembly, the few Liberal members of the Chamber of Deputies actually impeded efforts to release funds. In an editorial commenting on the May 14 debate over a two thousand *conto* credit for drought relief, the establishment *Jornal do Comércio* said that relief had fallen prey to "partisanship and political intransigence," and lamented that in this "terrible calamity" the opposition Liberals' desire to speak had exceeded their compassion.[61]

That both national and provincial politicians saw the drought in terms of opportunities for patronage and political advantage—with many local politicos adding personal profit to that mix—reflected the political culture of imperial Brazil. Patronage stood at the heart of this culture. In the words of Richard Graham, "as the decisive tool in nineteenth-century Brazilian politics, as predominant expectation, as unselfconscious pattern of action, patronage provided the major link between society and state."[62]

Patronage invoked a continuing calculus of social status. A successful career path through the imperial administrative hierarchy depended on loyalty and trustworthiness. The astute official kept his eye on the next preferred post and understood that the most important judgment of a job well done would be made by occupants of those higher levels of the hierarchy to which he aspired. This fundamental social knowledge ranged across all levels of the imperial bureaucracy, from humble posts to the highest offices.

DROUGHT POLICY

During the various smaller or "partial" droughts that periodically had beset the north over the past several decades, provincial presidents normally had recourse to credits on the imperial treasury budgeted under public relief. In keeping with that past practice, when the true "winter" rains failed to follow the sparser December rains, northern presidents in several provinces opened small credits for relief. In April 1877, Minister of the Empire Antônio da Costa Pinto e Silva advised provincial presidents to secure the government's permission before opening any additional credits. He also attempted to make Rio de Janeiro the source of all purchases for food relief, working through a private firm, Francisco de Figueiredo & Company.[63] He decentralized relief only to the extent of authorizing a regional distribution role for a Central Relief Commission in Recife, a decision reflecting that city's position as the area's leading port and commercial entrepôt.

In June, 1877, approving two thousand *contos* for public assistance, the government advised presidents to spend only on transporting food to people in need. Through the remainder of the year, save for ruling on additional credits or expenditures, the imperial government essentially left implementation of relief to the provincial presidents. They responded to the emergency by setting up several depositories or warehouses for storing and distributing relief supplies. Presidents also organized central relief commissions in provincial capitals and instructed local authorities to establish their own commissions to coordinate and oversee relief efforts. All of the provinces, therefore, had multiple relief commissions that in theory—though not always in fact—remained subordinate to the central commission in their respective provincial capitals.

As the "winter" ended, yielding to the normally dry "summer," the gravity of conditions in the provinces of the north increased, exacerbated by the relative sparseness of previous year's rains. Provincial presidents regularly corresponded with the minister of the empire pointing to difficulties in reaching the people most in need, those residing in the "high" or remote backlands (*alto sertão*). In July, 1877, for example, Ceará's Estelita noted that bad roads and inadequate transport made it impossible to get relief to certain localities.[64] The drought's persistence further complicated matters. Large-scale migrations from the backlands began as *sertanejos* sought areas where water and food were available. Soon, thousands of these *retirantes* lined the banks of the São Francisco river. Coastal capitals, smaller littoral towns, and various drought-free oases at higher elevations (*brejos*) also received large numbers of *retirantes*. As a result, even areas not directly affected by drought found themselves struggling with its impact. Migrants moving back and forth across provincial boundaries further complicated relief efforts and spread the effects of drought. And when *retirantes* crowded into locales ill-equipped to deal with them, various epidemic diseases broke out.

When Sinimbu took over as prime minister in January 1878, along with the ongoing drought and the vexing issue of electoral reform he inherited a fiscal emergency. Every fiscal year from 1870 to the outbreak of the Great Drought had witnessed budget deficits.[65] With a nearly thir-ty-four thousand *conto* deficit from the previous year, he faced the prob-ability that fiscal 1877-78 would produce a similar short fall. Furthermore some £225 on a foreign loan would come due in 1879.[66] Throughout his administration, Sinimbu focused on achieving electoral reform. He also wanted to restore balance to the nation's finances. The drought remained a secondary concern, an unwelcome complication that detracted from his ministry's primary mission. But, his administra-tion could not ignore the drought.

In March and April 1878, at special meetings of the Council of State, Sinimbu sought authorization for a substantial emission of nonconvert-ible paper money, arguing that prevailing conditions made it unlikely that an advantageous foreign loan could be secured and noting the need for increased expenditures for drought relief.[67] He also called for a new legislature on the grounds that the current Chamber of Deputies was not likely to approve the paper money issue.[68]

The emperor backed these requests. On April 11, 1878, he dissolved the legislature, setting December 15 of that year for the inaugural of a new Assembly.[69] Four days later, with no sitting Assembly to object, the finance minister received authorization to emit up to sixty thousand *con-tos* over the fiscal years of 1877-78 and 1878-79, officially earmarked for "drought expenses and other obligations of the treasury."[70] Between March and October of 1878, the government issued credits totaling twen-ty-six thousand *contos*, a sum approximately three times larger than the total budget authorized for the ministry of the empire for that year.[71] The fiscal year 1878-79, witnessed the greatest amount of government expen-diture on the drought, nearly fifty thousand *contos*, which represented about 75 percent of all expenditures on relief.[72]

As the rains continued to fail during the "winter" of 1878, the impe-rial government granted provincial presidents authorization for numer-ous relief projects. One favored approach was to resettle *retirantes* in agri-cultural colonies where, at least in theory, they would be able to provide for their own needs. Alagoas, Paraíba, Pernambuco, and Rio Grande do Norte all experimented with such colonies. *Retirantes* also worked in agricultural colonies that were set up in Amazonas, Pará, Maranhão and Bahia.[73] Colonies offered profitable opportunities to well-connected sup-pliers and merchants who provided the seeds, tools, clothing, foodstuffs, and other goods needed to sustain the colonists until they could bring in a harvest.

Public works, justified by both their present and future impacts, also received support. Roads would provide labor opportunities for *reti-rantes* and improve the flow of relief goods within provinces. They also would enhance the region's infrastructure, thereby promoting economic growth and alleviating problems caused by future droughts. That rationale also held for the construction of *açudes* (small dams or weirs) and reservoirs, as well as railroads. Throughout the provinces of the north, then, the years of the Great Drought saw the development of numerous hydraulic projects and the inception or extension of railroad lines.[74]

As early as September 1878, however, Sinimbu's ministry began pressuring presidents to limit expenses and encourage *retirantes* to return to their homes, a stance reflecting the relative unimportance of the drought for Sinimbu as opposed to electoral reform and fiscal balance.[75] Writing in March 1878 to the incoming president of Alagoas, Sinimbu had identified the nation's economic difficulties as one of the main concerns of the ministry and observed that this made the expenditure of public funds a particularly important issue.[76] In October of that year, Sinimbu applauded various measures the president had taken to end drought expenditures and concluded by remarking, "We have spent a fabulous sum."[77] On the fourteenth of that month, Minister of the Empire Leôncio de Carvalho sent a circular to provincial presidents in the drought region instructing them to encourage *retirantes* still being maintained by public funds to return to their homes. It further advised presidents to authorize only those expenditures that "had the most intimate link with the drought."[78]

But the new National Legislative Assembly that convened in the flush of Liberal victory expected the usual patronage rewards, which certainly could not be realized if the government turned off the flow of funds. Minas Gerais and Bahia, two powerful provinces that also experienced some of the Great Drought's impact, added further weight to the demand for assistance. Furthermore, in the quid pro quo of imperial politics, support for northern drought relief would result in favorable votes for projects in the south.[79] And, finally, whether at the national or provincial level, the politics of patronage made demands of its own. Francisco de Figueiredo, for example, lauded for his charitable efforts on behalf of the drought migrants, headed a national steamship company as well as Rio de Janeiro's leading commercial association. His control over the expenditure of funds for relief both reflected and further enhanced his status.[80] Strong ties existed between government leaders and key members of Rio de Janeiro's commercial and financial communities. The drought gave the administration an opportunity to award lucrative contracts to *amigos* and to cultivate new relationships with other members of the national elite. In the course of the Great Drought, only Ceará received more direct expenditure of imperial funds than did Rio de Janeiro.

Once cranked up to deliver the goods, the relief system itself would gain additional sources of momentum, developing supporting constituencies as it was brokered through the political system. Furthermore, despite the shaky state of national finances, the paper money emission provided the new administration with a ready source of cash. As a result, for a time a paradoxical situation held sway. An administration that saw the drought as an annoying distraction from its central mission of electoral reform and fiscal responsibility wound up authorizing large sums to provide relief to a group of provinces that collectively held relatively little political power.

Meanwhile, Sinimbu experienced major difficulties in trying to resolve the question of electoral reform, encountering resistance not only from the Conservative-dominated Senate, but from dissident Liberals in the Chamber of Deputies. At the same time, mounting relief expenses further imperiled the nation's already shaky finances. As expenses rose and drought persisted, relief became a target of convenience for Sinimbu's enemies, and they relentlessly critiqued its failures. In the imperial system, a prime minister who could not command clout sufficient to gain approval for major legislation lost all political viabilty. Toward the end of February 1880, then, Sinimbu wrote to long-time Liberal leader José Antonio Saraiva asking if he would be willing to head a new Liberal government.[81] Saraiva, who took over in March of 1880, moved quickly to end relief. Averring that "abundant rains" had fallen, he opined that the necessity for all relief would "end shortly." The following month, his minister of the empire ordered the return of all *retirantes* to their former homes and an end to all spending for the drought save for that required to "liquidate works in progress."[82]

On May 3, 1880, the emperor directly affirmed the drought's end, and government decree then proclaimed this as official reality on May 9.[83] Implementation of that decree fell to new provincial presidents, all of whom understood that so far as the imperial government was concerned, the Great Drought no longer existed. In the Chamber of Deputies that sat in session during the first months of the Saraiva government, neither the minister of the empire nor the minister of agriculture received a single inquiry regarding the drought. In fact, the only discussion of water related to damages to a reservoir that supplied the city of Rio de Janeiro.[84]

The silence of these legislators clearly bespoke a lack of consonance between government policy and the needs of a still-prostrate north. During three years of massive deaths and *sertanejo* migration, elites had constructed their own drought, one that reflected their common mental universe. By consensus and decree, then, they ended that imagined drought.

THE IMAGINED DROUGHT

As *retirantes* streamed out from the parched backlands, many of the empire's most distinguished scientists assembled at Rio de Janeiro's Polytechnical Institute (*Instituto Politécnico*) to discuss the problem of northern drought. The Conde d'Eu, Pedro II's son-in-law, lent his august presence as presiding officer.[1] Those attending the series of meetings in October 1877 at the Polytechnical included such luminaries as Viscount Henrique de Beaurepaire Rohan, whose 1873 *Carta Geral do Brasil* (General Map of Brazil), prepared for the Universal Exposition in Vienna, remained the standard for some fifty years. Rohan had served as provincial president of both Pará and Paraíba, and as minister of war in the 1864 cabinet.[2] Other distinguished participants included two engineers from the provinces of the north, João Ernesto Viriato de Medeiros, from Ceará, and Manuel Buarque de Macedo, from Pernambuco, both of whom soon would take up seats in the new Chamber of Deputies.[3] Unable to attend those meetings, Baron Guilherme Shüch Capanema, a childhood playmate of the Emperor and a founder of the Brazilian Statistical Society (Sociedade de Estatística do Brasil) sent a formal memorandum to the gathering.[4]

Various other of imperial Brazil's learned societies also considered the issue of drought, including the Brazilian Acclimatization Society (Associação Brasileira de Acclimação), National Industrial Aid Society (Sociedade Auxiliadora da Indústria Nacional) and the Imperial Fluminense Agricultural Institute (Imperial Instituto Fluminense de Agricultura) as did some provincial improvement societies and commercial associations. The national associations really functioned as "societies of the Court."[5] The ranks of their memberships included the emperor, a self-styled patron of science and learning, and he often graced their

1

meetings.[6] Rather than narrowly bounded academic conferences, then, gatherings of the learned were elite social events. On a lesser scale, provincial associations replicated that pattern.

Their deliberations and debates typically found expression in the capital's newspapers and, to a lesser extent, in those of the provinces, and continued as well in a number of books and pamphlets. This "scientific" production remained highly accessible to the national political elite—in part because of the relatively non-technical, unsophisticated nature of those publications, and in part because many political figures themselves were "men of science." As a result, discussions of drought and drought policy in the National Legislative Assembly often included direct references to that scientific literature, or, less directly, reflected its influence.

Though a unitary phenomenon in climatological terms, the Great Drought had multiple, mutable, and negotiable meanings for the elite of imperial Brazil. In various gatherings and publications of leading imperial scientists and national and provincial improvement associations, the drought became a symbol of Brazilian backwardness, a metaphor for the range of problems that impeded national progress. Political discourse initially represented the drought as a human tragedy, defined in terms of an unavoidable natural calamity and the suffering of an afflicted region and its people. By drought's end, charges of waste, fraud, and corruption had displaced that image. The formerly innocent *retirantes* had become idle loafers, morally deformed by public relief, and the drought naught but an artifice maintained by profiteers and corrupt politicos.

The imagic reality of drought reflected varying agendas: political figures from the provinces of the north used the drought as a platform to express regional grievances; it provided other politicians with a convenient vehicle to express partisan critiques of their national and provincial opponents; and it gave scientists, especially engineers, an opportunity to assert claims to authority.[7] In expressing these varying agendas, however, elite representations of the drought invoked common themes and concepts, and through them we can glimpse the representational world of imperial elites and view the constructed reality of drought.

As elites spoke and wrote of drought, they invoked specific images regarding its causes and the nature of the *sertão* and its inhabitants that both defined the drought and helped structure policy. This chapter focuses on policy discussions in the National Legislative Assembly. It identifies the key conceptual categories and issues that framed debates about relief policy, and analyzes them in terms of that broader elite discourse. In so doing, the intent is not so much to discuss the validity of the various "truths" asserted, as to provide a sense of the shared world view of those persons responsible for developing drought policy.

INITIAL IMAGES AND DISCURSIVE TENSIONS

During the failed "winter" of 1877, government policy became an issue in the national legislature, occasioning a lengthy exchange in the Chamber of Deputies in August 1877 between Martim Francisco Ribeiro de Andrada, a Liberal from São Paulo, and Minister of the Empire Antônio da Costa Pinto. If at one level their discourse simply represented the partisan sniping that typified political exchange among parties and factions in imperial Brazil, at another it presented both general themes and specific language that remained central to subsequent discussions of relief policy. These include an assessment of the government's response to the drought, judged in terms of compassion and approach; the nature of *retirantes*, particularly their moral character as manifested through a disposition toward labor; and the workings of relief at the provincial level, especially with regard to effectiveness and honesty. In sum, had the government acted properly and fulfilled the demands of conscience and constitution; had provincial officials been true to their office; and, had the *retirantes* behaved responsibly?

Martim Francisco began by pointing to news stories describing horrid conditions in the provinces of the north, noting especially reports that four children had died of starvation. He affirmed that this proved the inadequacy of government policy, which to date could be summarized as nothing beyond "the shipment of some foodstuffs." He also identified a basic flaw in the administration's approach: "Between giving of alms, which can produce the habit of laziness and inertia, and assistance given in return for labor, there is an immense difference." Martim Francisco urged a policy of government-funded public works so as to promote the moral benefits of remunerated labor, while also creating infrastructure that could reduce problems arising from future droughts. With regard to this latter, he raised the possibility of adopting the "modern discoveries of the most advanced nations," and pointed to England's ability to overcome water problems during the Abyssinian campaign. Finally, he spoke of the benefits that would come from resettling drought victims on agricultural colonies, noting the vast sums already spent by the imperial government—with little tangible benefit—on establishing such colonies with foreign immigrants. He concluded by urging the government to "redouble its energy and solicitude so that the numerous populations threatened by a horrid death will be saved and maintained for work, for family, and for country."[8]

Costa Pinto offered a spirited defense of his government's policy. He granted that as the backlanders journeyed toward areas with greater resources, "it is inevitable, gentlemen, that among so many *retirantes* one or another will suffer.... It is even possible that one or another may have succumbed to disease." But, he assured the assembled delegates, "none however has died from hunger."[9]

Costa Pinto minimized the dimensions of the crisis. He asserted that rains had fallen in various portions of Pernambuco, Paraíba, and Rio Grande do Norte. Furthermore, due in part to government shipments, and in part to large surpluses recorded in Pernambuco's harvest, ample supplies existed throughout the region. The locations of food warehouses in the afflicted provinces, said the minister, were well publicized so *retirantes* knew precisely where they needed to go to secure supplies, and no provincial president had complained of lacking relief supplies. As for modern science and the building of reservoirs and the like, Costa Pinto pointed to the cost and time factor in creating and completing large-scale works. He declared that the government's main concern was to meet the pressing immediate needs of the people of the provinces of the north. Costa Pinto also averred that both the government and provincial presidents had attempted to "call the *retirantes* to labor." However, he reminded Martim Francisco that "many *retirantes* refuse to work, they do not wish to subject themselves to this, and how can one force them?" And, he drew an additional distinction regarding the question of government hand-outs: "It is not the government that gives alms; it is the nation that provides relief to citizens in need."[10]

Martim Francisco had framed his attack on administration policy in terms of the adequacy of public assistance and the appropriateness of the methods the government used to provide relief. As a measure of adequacy, he raised poignant images of suffering *sertanejos* and dying children. Costa Pinto accepted that same yardstick—though his measurements yielded a different reality. As symbols, suffering *retirantes* invoked society's moral obligation to succor the innocent needy. No public policy in imperial Brazil could deny the just claims of such people. The main lines of Costa Pinto's portrayal—a caring, compassionate government that spared no effort in its successful attempt to relieve the suffering of innocent people—was echoed by the successor Liberal government, and asserted once more by Pedro II at drought's end.

But if the obligation to provide assistance to those in need formed a point of consensus, what form ought that assistance take? Martim Francisco emphasized the positive moral benefits of work relief, while pointing to the negative consequences of government hand-outs. Costa Pinto countered by suggesting the difficulty of compelling reluctant *retirantes* to labor. This captured a fundamental discursive tension that ran throughout the Great Drought: did *retirantes* truly belong to that class of "deserving" poor entitled to public charity, or were they simply idlers who refused to work?

The exchange between minister and deputy also suggests that the drought as represented differed considerably from the drought as experienced by the provinces of the north. Costa Pinto remarked the absence of complaints by provincial presidents, asserted that *retirantes* knew the locations of the government storehouses, and denied the actuality of any *retirante* deaths from starvation. Taken at face, these statements suggested that those in need had little difficulty obtaining relief. But at the very time that he so confidently referred to the provincial presidents' satisfaction, his ministry already had received numerous communications, especially from Ceará, expressing real concern. As for the location of government warehouses, given the rudimentary communications infrastructure and the wide dispersal of *sertanejos* throughout the province of the north just how were *retirantes* to quickly learn this information? And even assuming they did, how were they to reach those locations? Similarly, while high levels of mortality might seem an undeniable aspect of the drought emergency, neither the Conservative nor Liberal administrations ascribed any deaths to failures of policy.

COMPASSION

Reflecting not only the constitutional provisions regarding relief, but the assumptions embedded in a patriarchal and paternalistic society in which elites ascribed to the tenets of Christian charity and a certain moral responsibility to provide for the needy and dependent, compassion proved an immediate and continuing reference point for public policy, a positive rationale for funding relief and a standard for judging government policy. It cast the *retirantes* as innocent victims of catastrophe, persons who suffered through no fault of their own.

In its attempt to promote a charitable response from both the public and the government, the *cearense* drought lobby always emphasized the dimensions of human suffering. In ongoing columns in the *Jornal do Comércio*, Liberato de Castro Carreira wrote heart-wrenching descriptions of conditions in his native province.[11] In a November 1877 column, for example, he likened the situation there to the suffering of Tantalus and observed that deaths from starvation and thirst were "a sad reality among the inhabitants of Ceará!" He appealed to the nation's government to fulfill its duty to "its brothers, victims of hunger and of misery."[12] *O Cearense*, the Liberal Fortaleza newspaper, wrote approvingly of Carreira's activities, and contrasted the government's minimal efforts with the outpouring of generosity from the Brazilian people themselves: "Among no other people, certainly, had philanthropy reached such a height."[13]

In June 1877 in the Senate, Ceará's Domingos José Nogueira Jaguaribe spoke against the relief policy of the Conservative ministry. His words held great weight due to his position as president of a committee organized by *cearenses* in Rio de Janeiro to secure charitable contributions for drought relief.[14] Arguing for imperial funding for a railroad in Ceará, he contrasted the government's spending on immigrant colonies with its reluctance to subsidize the employment of native Brazilians: "Come now, when so much money is spent to import labor, it seems painful to me that we allow our workers to perish for lack of funds."[15] Viriato de Medeiros similarly advocated improving transportation in the north. He wrote poignantly of the long and arduous journeys of *retirantes* who "barefoot, hatless, scarcely clothed, and breathing scorched air set out on the fatal road."[16]

When the new National Legislative Assembly began its work in January 1879, representatives from the provinces of the north relentlessly pushed the moral demands of charity. João Florentino Meira de Vasconcelos, a deputy from Paraíba and chief of its Liberal party, acknowledged the government's good intentions, but suggested the need for a much larger relief operation.[17] The suffering of the people had been great and prolonged, as disease and death stalked the land. He drew an analogy between government relief and the actions of individuals in aid of those less fortunate. Both "found their inspiration in heartfelt generosity" that in turn was strengthened "and derived legitimacy from the duties of conscience, of eternal justice, and moral depth that commands us to succor with dedication—and even with sacrifice—those who suffer."[18] He also reminded his colleagues that only those who were sons of the provinces of the north could truly appreciate the torment of drought—"the cruel suffering of these regions condemned, over two years to death by the horrors of hunger and plague."[19]

After establishing this moral justification for relief, Meira de Vasconcellos focused more directly on conditions in Paraíba, underscoring how the drought had deprived the province of its harvest and normal sources of revenue. He presented figures from the inspector of the provincial treasury indicating a large budget deficit for the fiscal year ending December 1877, and a predicted increase in that deficit through 1878 to total one thousand *contos*. Furthermore, the inspector had estimated that the province's revenue scarcely sufficed to make the interest payment due on its loan from the *Banco do Brasil*. Following this graphic detailing of the "penury and poverty" of his province, he concluded with an appeal: "I am not here asking for money, nor for aid for works and material improvements . . . but I am asking for help and aid for the public coffers of the province, in order that it might live and subsist, save its credit and maintain its integrity and its autonomy. Its abandonment will bring total annihilation. It is not only the province that protests this abandonment, but the very integrity of the empire requires that Paraíba be saved."[20]

Meira de Vasconcellos's expressive language portrayed a suffering and prostrate Paraíba, laid low by natural disaster, and abandoned by those who had a moral as well as legal obligation to provide support. His discussion of the province's dire financial circumstances, which noted that Paraíba had been a poor province even before the drought's devastation, cast Paraíba in the category of deserving poor.

Ceará deputy Antonio Joaquim Rodrígues Júnior also supported the necessity and justice of authorizing additional credits for relief. He charged that the province's former Conservative president had contributed to the suffering of the people. That president's failure to provide adequate relief to the interior had provoked—indeed encouraged—*sertanejos* to leave their homes and migrate out of the backlands to the littoral. As a result, Fortaleza had become home to over one hundred thousand *retirantes* who endured deplorable conditions. The people of Ceará, Rio Grande do Norte, Paraíba, and other provinces suffered not because of any action on their own part, but because of exceptional circumstances totally beyond their control, exacerbated by poor policy decisions made by those who held the duty and responsibility to care for them.[21]

A few months later, during the May 1879 legislative session, when several deputies charged that serious improprieties in the use of relief funds had occurred, Rio Grande do Norte's José Moreira Brandão Castelo Branco responded by reminding his colleagues of the horrible suffering caused by the drought. He quoted various authorities who suggested the moral imperative to succor the needy, and then closed this point by noting that the people—the Brazilians—who suffered were victims of a disaster that was "unpredictable and inevitable."[22] José Basson de Miranda Osorio of Piauí asserted that giving money in return for labor to "a hungry naked emigrant," seemed an appropriate use of public funds.[23]

Sinimbu's minister of the empire, Leôncio de Carvalho, began his year-end summary of the new ministry's approach to the drought by acknowledging the moral dimensions of this tragedy and the concomitant demand for a charitable response. He defined the drought as a terrible natural disaster that catapulted into misery thousands of people who lived off the rich fertility of the northern provinces. Forced to wander far from their homes in search of "the bread of charity," they endured yet more misfortune, castigated by epidemics.[24] The government, feeling as all Brazilians did, pain and anguish at the prospect of such suffering, rushed to provide assistance. Leôncio also lauded the charitable efforts of the royal family as well as those of private individuals. He placed the government in that same moral light, asserting that its desire to save the lives of its suffering citizens held primacy in relief policy.[25]

And, facing entrenched Senate opposition and the impending collapse of his ministry in October 1879, Sinimbu attempted to defend his relief policy on those same grounds of compassion. At any other time, said Sinimbu, given the state's shaky finances such massive expenditures would have been out of the question. But, he asked, how could the government allow people to die just to avoid spending a little more money?[26]

THE MORAL VALUE OF LABOR

For the deserving poor to merit compassion, they had to behave appropriately, displaying the virtues of honest poverty. According to that standard, all able-bodied *retirantes* ought be willing to labor. Jaguaribe, pointing to the benefits of hard work and dangers of the dole, waxed eloquent on this point in the Senate session of June 26, 1877: "We know that giving alms to the able-bodied lowers their self-respect; it takes from them certain stimuli, a certain moral force that they ought have as heads of the family. As a result of this, how many unfortunate consequences! How many prostitutions, how many miseries! But labor preserves a man's dignity and moral force; their families know that their heads (*chefes*) work to support them."[27] His Conservative Ceará colleague, Senator Jeronymo Martiniano Figueira de Melo, echoed these sentiments, making an especially forceful defense of the moral character of his province's inhabitants. "*Cearenses*, in the depths of their hearts, in accord with their understanding of the dignity of man, reject . . . these hand-outs; it embarrasses them to extend their hands to receive charity to sustain them. On the contrary, as men of courage, they wish to maintain themselves through labor, with the sweat of their brow."[28]

This inherent *cearense* quality received prominent mention in discussions regarding *retirante* agricultural colonies established in Pará and Amazonas. For example, in that same February 1879 Chamber of Deputies, Ceará's Francisco de Paula Pessoa Filho had assured his fellow deputies that, given land to cultivate and conditions of climate and soil similar to those of their native province, *cearenses* had performed exceedingly well.[29]

Throughout the discussions of the drought, deputies and senators continuously invoked the importance of a policy of compensated labor rather than direct relief. Rodrígues Júnior, for example, said that one "fatal error" of relief policy—begun by the Conservatives, but still continuing—was that it had distributed relief without demanding labor from the able-bodied. Relief granted with no requirement for labor produced "idleness with all its consequences, which always are disastrous."[30]

The myriad negative consequences of idleness included a propensity toward violence. When gathered in large numbers without adequate supervision and the discipline of labor, masses of *retirantes* were invariably seen as threatening. In July 1879, for example, Senator Anbrosio Leitão da Cunha pointed to serious problems in his native Pará. The provincial president there had requested additional troops to deal with the potential threat to public safety posed by the thousands of *retirantes* at the agricultural colony of Benavides. These clearly were not the "hard-working men" spoken of by "the honorable senator from Ceará," but "idlers."[31]

Disturbances of public order by *retirantes* stood as one of the most serious threats possible to the imperial elite. One pillar of the imperial system was its ability to maintain order, which required in turn that the masses remain disciplined and controlled. Leôncio de Carvalho's *relatório* specifically noted incidents of disorder involving *retirantes*: they responded to any proposed cuts in relief with the threat or actuality of violence. Leôncio explained this debased moral character as the natural result of living so long on the dole. He stressed the government's resolve to end such disturbances and get those *retirantes* working again so they would return to the "peaceful and industrious nature" of Brazilians. And he summarized the thrust of administration policy as designed to achieve two goals: providing "moralizing and pacifying" labor for the *retirantes*, and freeing the treasury from demands arising from the drought but "aggravated by idleness."[32] He also affirmed that "habits of labor" were the only thing that could assure *retirantes* "days of happiness and ennoblement."[33]

This emphasis on labor and idleness reflected a broader elite assessment of the masses, one fueled in part by the *decadência* or decline in export agriculture. So, for example, concerns centering on the work ethic peppered the discourse of those attending agricultural congresses held in Rio de Janeiro and Recife in 1878. A memorial to the Rio de Janeiro gathering called for stricter vagrancy laws, and advocated forcing the masses into agricultural colonies so they would "acquire work habits."[34] That congress's official response to the question of providing adequate plantation labor suggested "prompt and severe execution of the laws that prohibit vagrancy," and establishing a "rural code" to regulate relations between landowners and workers.[35] Participating in the Recife meeting, Joaquim Alvares dos Santos Souza, an engineer and member of a provincial improvement association, advocated better laws against vagrancy and the establishment of agricultural colonies for the "children of proletarians who presently wander about in the streets and roads."[36]

Concerns relating to questions of labor were also sparked by the impending "disorganization of labor" presaged by the 1871 *Ventre Livre*, or Law of the Free Womb, which declared the freedom of all children henceforth born to slave mothers.[37] Slave labor still accounted for a preponderance of Brazil's agricultural exports. Beyond its economic importance, slavery also functioned as a system of labor relations and as a fundamental element of social hierarchy. As planters increasingly relied on free labor—or even contemplated that prospect—they saw control as a fundamental issue. Brazilian elites expressed deep concern about free Brazilians as workers and saw them, says Lucio Kowarick, as "a useless rabble that preferred idleness and vagabondage, vice, and even crime to disciplined labor on the *fazendas*."[38] According to Kowarick, doubts about the capacity of the Brazilian worker, and assertions of their idleness and aversion to sustained toil as inherent characteristics characterized an ideology of *vadiagem* espoused by Brazilian elites. And George Reid Andrews remarks that planters took as axiomatic that "slaves and free workers alike were *vadios*, bums and vagrants, who would not work except under the threat of extreme force—and often, not even then."[39]

New currents of thought further buttressed elite concern with the nation's idle masses. The nineteenth-century European world celebrated labor as an ethical good, and defined it as productive in terms of regular and regulated patterns that contributed to the expansion of capital and progress. The importance of inculcating a work ethic had become "common sense." If all these varied idlers could be brought to labor, Brazil would "advance to its proper place in the forefront of civilization."[40]

Rhetorically justified by the importance of providing productive employment for displaced *sertanejos*, work relief became a central feature of Sinimbu's drought policy. And here, the celebration of hard-working *cearenses* had powerful implications. It functioned as an idealized stereotype of appropriate behavior that was used to justify exploitative labor practices, draw invidious distinctions between deserving and undeserving *retirantes*, and minimize relief expenditures. Clearly, no moral claim could be made by *retirantes* who had "lost all the virtues of honest poverty."[41] If, as in Figueira de Melo's formulation, "men of courage" refused to accept handouts, then a refusal to work, even if such refusal reflected an unwillingness to accept excessively onerous, exploitative terms, could be defined as evidence of moral failing. That *retirantes* could provide for their own sustenance through supervised labor seemed an ideal solution, one that promised to protect society as a whole, while bringing real benefits to both the backlanders themselves as well as the provinces of the north.

TROPICAL ABUNDANCE

Elite representations of the idle masses often invoked the richness of Brazil's land as an explanation. The masses never developed a work ethic because the land's prodigious production made for an easy life. This image of abundance and fertility—with roots dating back to the colonial period—remained beyond question, virtually constituting a national myth.[42] For example, an 1877 article in the journal of the National Industrial Aid Society said: "Brazil has an immense territory, extensive coasts, the greatest rivers in the world and majestic forests; it has fertile soil and rich mines."[43] The Fluminense Institute's director opined that "all those who knew Brazil . . . rightly considered it the richest part of the world because it has the most desired natural resources."[44]

A Conservative deputy from Maranhão, Augusto Olímpio Gomes de Castro, affirmed that "the lowest portion of our population . . . has no needs other than the natural ones, and those are the very ones the climate and fertility of the soil make easily obtainable."[45] Henrique Milet, a Pernambucan engineer, economist, and one-time sugar mill owner, who helped organize the 1878 agricultural congress in Recife, advanced the same analysis: "In a vast country like ours, where the sea, rivers and fields in return for very little labor give that which is necessary to satisfy the primordial needs of humanity, it is natural that only a small number of free men would subject themselves to a regime of constant labor."[46] Phrasing this conception more concretely, Milet remarked that he many times had heard "his fellow agriculturalists lament that there were shellfish in the reefs, crabs in the swamps and game in the bush."[47]

The discourse of elites, then, represented the provinces of the north, and especially Ceará, as enjoying an advantageous natural environment. Antonio Marco de Macedo, the author of an 1871 book about drought in Ceará, asserted that inadequate rainfall, not an absence of soil fertility, had caused people in the high *sertão* to engage in stockraising instead of agriculture. The soil, he said, had "prodigious fertility," so much so that "often a single rain in a year sufficed to assure prosperity for their pastoral industry, and even for their small gardens to produce corn and other vegetables."[48] An imperial senator explained that the province's inhabitants had paid little attention to anti-drought measures because the land recovered rapidly with the onset of rains.[49] Guilherme Shüch Capanema spoke of Ceará's "proverbial healthfulness," and Viriato de Medeiros affirmed that the province always would be "an exceedingly fertile country." [50]

This conception provided not only a ready explanation for the backlanders' habitual aversion to toil, but a basis for seeing *sertanejos* as culpable, as contributors to the region's problems. They had failed to manage the land properly, and because of their improvidence and ignorance, the drought had caught them unprepared. This further justified the centrality of work relief and an ongoing concern with developing anti-drought public works projects. It also provided a rationale for seeing *retirantes* as something other than deserving poor who merited compassion. Furthermore, if a supremely fertile and healthful land could quickly regain what Leôncio de Carvalho termed its "exuberant fertility," then the simple onset of rains might suffice to end the need for assistance.[51] In turn, if living off public support had made the *sertanejos* reluctant to return to their former homes, a moral, responsible government ought to force them to do so. Back in their natural environment they would either "recover" their normal good habits, or continue to live easily off nature's bounty. In a country where the lands "so amply and generously compensate whatever labor of man," no former *retirante* would want for food or shelter.[52]

PROGRESS

Reflecting on droughts, floods, and other disasters of a "periodic character," Leôncio de Carvalho noted that typically humankind drew beneficial lessons for the future from past misfortunes. This, he asserted, seemed not to be the case in Brazil. As soon as the emergency ended, so too did all concern. Hence, the same problems once again arose, and once again government and private charity rushed in. Charity resolved immediate needs but not underlying causes, so the cycle of emergencies continued.[53] Manuel Buarque de Macedo echoed this sentiment, characterizing Brazil as "a country in which enthusiasm, even for useful things, does not last for more than twenty four hours."[54] Alvaro de Oliveira, a native of Ceará and professor of chemistry at the Polytechnical School, argued that indolence characterized all Brazilians, especially the nation's governments, "which only begin to deal with a problem when it is already too late to solve it."[55]

If drought itself remained unavoidable, informed human action could have an ameliorative effect. Leôncio de Carvalho noted measures suggested in the report submitted to him by an 1877 engineering commission sent to Ceará to investigate the problem of drought. These included construction of *açudes*, which would promote irrigation. At the same time, if stocked with fish, large *açudes* would introduce another element of subsistence for the region's people. Improved transportation infrastructure, especially railroads, also figured in the commission's report.[56]

Many of these suggestions, which were aired again in the Polytechnical gathering, harkened back to reports of an earlier commission sent to Ceará in 1861, which had among its members Guilherme Shüch Capanema and geographer Giacomo Raja Gabaglia.[57] The latter wrote a series of newspaper articles that were republished as a book in

1877.[58] Its title, "Essays on Some Improvements Tending toward the Prosperity of the Province of Ceará," suggested his outlook, for Gabaglia saw drought in terms of a broader *problematique*, one susceptible to solution through human action. He attacked what he saw as the two existing paradigms. One viewed Ceará as "the Job of the north, condemned by phenomena superior to the will of man," with flight in time of disaster as the only possible response.[59] In the other, all ameliorative measures awaited the onset of an emergency situation, with the government then "becoming like the generous father who opens his wallet for the prodigal son, who . . . has given no thought to the future."[60]

The scientists who wrote about drought typically saw it as an easily remediable problem. Viriato de Medeiros, who touted meteorological stations as a means of forecasting drought and thereby minimizing its devastating impacts, asserted that rather than climate, "inertia, ignorance, and lack of faith in science" constituted the real problem.[61] Capanema characterized the droughts as natural, unalterable periodic phenomena. The significant question, then, was how to attenuate the negative impacts of drought. The solution consisted of steps that "could easily be carried out with predictable results."[62] Elaborating on this theme in an article in the *Jornal do Comércio*, Capanema again stressed the relative simplicity of the issue, averring that it required nothing more than "foresight, perseverance, and common sense."[63] André Rebouças, an engineer and reformer who had also attended the Polytechnical gathering, cast the larger solution to the region's problems in terms of an obvious answer to an obvious question: "If in the province of Ceará, droughts alternate with floods, is not Nature clearly teaching us that it is necessary to create works so that superabundant rains will not cause damage, and to collect and maintain excess water for the years of drought?"[64]

The scientists suggested projects that ranged from the audacious—irrigation works involving canals, giant reservoirs, and diversion of the waters of the São Francisco River—to the ludicrous, as in planting so-called "rain trees" said to produce more atmospheric water than they took from the soil.[65] But they all viewed the problem as solvable through informed, rational actions, and stressed the importance and possibility of producing positive change. So Viriato de Medeiros suggested that a policy stressing improved ports, paving of city streets, and construction of railroads would see Ceará emerge from the drought better able to cope with future problems.[66] Similarly, André Rebouças opined that with implementation of a progressive policy, the drought of 1877 would be remembered by future generations as a "providential revolution, the alpha of all the reforms needed to elevate the region between the Parnahyba and the São Francisco to the highest level of prosperity."[67] In sum, said Rebouças, the nation would "reconquer the sertão."[68]

Sinimbu defended his administration's policy on that very basis of funding projects that promised future benefits. In a Senate session on October 23, 1879, commenting on imperially backed railroad construction, he remarked: "I already have had occasion to tell the Senate that it was not for the sake of mere luxury that . . . such roads were authorized, but under the pressure of an inevitable and urgent necessity to look to the future." [69]

This emphasis on progress and civilization, key concepts of nineteenth-century European thought, reflected tenets of the "Brazilian Enlightenment," which challenged the traditional "Catholic-conservative" outlook and stressed the use of science and education to transform the national reality.[70] Viewed broadly, its goal was to narrow the gap between Brazil and Europe, to "bring Brazil to the level of the century."[71] Evincing a new "critical spirit," Brazilian elites spoke knowingly of evolutionism and positivism and celebrated the promise of modern science. The intellectual appeal of the new currents of thought lay in their exposition of universal laws that guided progress. Both at home and abroad, the desire was to project a new national image of Brazil as a "modern, industrious, civilized, and scientific nation."[72]

Progress placed a premium on what was commonly understood to be a "rational" or "scientific" outlook, and elite discourse reflected both implicitly and explicitly many of the central understandings of a "scientific" point of view. Science provided the tools of mastery that enabled people to overcome the limits of their natural environment as well as to exploit more efficiently its resources. The dividing line between civilized and savage rested on the use of technology, machinery, and inanimate energy sources to "triumph" over nature. Uncivilized people lived off nature's bounty and remained entirely subject to the vagaries of climate. The observations of Milet and Olímpio de Castro regarding the "primitive" life style of the Brazilian masses clearly reflected this dyad, as did the critiques of Gabaglia and Capanema.

Brazilian intellectuals embraced, indeed appropriated, European developmentalist assumptions in part because these represented a communication code, a common language of the "civilized" world. At the same time, its appeal rested on its provision of scientific confirmation for a long-standing elite view of the masses. To many among the Brazilian elite, then, the drought evidenced the nation's backwardness, defined in part in terms of the uncivilized nature of the backlands and its people. For example, José Americo dos Santos, another of the Polytechnical participants, saw the *sertanejos* as living "a sort of nomadic existence," which caused them to have little concern for the material conditions of their life in the backlands. Their dwellings and other constructions gave the appearance "of great backwardness or of a very primitive civilization, if not an aspect of complete decadence." And even the normal dry seasons caused hardship, he said, as *fazendeiros* set their livestock loose on the *zona da mata*, and the *"matutos"* of the *sertão* set off to work on the sugar harvest.[73]

Americo dos Santos saw the masses' "indifference" as a major obstacle to national progress. This, combined with their ignorance and superstition, constituted a formidable barrier against which "the most well-founded arguments of men of science and philanthropy have to batter infinite times in order to open a breach, and convince them of the efficacy of the measures that are suggested to them for their own well-being."[74] Raja Gabaglia had an even harsher critique of the drought-stricken *cearense* backlanders,"up to their ears in misery and hunger, without any education through labor, accustomed to ease in feeding themselves, and dominated by religious fanaticism."[75] Americo do Santos believed that this barbarism argued for railroad construction: "It could be said almost without fear of error that for every kilometer a railroad advances into the interior, civilization penetrates ten kilometers."[76] André Rebouças's phrase reconquering the backlands partook of this same outlook. "Conquered" previously—that is, wrested from their original barbarous indigenous inhabitants—the still primitive, unproductive backlands required the civilizing influence of modern scientific practices.

FRAUD AND FINANCES

From the earliest days of the Sinimbu administration, the linking of fraud and expenditures for drought relief had formed a consistent thread in drought discourse. Defending his circular of October 14, 1878 that ordered limits on relief, Leôncio de Carvalho affirmed that it was not intended to end relief to "those unfortunate persons whose penury made them truly worthy of it." Rather, it aimed at those who "under the pretext of aiding the poor, . . . undeservedly, indeed scandalously" used relief funds for their personal gain.[77] His *relatório* also expressed outrage at the behavior of these venal profiteers, and noted his administration's stern advice to the provincial presidents to employ careful accounting and oversight.[78] And speaking to the National Legislative Assembly, Leôncio referred to the lack of probity among some provincial relief officials and characterized those individuals as "frock-coated thieves in kidskin gloves."[79]

In January 1879 the Chamber of Deputies moved to consider an additional credit of forty thousand *contos* "to aid the provinces scourged by the drought."[80] Martinho Alvares da Silva Campos, a deputy from Minas Gerais, acknowledged the government's obligation to do everything possible to aid the "unfortunate inhabitants of those provinces," but he also asserted the necessity of strict supervision and inspection, especially given the shaky state of the nation's finances.[81] He expressed concern regarding statements made by Leôncio de Carvalho that "revealed serious abuses in the distribution of relief," abuses that had been noted as well by the press. Campos remarked that if "frock-coated thieves" had been "feeding off the drought calamity," they ought to be brought to justice and forced to return "the fruit of this rapine."[82] How could the Assembly vote on new credits without first learning from the minister of the empire what steps had been taken to end such abuses? He also alluded to an assertion by Jaguaribe regarding colossal fortunes being made from relief in Ceará. Expounding further on this theme in a subsequent session, Campos declared that the government was in grave difficulty and had no funds other than paper money. He concluded by demanding an accounting for expenditures made in Ceará.[83]

Speaking in response, Ceará's Antonio Joaquim Rodrígues Júnior strongly supported the forty thousand *conto* credit, but nonetheless criticized the government for failing to monitor the relief process and to establish enforcement mechanisms to correct abuses. Abuses left unpunished, he warned, simply encouraged more fraud.[84]

Over the next few months, chaotic conditions in Rio Grande do Norte and persistent reports of fraud led Finance Minister Silveira Martins to send a treasury agent there. That agent soon became locked in battle with provincial officials, including the sitting president and the vice president who succeeded him.[85] Later, as accusations of improprieties in Rio Grande do Norte continued, along with denunciations of similar problems in Ceará, the finance ministry, now headed by Afonso Celso de Assis Figueiredo, stepped up efforts to contain ever-mounting relief expenditures. In April 1879, he sent Fabiano Alexandrino dos Reis Quadros to Ceará to check the books. Quadros found exaggerated amounts allotted for food relief and noted various public works projects that seemed unrelated to relief. Afonso Celso then informed Leôncio de Carvalho that Quadros had concluded that works were being carried out in Ceará that would have no justification even in times of prosperity.[86]

Several months later, questions of fiscal impropriety resonated throughout the sessions of the National Legislative Assembly. Speaking in the Chamber of Deputies in May 1879, Manuel Buarque de Macedo referred to news stories regarding public works that seemed inappropriate uses of relief funds.[87] Pointing to the large sums already spent and the prospect that these would continue to grow, Buarque de Macedo expressed concern that if matters continued apace, the nation soon would run out of funds. So, while acknowledging the dominant truth that so long as there were drought and people in need the government had an obligation to respond, he observed: "If we are condemned to sacrifice ourselves because of those sad events in the provinces of the north, then we all will sacrifice ourselves, but let us at least be certain that there is no way to minimize those expenses."[88]

The possibility of realizing savings without sacrificing the needs of the provinces of the north also animated Minas Gerais deputy Felicio dos Santos who applauded Buarque de Macedo's position as a welcome effort to see the drought through a "prism other than sentimentality."[89] He pointed subsequently to the sixty *contos* already expended on the drought and stressed the importance of gauging to what extent these expenses had been necessary. Here, he noted that each of the provinces had received in relief much more than they produced. In fact, Ceará and Rio Grande do Norte had realized through imperial relief funds more than three times the income they produced for themselves during their best non-drought years![90]

Even Finance Minister Afonso Celso de Assis Figueiredo argued that current levels of drought spending could not be maintained without jeopardizing the nation's finances for years to come. He also acknowledged that fraud certainly had occurred, though he minimized its dimensions. And, finally, he suggested that if drought expenditures did not soon end, those provinces presently sacrificing to send relief to the north would themselves be in need of assistance.[91]

REDEFINING THE DROUGHT

By the time of the October 1879 legislative sessions, with electoral reform still unresolved and the future of his ministry hanging in the balance, Sinimbu found himself forced to request additional credits for relief, despite several official cut-off proclamations. Senate discussions of the drought increasingly turned on a cost/benefit assessment of government relief. Pernambuco's João Alfredo Correia de Oliveira noted a credit first set at ten thousand *contos* in February, 1879—a time when the government averred that the drought was diminishing—that the Chamber of Deputies doubled when it considered the proposal in May. When the relevant Senate commission took this up in August, it approved the increase, but noted that expenses had already exceeded that amount. Correia then related the commission's concern regarding defalcation of relief funds due to inadequate supervision, and its belief that relief would have required far less money had the administration exercised more careful oversight.[92] To general laughter, he also derisively observed that Ceará had a "treasurer general of public relief."[93] Also engaging in the heated discussion regarding additional relief credits, Rio Grande do Norte senator Diogo Velho de Cavalcanti read from some public documents detailing an enormous train of abuses at a *retirante* colony in that province and charged that it represented "officially organized misery, regularized abuse . . . [and] documented administrative scandal."[94]

Jaguaribe, who long had been scorning the administration's efforts at exercising oversight and its failure to clean up the relief process, added his voice to this discussion. Speaking now of the various problems adduced by Diogo Velho, especially those related to the probity of relief officials, Jaguaribe asserted that the government's response had produced only cosmetic changes: "There was simply a change in personnel; in all these lodging places the large scale diversion of public monies proceeded."[95] The senator concluded by asserting that persons who one day were beggars, the next became wealthy.[96] This formulation inverted one that Jaguaribe himself had employed earlier in the drought in arguing in favor of relief, when he suggested that once wealthy families had become reduced to penury. So, if the drought itself had reduced formerly respectable elements of society to misery, drought relief had unjustly elevated the formerly miserable!

The Senate session of October 23, 1879, which continued the discussion of additional credits, witnessed a thoroughgoing attack on administration policy by powerful Conservative senators, including Jaguaribe and Correia, joined by the Goiás Liberal José Inácio Silveira da Motta. The terms of their critique clearly evidenced a redefinition of the drought emergency and government relief. Correia styled the constitutional guarantee of aid a "magnanimous provision" but questioned what this had meant in practice. Drought relief, said Correia, had become "the expenditure of enormous sums of money without any oversight." This had destroyed the budget and necessitated new taxes. The further result of this supposed humanitarian assistance, said Correia, "to judge by what I have heard in this house and read in the press, has been to enable some people to become wealthy."[97] He attacked as well the practice of provincial presidents' opening credits on their own authority, then funding public projects of dubious validity. After detailing some examples from Ceará and Rio Grande do Norte, he again drew a distinction between those types of relief expenditures that did indeed conform to the intent and spirit of the constitution, and those that simply lined the pockets of dishonorable individuals.[98] Correia concluded by asking: "what are the fruits that we have harvested from the government's manner of proceeding in this question of public relief?" And in answering that question, he stressed not only the fabulous sums of public money "hurled into the whirlwind" but also the "agglomerations of large numbers of *retirantes* at various points of the Empire, threatening public safety."[99]

At that point, Silveira da Motta joined the fray. Like Correia, he pointed to the disastrous impact of drought expenditures on both the nation's finances and its ability to craft a reasonable national budget. He warned that continued heavy relief expenditures would produce commercial and industrial crises, "with all their vile aspects."[100] He also noted the fundamental imbalance of the present situation. The continuing flow of government monies to the north necessitated new taxes. People would tire of paying these heavy imposts, he predicted, recognizing that it simply was not right to impoverish an entire nation "because of two or three provinces where the improvident government has not known how to distribute public relief."[101] He further questioned the efficacy of government policy by focusing on its results, repeating Correia's assertion that years of throwing public money into drought relief had produced potentially dangerous masses of *retirantes* in the littoral.

Expounding on this point, Silveira da Motta directly ascribed this situation to the cupidity of those who profited from supplying the *retirantes*. He noted that the government itself, mindful of the large numbers of *retirantes* in the littoral, had cited the threats and actuality of *retirante* uprisings to argue against an abrupt cessation of relief. Silveira da Mota claimed that dealers in relief supplies had deliberately maintained those populations because they profited so mightily. Confronted with the prospect of losing this rich source of income, they actually incited *retirantes* to engage in these disorders. "The true mutineers of the *retirantes*," he declared, "are the potentates of Ceará and of the [other] provinces where relief is distributed."[102]

That the whole nation had borne enormous sacrifice for the sake of a few provinces assumed the status of conventional wisdom in the later days of the drought. Comments about the outrageously high level of these expenses increasingly punctuated discussions of government policy. Cândido Mendes de Almeida, a senator from Marnahão, remarked, "Paraguay is being substituted by Ceará," likening the empire's expenses for *cearense* relief to those the nation had borne in the War of the Triple Alliance.[103] Another Senator subsequently picked up the analogy, observing that the nation already had spent a fifth of what that war had cost, to which Mendes de Almeida quickly added, "and the remainder is on its way."[104] Jaguaribe asserted that in one year's time the drought had absorbed almost the entire revenue of the nation. And, he thundered, "it is imperative to put an end to this state of affairs."[105]

Both Silveira da Mota and Jaguaribe also spoke of the negative social impacts of drought relief. Silveira da Mota noted that the fraudulent use of relief funds had enabled many lower class people to gain wealth. Jaguaribe again spoke of "men who prior to the drought lived in extreme poverty, who today are wealthy, flaunt luxury, and take pleasure trips."[106] He further expressed concern that if unchecked, continued relief would create an "official proletariat," a group that to this day "happily never existed in this country," but had been known in ancient Rome, and continued in the present in England in the class known as paupers.[107] Silveira da Mota shared that specific fear of a class permanently maintained by government funds, for already the *retirantes* had become accustomed to that kind of existence. Furthermore, this occurred "through the expenses of those classes that have worked, and through their labor accumulated capital."[108]

Senators also hit hard at issues of electoral fraud, a particularly damaging indictment of the Sinimbu ministry given its mission of electoral reform. Jaguaribe charged that the administration maintained Ceará president José Julio de Albuquerque Barros because of his "talent for converting the dead and ambulatory mummies into electors."[109] And Silveira de Mota remarked that while the administration of relief services in Ceará had been poorly organized, the "electoral service had been well organized indeed."[110]

A DELICATE DISCURSIVE BALANCE

As the drought dragged on and the demand for additional relief credits and expenditures became a constant feature of legislative sessions, the delicate discursive balance shifted ever more strongly away from its early emphasis on the constitutional and moral necessity of compassion. To be sure, tales of suffering *retirantes* might still be recounted, and the deaths of *sertanejo* women and children retained their emotive power. However, counter images gained increased force. Long after his departure from the ministry Leôncio de Carvalho's reference to "frock-coated thieves" remained a popular rhetorical device. So too, the initial reports of fraud in resettlement colonies later served as handy symbols for a corrupted relief system. At the same time, new revelations of waste and fraud, joined to accusations that some provincial presidents had thoroughly politicized the relief process at the expense of the legitimate needs of *retirantes*, commanded increased attention in the National Legislative Assembly. And the sacrifice of the nation on behalf of the stricken provinces of the north, it was said, had become far greater than that endured by the region's inhabitants.

In many cases, representatives of the provinces of the north themselves launched the most severe critiques of drought relief. Throughout the drought, as native sons of the region they had laid special claims to authority. For example, a representative from Piauí speaking in the Chamber of Deputies in 1879 asserted that "those who had not themselves directly seen the horrors . . . cannot imagine the degree of misery unleashed."[111] Now, in speaking out against the relief process, they gave greater credibility to the proposition that relief had outlived its usefulness.

These shifting stances formed a delegitimizing discourse that issued from opponents of continued relief. While acknowledging the state's obligation to the deserving poor, they portrayed the mass of *retirantes* as idlers and, even worse, as threats to public order. Powerful expressive words and phrases peppered this new discourse. Frock-coated thieves, drought-spawned "nabobs" and voracious purveyors of goods became stock expressions that captured and communicated the perversion of what had begun as a well-intentioned effort to aid the unfortunate victims of drought. Inveighing against corruption and the defalcation of public funds, these critics suggested that government policy brought benefits to unworthy elements while failing to serve those *sertanejos* who truly merited support. Stress on the fabulous amount of money absorbed by the relief process and the degree to which this imperiled the nation's finances minimized the moral basis for relief, for it decentered the hardship and sacrifice of *retirantes*. Sacrifice instead became the lot of the entire Brazilian nation, which had responded generously and selflessly, but now found itself verging on bankruptcy. Surely the needs of the entire nation took precedence over those of a single region.

The political elite's new representation even called into question the very existence of the drought. Rather than the product of climate, it had become an artificial emergency. Early on, Jaguaribe had suggested the possibility that in the future there might be attempts to "invent a drought," so profitable had this one proven to certain provincial interests.[112] Others now embraced that concept. Silveira da Mota asserted that drought relief represented naught but an artifice to drain imperial funds, and that the situation of many *retirantes*—certainly those lodged in colonies and congregating in littoral locations—was artificial, rather than an inevitable or natural result of the drought. Senator Cruz Machado now suggested that the volume of drought funds varied in keeping with electoral needs in various of the provinces of the north. Indeed, he asserted that eliminating elections would quickly end the drought![113]

CHAPTER 2

ANOTHER NORTHEAST

An almost ritualized invocation of the healthful, exuberantly fertile backlands marked the discourse of legislators, imperial officials, and scientists who focused on problems of drought and development in the provinces of the north. So too did an emphasis on the resulting ease of existence for the area's inhabitants, seen as generating habitual patterns of idleness, an aversion to sustained, productive toil. Against the bedrock of these representations—an imagined *sertão*, and an imagined drought—members of the Cabinet and Legislative Assembly had both developed, critiqued, and ended relief policy. The failures of relief gained explanation through a set of stereotypical characters: profiteers; corrupt bureaucrats; venal local politicians; and lazy, immoral *retirantes*.

This chapter assays the Great Drought from a different perspective, one that measures the *sertão* of the legislators and scientists against that of the *sertanejos*. It revisits drought relief policy at this other level of reality and views its functioning in the context of the constraints—both physical and institutional—of a land of harsh soils and irregular climate, with masses of people, frequently malnourished and disease-ridden, living in relations of production that mostly provided but a marginal existence. In so doing, the discursive reality of elites, whether explaining policy problems in terms of lazy, immoral *retirantes*, or celebrating policy success in averting starvation and providing relief to those in need, emerges as both flawed and self-serving. The ease of coping with the massive problems generated by the Great Drought and effecting change, so dominant a strain in the proposals of scientists, seems hopelessly naive. It becomes evident as well that the discourse of provincial elites mirrored that of the national elites in Rio de Janeiro, especially in constructing a reality that promoted the ruthless exploitation of *retirante* labor.

A LITTLE-KNOWN LAND

In the national legislative assembly, representatives of northern provinces had declared that only those who actually had seen a drought close up could speak knowledgeably about it. Some scientists had also stressed their own first-hand experience in one or another northern locale.[1] But even those who lived in the provinces of the north were not fully acquainted with the region's climate and natural endowment. Available meteorological information consisted of a few rainfall series for littoral locations in Ceará and Pernambuco.[2] Henrique de Beaurepaire Rohan pointed out that many of the rivers indicated on maps and included in published books really had no natural source feeding them, nor a permanent course.[3] No comprehensive geological surveys existed and the topographic mapping of the nation remained incomplete. Cândido Mendes de Almeida, compiler of the nation's 1868 *Atlas*, lamented the "deficiencies of topographic studies" in Brazil.[4] Even "scientific" estimates of the nation's total area varied considerably.[5] Not surprsingly, then, so too did estimates of the area of individual provinces.[6]

In his *Ensaio Estatístico*, Thomaz Pompeu de Souza Brasil, the leading authority on land formations and climate in his native Ceará, identified three climate zones in the province: the humid littoral; the cooler but less humid mountains; and the hot, dry *sertão*—a division subsequently followed by all those writing about Ceará's climate.[7] By extension, it stands as the base of the common tripartite classification of northeastern climate zones and land forms: the *zona da mata*, *agreste*, and *sertão*.

Although Pompeu's geography noted the existence of elevated *brejos* and moister river valleys, at the time of the Great Drought neither the term *agreste* nor its identification as a separate climate or cultural zone had become well established.[8] The term *"agreste"* did surface occasionally in official reports, but elites conceptualized the drought provinces largely in terms of *sertão* and littoral. Better known because of its historic role in the process of settlement and its economic importance for the *grande lavoura*, the littoral or coast housed the region's few major cities, and enjoyed reasonably rapid and secure sea-borne communication with Rio de Janeiro. The *sertão*, remote and isolated, remained more of a mystery.

Complexity and contrast mark the vast expanse of the provinces of the north. Even the tripartite zonal division of the northeast masks the variation within each of the zones and their varying extent within each province. An outline of some of these differences among the provinces of the north with regard to land and climate is a necessary corrective to the grand generalizations of the imperial elite.[9] The nature of that land itself, both in terms of climate—especially patterns of rainfall—and the fertility of its soils also merits attention, for here, too, physical reality diverges sharply from the imagined north of the national elite.

AN INITIAL ORIENTATION

In general, moving inland from the coast rainfall diminishes and elevations rise. The most significant of the mountain systems is the Borborema, about one thousand meters at its greatest height, which breaks the coastal zone of Paraíba and Pernambuco.[10] Other significant uplands are the *chapadas*, high plains with a more limited extent than true *planaltos* like the Borborema.[11] Agricultural settlements dot various of these smaller uplands, serving as refuges from the harsh conditions of the dry *sertão*. At some high elevations, moist southeastern air produces levels of humidity and rainfall that approximate those of the *zona da mata*.[12] These areas are known as *brejos*, a word also applied to low-lying marsh lands.[13]

As Beaurepaire Rohan noted, maps indicated the existence of numerous rivers in the provinces of the north, but the "true" rivers, those fed by perennial sources numbered only three, the Parnaíba, Jaguaribe and São Francisco. The Parnaíba, with some 668 kilometers of navigable waters, marks the western boundary between Piauí and Maranhão, "flowing for most of its course through level, more or less swampy lands, grown up with thick bushes and groves of carnahuba and piassaba palms."[14] The Jaguaribe, which figured in the ambitious irrigation schemes of several scientists, meanders in a northeasterly fashion across eastern Ceará, flowing past the city of Aracatí into the Atlantic. Greatest of the three, and Brazil's third ranking river in terms of navigable waters, the São Francisco originates in the highlands of Minas Gerais. The course of its 2,700 kilometers flows in a northeasterly direction through Bahia, then more sharply east through the southwestern limit of Pernambuco and curving south to mark the border between Alagoas and Sergipe.

Even those three "true" rivers experienced decreasing water levels during normal dry seasons, dropping still further during periods of extended drought.[15] For example, the São Francisco's water level could drop by some nine meters. Furthermore, during the dry season in the sertão, "all of its affluents" there dry up.[16] The pattern of rising and drying proves more dramatic with the various rivers whose existence derives solely from seasonal rains. Andrade calls attention to the valleys of the "*sertão* rivers," like those of Rio Grande do Norte's Mossoró and Açu rivers, and the Acararú in Ceará. Their beds dry most of the

25

Map 2. The Drought Provinces: Climate Zones

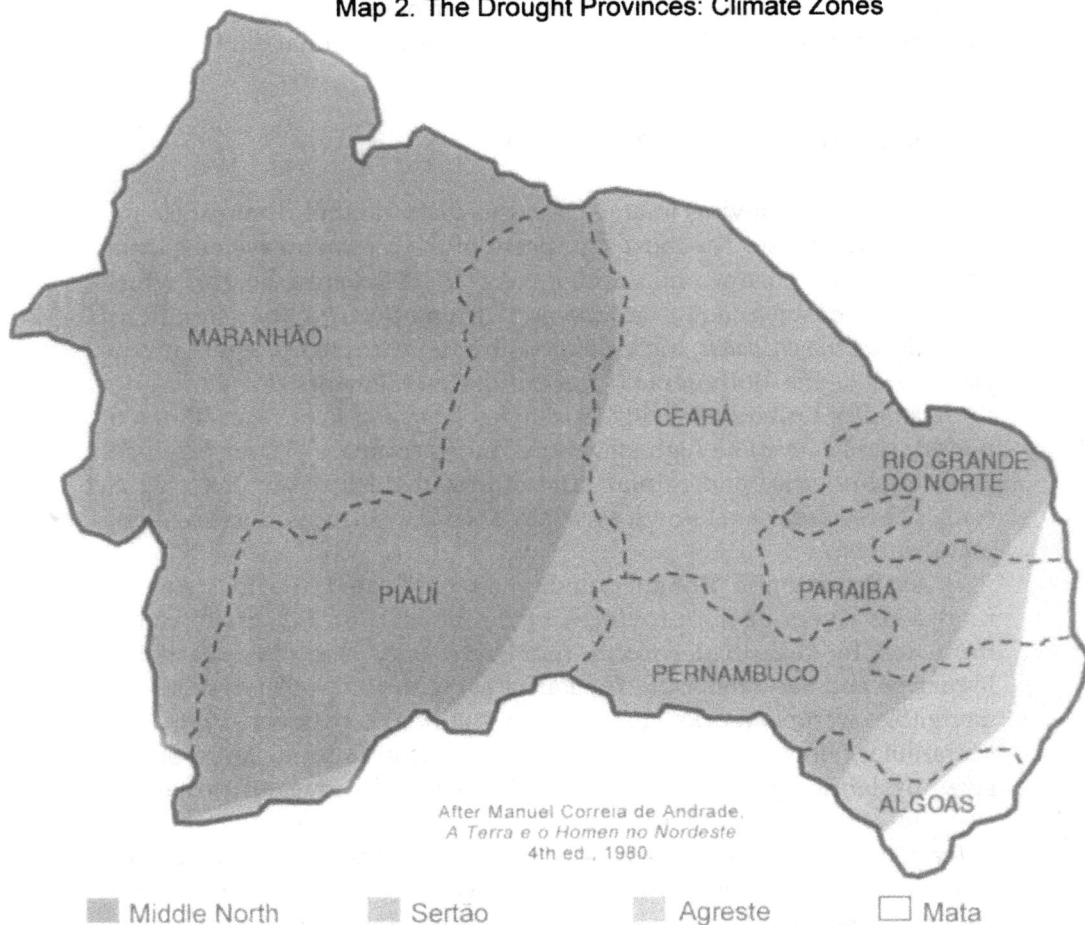

MARANHÃO

CEARÁ

RIO GRANDE
DO NORTE

PIAUÍ

PARAÍBA

PERNAMBUCO

ALGOAS

After Manuel Correia de Andrade,
A Terra e o Homen no Nordeste
4th ed., 1980.

▓ Middle North   ▓ Sertão   ▓ Agreste   ☐ Mata

year, when swollen with rain they might rapidly overflow, with "valleys . . . up to 10 kilometers in width . . .[and] depressions transformed into lakes."[17] Although flooding often posed a serious threat, it also enriched submerged areas. As the waters receded, they left *vazantes*, moist areas suitable for agriculture.

RAINFALL AND CLIMATE ZONES

The absence of normal rainfall defined drought. And, as we will see, at various times during the years of the Great Drought, when rains did fall, they were seen as signs that drought was at an end. Yet, beyond the general perception of the existence of alternating wet and dry seasons, the actual patterns of precipitation in both the *agreste* and *sertão* largely remained unknown.

As northeastern Brazil is an equatorial area, seasonal variation witnesses little change in temperatures, but significant alternations in rainfall. It becomes important to remember that during times of normal weather, the interior of northeastern Brazil always passes through a period where rains are relatively sparse or almost entirely absent. Drought, then, refers to the failure of precipitation during the rainy season. Hence, a single season of drought sums to a full 18 months without rain (the drought season sandwiched between two normal dry seasons). This alone suggests how serious an impact even a single season of drought would have, let alone the mutiple failed rainy seasons that defined the Great Drought.

The hot, humid, coastal zone receives annual precipitation in excess of two thousand millimeters. The rainy season usually begins in October with the light rains known as the *chuvas de caju* (cashew rains), with heavier rains falling from December through April. Varying in width from one hundred to two hundred kilometers, the coastal zone runs from Rio Grande do Norte through Alagoas.[18] Its greatest width is in Pernambuco.[19] To the north, in Paraíba and Rio Grande do Norte, river lowlands mark the narrow limits of this zone and of sugarcane. Moving slightly further north and then westward from Natal, both the *zona da mata* and the *agreste* end. In other words, much of Rio Grande do Norte and all of Ceará have no true *zona da mata*.

The *agreste*, which marks the transition between the *zona da mata* and *sertão*, "occupies the eastern portion of the Borborema Plateau, and extends toward the mountains of Rio Grande do Norte and the southern part of Alagoas."[20] Delineated by the Borborema, the *agreste* parallels the north-south extent of the *zona da mata*, ending to the north of Natal. As the term "transition" implies, the *agreste* is heterogeneous:"what characterizes the Agreste is the diversity of landscape over short distances; it is almost the Northeast in miniature, with very dry and very humid areas."[21] So, for example, not all high elevations enjoy good rainfall. While the eastern or windward slope of the Borborema is an area of *brejos*, the leeward slope becomes dry *sertão*.

Colonized initially by cattle ranchers, the *agreste* became an area of small holdings and mixed agriculture, including cotton cultivation. Since the *agreste* is defined as much by economic activity as geography, its spatial extent remains subject to change.[22] At the time of the Great Drought, some portions of today's agreste were seen individually in terms of *serras*, or mountains, while the balance largely belonged to the *zona da mata*.

By far the most extensive of the three zones, the backlands area embraces almost the entirety of Ceará, all but a thin eastern portion of Rio Grande do Norte, and those parts of Pernambuco, Paraíba, and Alagoas extending from the western slope of the Borborema. Among these latter three, Pernambuco's *sertão* is the most extensive, followed by that of Paraíba. Alagoas's *sertão*, smaller and moister, offers better possibilities for agriculture. Because of that, it has been dubbed the "fillet of the Northeast."[23] In Ceará and over much of Rio Grande do Norte the *sertão* reaches almost to the coast. Andrade notes that Mossoró, 50 kilometers from the coast, "is a city of the Sertão, the inhabitants consider themselves sertanejos, and the landscape of the area is typical of the Sertão."[24] He points as well to the late nineteenth-century *cearense* scholar Rodolfo Theophilo's observation: "that part of the interior that is not made up of mountains is called *sertão*."[25]

The *sertão*'s rainy season runs from January through early July, but most precipitation occurs between February and April. Rains "fall chiefly in the form of great cloudbursts," producing floods and soil erosion.[26] The general aridity and high temperatures quickly evaporate rainwater, thereby minimizing its utility for agriculture.

Cattle ranching had settled the *sertão* and provided a stimulus to agricultural production in the *agreste*. The need to drive cattle to market created trails out of the backlands toward the coast, thereby tracing the basic overland road system of the region. That same cattle drive sparked the development and growth of *agreste* towns as way stations and as regional fairs or markets. Cattle raising itself also took place within the confines of the *agreste*, again indicative of the diversity of that zone. In the *sertão*, due to the greater aridity, livestock raising occurred on a more expansive scale than in the *agreste*.[27]

The cowhands of the north wore long leather coats and chaps, as well as leather boots and hats to protect themselves from the spiny cactus-like caatinga, a scrub vegetation often referred to as "thorn forest." Their distinctive appearance in towns and markets further buttressed the perception of a "leather civilization," as characteristic of the *sertão*.

The perceptual absence of an *agreste* combined with the imagic power of ranches and leather-clad *vaqueiros* (cow hands) deemphasized the importance of agriculture to the lives of the backlanders.[28] One attender of the Recife agricultural congress explained the laziness of the *sertanejos* as an inherent product of cattle raising. He pointed out that save for some few times in the year, for example, round-up, *vaqueiros* had nothing to do.[29] At that very time, however, the majority of non-coastal dwellers in the provinces of the north engaged in subsistence farming rather than ranching. Since rains insufficient for agriculture could produce adequate pasturage, the perceptual importance of cattle raising may have minimized a sense of drought's real damage.

The unitary elite image also masked the reality of multiple *sertões*. Pediplains marked by caatinga constitute the most extensive area of the *sertão*.[30] River valleys, plateaus, and mountain peaks break these pediplains. Some of the mountains receive good rainfall, and their cooler temperatures reduce moisture lost through evaporation. For example, in the midst of a dry, caatinga-covered pediplain in Paraíba, the Teixeira mountain has lush vegetation.

In all those moister areas, agriculture formed a significant activity for the *sertanejos*. This included cultivation of manioc, the tuber from which they made *farinha*, the flour that along with beans and maize formed the major staples of their diet. Sugarcane cultivation and production of raw sugar also took place in some of these climatically advantaged areas of the *sertão*. As Andrade reminds us, small mills, typically animal-driven, "were crushing creole cane in the Cariri of Ceará" in 1731. And, "almost all the Sertão mountain area," as well as lands bordering the São Francisco, "excelled in this kind of raw sugar production."[31] Around the mid-nineteenth century, moist areas within the *sertão* also supported the growing of cotton and coffee.

The dominant perception of a rich, fertile land did not accurately capture the physical reality of the drought region. Indeed, rather than a land with prodigious soils that quickly recover from drought, in the words of a contemporary expert, this "region is a parched upland, with bare rock pavements and coarse soils which for the most part are saline."[32] The soils' salty nature is another indication of the harsh climate regime. With rates of potential evapotranspiration exceeding annual rainfall, "upward percolation of water in the soils . . . is more common than is downward movement of rain water," and thus salts are brought up to the surface.[33] Salts naturally occur over a broad swath of the *cearense* and *riograndense* coast, a product of climate and tidal variations. Though salting of beef became an important economic activity in the area, the sandy soils, wind-blown dunes, and narrowness of the coastal strip hampered agriculture, limiting it to the river banks.[34]

Over large portions of the *sertão*, the presence of extensive rocks and cobbles reduced the utility of plows, as did the thinness of the soil, which also contributed to high rates of erosion.[35] To some extent, then, the traditional *sertanejo* practice of clearing the land by burning and using the hoe rather than the plow proved well-suited to the soils of the *sertão*. Burning added some fertiliizing nutrients to the soil. Deep plowing would have promoted erosion of the fertile top layer. Similarly, free-range grazing of cattle arose in part because of the *sertão*'s lack of fertility. It was the only economically viable activity in that harsh environment.[36]

LAND HOLDING

Of the agriculturalists in the *agreste* and *sertão*, probably fewer than 5 percent were independent small-holders. The rest worked land owned by others under a variety of exchange relations.[37] *Agregados* had the most precarious position, for only the estate owner's volition allowed them access to the land. *Agregados* fulfilled the social function of retainers, symbolizing the power and prestige of landowners. Landowners used *agregados* as agents of violence for both economic and electoral purposes and as a pool of available labor. *Moradores*, though defined officially as renters, in most respects differed little from *agregados*. True renters, *rendeiros* and *foreiros*, might possess some capital, though not enough to purchase an economically viable holding. But with access to large properties through rent, they could enjoy at least a middling economic standard and might themselves have other landless people working for them. In other cases, however, those "renters" might be naught but sharecroppers. Other nomenclature for the landless—including *parceiros* and *meieros*—indicates various types of dependent situations characterized by sharecropping or labor exchange.[38]

Whatever the terminology, dependence remained the key feature, for ultimately all such arrangements existed at the pleasure of the landowner, who, as a member of the elite, controlled not only his own land, but access to the legal system as well. Securing redress for breach of contract by a *fazendeiro*, assuming that a formal written agreement existed, remained a virtual impossibility for non-elite members of society. Conversely, powerful landowners could engage in heinous acts without penalty. In 1877, for example, João de Albuquerque Maranhão Cunhaú went with a group of thirty armed men to dislodge *moradores* from his property in Baía Formosa in Rio Grande do Norte. The *moradores* resisted, shots were exchanged, and deaths resulted. Cunhaú, brought to Natal to face justice, walked away a free man.[39] With that type of hierarchy as a fundamental societal principle, even times of economic prosperity might fail to produce any leavening effect on the conditions of the masses. For example, as pointed out by Linda Lewin, the 1860s cotton boom produced a system known as *sujeição*, literally "subjugation," which worked against freeholding and made traditional dependent labor arrangements even more onerous.[40]

Beyond their obligations to landowners, subsistence farmers had to provide for their own survival. The *sertão*'s poor soils and unreliable rainfall certainly conspired to limit surplus. While *brejos* and *vazantes* offered better physical conditions, the land tenure system still restricted productivity, especially in that owners often rented out the most marginal of their lands. Elites emphasized knowledge base and outlook as essential to the use of improved agricultural techniques, but prevailing class relations kept both knowledge and capital beyond the reach of the dependent masses. Precarious tenure on the land further militated against investments that elites saw as rational. Even assuming the availability of resources, what sense did it make to improve a property that could be taken away by the locally powerful?

Portraying the nineteenth-century socioeconomic structure of the important and relatively prosperous market town of Campina Grande in Paraíba, Joan Meznar suggests that those of "middling wealth" perhaps made up the majority of the population. But her description of this group clearly indicates the rather minimal levels of their middling existence. They "either owned or rented small plots of land from which they coaxed their family's sustenance and a small surplus to sell at the local markets."[41] Not surprisingly, then, Meznar also tells us that "most nineteenth century *campinenses* were poor."[42] Given low levels of productivity and labor obligations to owners, the "primitive" life style of *sertanejos* reflected the reality of deprivation and dependence rather than the volitional expression of "uncivilized" or "indolent" people. People best described as "impoverished dirt farmers" were not comfortably living off the fat of the land.[43]

Even *vaqueiros*, who by many measures enjoyed considerable freedom and a measure of economic success, scarcely enjoyed an easy existence. The imagic view of free-ranging cattle with the round-up and drive as the only times of sustained labor ignored the myriad tasks involved in ranching and the fact that *vaqueiros* also might have to engage in subsistence agriculture. It further failed to recognize a key aspect of the cattle business as practiced at that time: a very limited number of *vaqueiros* cared for an exceedingly large number of cattle. Even with the minimal nature of that care, the task as a whole remained challenging, especially considering the difficulties imposed by travel across difficult terrain. The common belief that the masses did not labor reflected erroneous assumptions about the nature of the land and people, and an elite definition of productive labor that stressed disciplined or controlled relationships where the worker remained dependent.

A HEALTHFUL LAND?

If the land was difficult and conditions of life reflected the harshness of that environment, what of its healthfulness? Here, too, questions of data, definition, and judgment come into play. In general, no reliable data for mortality or total incidence of disease existed. Isolation, absence of health professionals, and a bureaucracy oriented toward patronage rather than service and record keeping conspired to render conditions in the *sertão* invisible even to coastal elites who lived in the provinces of the north.[44] For the intelligentsia of Rio de Janeiro, the *sertão* remained more a construction of imagination than of fact.

It seems likely, then, that characterizations of the *sertão* as a healthful environment rested mostly on prevailing assumptions regarding the relationship between climate and disease. Nineteenth-century medicine upheld the inherent unhealthfulness of tropical climates. The experience of western Europeans in Africa, where heat, humidity, and high mortality from yellow fever and malaria accompanied one another caused them to dub that continent "the white man's grave."[45] It led them to assume a causal link between such climates and both disease and lower levels of development. Since epidemiology had not progressed to the point of isolating the causes of those tropical diseases, any number of theories abounded. Nancy Stepan points out that "because yellow fever often occurred with the arrival of European ships from cold climates, the hot climate of Brazil was believed to be one cause of the disease."[46] European climates, cooler and dryer, clearly seemed superior. Though the *sertão* certainly experienced high daytime temperatures, it enjoyed cooler, pleasant evenings and, at all times, low humidity.

Another basis for the presumed salubrity of the *sertão* rested on its seeming immunity to the epidemic diseases that frequently visited coastal settlements. When outbreaks of smallpox, malaria, and tuberculosis occurred, many wealthier inhabitants abandoned coastal settlements choosing, by preference, the cooler, less humid, and therefore healthier highland locations. Pedro II's summer palace in Petrópolis, only sixty-six kilometers from Rio de Janeiro, but some eight hundred meters higher in altitude, exemplifies this belief in the restorative power of cooler climates. Having built the Petrópolis palace in 1844, the emperor doubtless saw graphic confirmation of his wisdom when five years later the first great yellow fever epidemic struck Rio de Janeiro, affecting over a third of the city's population.[47]

Cooler airs were cleaner airs. One prominent school of medical thought, the infectionists, ascribed the incidence of numerous fevers and ailments to foul air and noxious odors. "Miasms," thought to be poisons "activated by the heat under conditions of crowding or dirt," held an important place in medical theory.[48]

Humid hot climates promoted decay and bad odors. In the *sertão*, however, the combination of aridity and high temperatures caused wastes to desiccate rather than rot.[49] The lower incidence of epidemic disease in the *sertão*, however, most likely reflected its lower population densities, scattered settlements, and isolation from the coast, all factors that would be altered radically by drought-spawned migration.

We ought also to question whether a healthful land automatically would produce healthy people. Even granting a lower incidence of certain highly visible diseases, it seems doubtful that the average *sertanejo* enjoyed good health. Nutrition and working conditions certainly factor into that equation. A variety of nutritious foods existed, including pumpkin and other gourds, as well as fruits, beef, milk, and vegetables. But, the seasonal nature of some foods and, above all, poverty, led to a heavy reliance on manioc flour, dried beef, and the clumps of coarse brown sugar known as *rapadura*.[50] Nutritional deficiencies resulted in stunted growth, reduced physical vigor, and short lives, while also producing high rates of beriberi, a significant cause of both infant and adult deaths. It seems probable, in fact, that the large number of infant deaths typically ascribed to various gastrointestinal problems really resulted from thiamine deficiency.[51] Drought further reduced the range of food choices, forcing an even greater dependence on *farinha* and *rapadura*, thereby increasing the incidence of conditions caused by vitamin deficiencies.[52]

Conditions of work and life, which included farming poor land, giving some days of labor to landlords, inadequate and unreliable supplies of water, no sanitary amenities, and an almost total absence of medical facilities and practitioners, certainly made for a difficult existence.[53] While elites saw the backlanders as healthy in comparison to the slaves and poor urban masses of the *zona da mata*, at best, "less impoverished" and "less disease-ridden" would seem more appropriate characterizations.

RESOURCES

The provinces of the north in general, and especially the small settlements of the *agreste* and *sertão*, certainly did not enjoy much fiscal health. The national government monopolized most sources of tax revenue, and in return provided funds to the provinces.[54] Politically powerful provinces usually managed to do well, while the weaker ones languished. Provinces that actively participated in national and internal commerce could supplement their incomes through taxes; those less developed commercially had few options. Save for Pernambuco, which in 1872 accounted for some 80 percent of their combined total income, the provinces of the north beset by drought enjoyed few resources beyond those provided by the national government.[55] Furthermore, by disorganizing agriculture and devastating livestock industries, the drought reduced provincial tax revenues.[56]

Whatever the levels of funding, capital cities took the lion's share. For example, Pernambuco's 1878 budget law authorized two-thirds of all funds budgeted for counties to Recife, even though it held no more than

11 percent of the province's population.[57] This pattern of domination evidenced itself in the developmental gap between provincial capitals—generally coastal, port cities—and the small towns and villages of the interior. So, for example, a resident from the interior of Pernambuco vividly expressed the contrast between his home town of Pesqueira, which had no real streets nor even a butcher shop, and Recife, replete with public lighting and streetcars.[58] Apart from those interior towns that served as sites of major *feiras* or markets, therefore, the various smaller localities scattered throughout the provinces of the north had neither the infrastructure nor the resources to deal with the devastating consequences of drought.[59]

Throughout the provinces of the north, when provincial presidents or central relief commissions sent instructions that rations ought be given only to the *retirantes*, local officials often noted in response that the vast majority of their populations were in need—whether *retirante* or regular residents. A county judge in Granito advised the president of Pernambuco, that excessive poverty existed there even before the arrival of *retirantes*.[60] A district judge in Pernambuco made a similar observation regarding the *municipio* of Salgueiro, noting that it had never been a "flourishing center," and that "almost everyone" among its population was indigent.[61]

RELIEF POLICY

If the confident assumptions of the scientists emerge as flawed when measured against the reality of the backlands, so too do many of the equally confident assertions of imperial government officials regarding the effectiveness of the relief effort. Viewed globally, commonalities in the experience of the several provinces emerge. The sheer magnitude of drought-spawned migration caused insurmountable problems. Even the best intentioned local relief commission could not compensate for an absence of the food, clothing, and medical facilities and practitioners needed to assure the lives of *retirantes*.

Consider, for example, the city of Penedo, situated in Alagoas on the banks of the São Francisco River. Steamers regularly stopped there, reflecting Penedo's active commerce with both Recife and Salvador, as well as its role as a market center for other settlements along the river.[62] In the words of United States naturalist Fred Hartt it was "quite a respectable little town of some 3,000 or 4,000 inhabitants."[63] In January 1878, the relief commission of Penedo informed the provincial president that five thousand *retirantes* had arrived within a single week![64] This new population element was desperately needy, and nearly five hundred *retirantes* were ill. Not surprisingly, the relief commission complained of supply problems and expressed concern because the *retirantes* "refused to leave."[65] In August 1877, Agua Branca, another *municipio* in Alagoas, found itself dealing with a sudden 20 percent increase in population, and it had no medical professionals to care for the sick.[66]

Various of the elevated areas in the *agreste* that enjoyed ample rain and, because of cooler temperatures, experienced less moisture evaporation, had gained population during the eighteenth century when drought migrants from the *sertão* decided to remain.[67] Such areas again became points for refuge during the Great Drought, as did the humid mountainous areas within the *sertão*. To the degree that a town enjoyed a "favored location" with regard to either the effects of drought or the presence of traditional routes from the *sertão* to the coast, it might find itself virtually invaded, not only by drought migrants from the remote *sertão*, but in a sort of domino effect, from nearby towns that were themselves experiencing difficulties.

Such was case of the village of Triumpho in the high Pernambucan *sertão* at about one thousand meters in the Baixa Verde mountain, some 450 kilometers from Recife, and near settlements in Paraíba and Ceará.[68] As the early months of the drought wore on, Triumpho received *retirantes* both from those provinces and from Rio Grande do Norte. By September 1877 almost no goods remained in its normally well-stocked public market. With harvest ended and in the midst of the normal dry season, the Triumpho relief commission struggled to maintain some warehoused foodstuffs against future adversity. But an even greater difficulty confronted the village. Desperate to save their own economic base, livestock owners from surrounding areas already denuded of pasturage had brought their cattle to Triumpho to graze. Those freely-grazing cattle were "destroying cane, manioc, and other plantings, reducing those who live exclusively from agriculture to the ultimate level of misery and despair."[69] Piauí's president reported his concerns about the province's condtion, and noted that the influx of *retirantes* from Ceará "grows daily."[70] Increased migration sparked by an ever-deepening drought narrowed an already thin margin of existence for many towns. As a result, the very resource base that had attracted *retirantes* to various "favored" locales incurred real damage. For example, in November 1878 Ceará's president remarked that several of the *serra* areas and river valleys continued to have sufficient water for farming, but the migration of so many *retirantes* to those places had caused "irreparable harm" to the remaining agriculture.[71]

As the direct impact of drought limited resources throughout an already poor region, relief supplied by the imperial government truly became a matter of life and death. In Ceará, toward the end of 1877 a county judge from São Matheus informed the provincial president that more than fifty people had died, and spoke of entire families being wiped out. He had been dispensing daily what little food he had at his disposal, "a little meat and some scraps of *rapadura*." There was no *farinha*, rice, or any other cereal, and as a result diarrhea had claimed many lives. He predicted that "without fail" by the month's end more than one hundred people would have died of starvation.[72] Writing in February 1878, the county council of Vila da Palma decribed the worthy poor as completely bereft of of any support, including private charity. Cattle-raising, the town's major economic activity, had been "destroyed" by the drought, and in desperation people were seeking survival by migrating. The council noted as well that there were several families whose little children "were dying of hunger."[73] Writing that same year, Ceará's president asserted that deaths caused by hunger had indeed occurred. Noting that children proved especially vulnerable, he remarked, "This is unfortunately a sad truth that cannot be denied."[74] Officials in Rio de Janeiro, however, consistently refused to accept that reality. At most they conceded that, weakened by their long journeys and affected by the difference in climate between their native *sertão* and the littoral, *retirantes* had more easily succumbed to disease.

PROBLEMS OF TRANSPORTATION

These bland assurances notwithstanding, government supplies certainly did not always reach those in need, and not only because of fraud or the actions of profiteers. Transportation proved a major problem throughout the provinces of the north. With only the São Francisco and Parnaíba providing riverine access, and the limited railroad network confined to Pernambuco and Ceará, the transport of goods to most non-coastal settlements involved travel along "roads" that in many cases were at best simply beaten dirt trails. The siting of many settlements further complicated travel. Writing in 1841 about his travels in Ceará, the English traveler John Gardner observed commercial goods moving by oxcart between the port of Aracatí and the interior city of Icó. From that point on to the more important *brejo* city of Crato, the hilly ground made the use of such carts impossible. Travel and commerce then depended on the use of pack animals.[75] Gardner recounted the problems he experienced trying to go south from Crato to Barra do Jardim, a distance of about fifty miles: "The road skirts along the base of the serra in a southeast direction for about five leagues, at the termination of which it is necessary to ascend it for the purpose of crossing to the other side. The ascent is far from good, it being left entirely in the hands of nature."[76]

Overland travel could prove arduous even along the littoral. In 1810, it took Henry Koster, traveling by horse, 16 hours to traverse a 70 kilometer stretch between Recife and Goiana. He followed a trail used by cattle drovers bringing herds to market in Recife. Koster noted that on level ground the road flattened out by the passing of cattle made for easy passage. The hills, however, remained another matter. "Instead of being carried round the steepest ascents, the trach has been made straight up and down or nearly so, and the winter torrents form deep caverns and ravines, the sides of which sometimes fall in and make the roads very dangerous." He warned that "unless well acquainted with a hill, it is by no means safe to ascend or descend by night, as one or two days of the usual rain of Brazil may have made a great difference, and have rendered the road impassable."[77]

In cruel irony, then, when rains did fall heavily in the littoral, and in those few interior places that remained relatively "drought-resistant," they washed out dirt trails and caused mud slides, making roads difficult, and at times impossible, to traverse. Since capital cities along the coast typically served as major supply centers during the drought, and often continued to experience winter rains, provisioning the interior proved difficult. *Agreste* towns, better positioned to supply the *sertão*, remained somewhat isolated from the coast. Indeed, the humid *agreste* had developed considerable self-sufficiency largely as a result of its elevation and rugged relief, which made transporting food difficult.[78] Since pack animals needed fodder and water, even during a normal dry season, the parched land made travel difficult. When rains did not follow that normal dry season, travel into the *sertão* became impossible, a jouney into a parched land bereft of fodder and water.

In April 1877, the county council of Russas, a Ceará town in the *Chapada* of Apodí near the Jaguaribe river, wrote to the provincial president detailing dire conditions caused by the drought, including the destruction of the *municipio*'s agriculture and livestock. He noted that roads had already become nearly impassable, and that they would deteriorate further over the next months. Hence, he opined, if relief supplies were not sent promptly, they might as well not be sent at all.[79] Similarly, in September 1877, a district judge in Villa Bella wrote of drought migrants passing through that Pernambucan town en route to settlements near the São Francisco river, and pointed to the difficulties of receiving the supplies needed to help these "starving and tattered bands of *retirantes*." The dearth of pack horses was such that, "notwithstanding the government's liberal assistance, from October on, nothing more could be sent."[80] Billy Jaynes Chandler recounts a story from *O Cearense* on November 11, 1877, that further underscores the difficulties of delivering relief supplies in Ceará: "The commission in charge of relief in Tauá contracted with an owner of pack animals to go to Quixeramobim to transport supplies sent from Fortaleza; all of the pack animals died in the course of the journey, the last survivors succumbing more than 60 kilometers from Tauá on the return trip."[81]

The village of Teixeira provides an example of how difficult the remission of goods could be, even to a well-situated *brejo* settlement that enjoyed a lively commerce as well as active agriculture and stockraising. Because this village was located only 170 kilometers from Campina Grande, the major relief center in Paraíba's *agreste*, the remission of goods would seem to have been a relatively easy matter. Despite these advantages, Teixeira was not "drought-proof." According to the parish priest, the vicar Bernardo de Carvalho Andrade, during the initial year of drought, relief supplies arrived sporadically, and Teixeira's population "became almost nomadic," as they sought sustenance in nearby areas. But those people always returned since they failed to encounter a substantially better situation. By May 1878, with Teixeira in the grip of another failed winter, Father Bernardo traveled to the provincial capital to secure help from the president. Out of their meeting there arose the idea of building a reservoir. Unfortunately, considerable time elapsed between the vicar's May visit and the actual arrival of supplies. Sent from the capital on July 16, they reached Teixeira nearly three weeks later. As drought's hold on the land grew, it became increasingly difficult to find people willing to transport goods from the capital. At one point, 45 days passed with no shipment. Supplies authorized for November 1878 did not arrive in Teixeira until January 1879.[82] Yet Teixiera represents a "best case" situation in terms of location, and the Vicar, given his standing, certainly received preferential treatment from government officials in the capital. Imagine, then, the lot of smaller, more distant towns that had no effective spokesperson to articulate their needs.

An engineering commission that had been sent to Ceará by the imperial government to investigate ways to prevent drought or minimize its impact also found travel through the real *sertão* daunting. Presided over by Beaurepaire Rohan, and directed by the well-known engineer Julio Pinkas, the commission arrived in Fortaleza in January 1878. The commission could not go into the *sertão* since the roads at that time were, in the words of the provincial president, "almost impassable," and no means of transport were available. The president recommended that Pinkas instead study ways to deal with winter flooding in Aracatí and help devise a system for increasing the supply of potable water to Fortaleza.[83] The Pinkas commission remained in Ceará through June. It did finally manage to travel into the interior, but accomplished little. As for the Fortaleza water supply issue, it turned out that the potential source identified in the *serra* of Maranguape could not fulfill even the needs of the small city located there.[84] Clearly, in the cases of both Teixeira and Ceará, the harsh realities of the backlands and the rudimentary system of roads and transport had defied the optimism expressed by the scientists and modernizers of Rio de Janeiro with regard to the ease of effecting positive change through the use of rational, modern methods.

Even water transport, by far the most efficient means available, posed problems. The region's seasonal rivers had dried up over the months prior to the drought. And since even the few "true" rivers declined during the dry season, they too could prove unreliable during the drought because of shoals and sand bars. The São Francisco river allowed steam navigation from its mouth all the way to Piranhas, but well before that point, just past Penedo, its course became more difficult, and its width narrowed. At the end of the normal dry season, lower water levels always decreased its navigability. With drought further reducing those already low water levels, conditions worsened. The Pernambucan Steam Navigation Company, for example, advised Pernambuco's president that two of its ships carrying relief supplies had been forced to stay at Penedo because of low water levels in the river.[85] To be sure, such supplies could be off-loaded onto smaller boats or barges. However, that process and the slower pace of such vessels would delay the arrival of relief shipments. Furthermore, any transfer of relief goods increased possibilities for loss through accident or, more commonly, theft, while smaller vessels plying the river remained more vulnerable to bandit attacks than did steamships.

Nor were ocean-going vessels always successful. Even Recife, the busiest port among the provinces of the north, scarcely offered ideal conditions for large ships. At times of lower tide the great sandstone reef that created a protected harbor there became a barrier. In fact, regardless of tides, larger ocean-going vessels usually anchored beyond the reef, their cargoes unloaded by shallow draft launches or by *jangadas*, the wooden rafts used by area fishers.[86] A reef also extended across much of the mouth of the Paraíba river, which was the access point to the provincial capital, Paraíba City (today, João Pessoa).[87] The port at Maceió in Alagoas had good depth but provided little shelter from southeastern winds.[88] Conditions in Piauí, Ceará, and Rio Grande to Norte presented greater difficulties. Piauí, with but 16 kilometers of coast, had only two small ports, the larger of which could accommodate ships with a draft of 3.5 meters.[89] At that time, the world's largest steamships required ports with a depth of nearly 10 meters.[90]

Ceará's extensive coastline was rough, and sandbars at the mouths of rivers created major difficulties.[91] Access along much of the coast remained limited to small launches. The province's two most important ports, Aracatí and Fortaleza, offered somewhat better conditions, and steamships of the Maranhão and Pernambucan companies regularly called at both locations. Even so, shifting sands caused some problems at Aracatí, and at high tide water depth was only four meters.[92] Fortaleza, the province's busiest port, had a large barrier reef that complicated docking. High tide and rough seas made using the port an adventure. Furthermore, it could accommodate very few ships.[93] Multiple studies had suggested improvements, but they remained naught but plans on paper.[94]

Docking in Natal proved an even more difficult enterprise, its reef forcing an entry both narrow and twisting into a river mouth that at some places had exceedingly low depths and presented dangers from shoals and rocks.[95] Writing in 1877, the province's port authority pointed to the urgent need for works to improve the port and noted that great masses of shifting sand dunes threatened its total obstruction.[96] At the time of the Great Drought, the twice-monthly appearance of ships from the Pernambucan Steamship company provided the only scheduled maritime traffic.[97]

Loaded with relief goods, an imperial transport arrived at Natal in May 1877. Its draft too deep for the harbor, it set anchor beyond the reef. Ordinarily, *jangadas* would have been employed to off load the cargo. In this case, however, more sophisticated vessels were available, for the Portuguese vice-consul had lent the use of some lighters. Still, rough seas almost capsized two of the vessels. Unable to complete the unloading, the warship went on to Ceará.[98] But even had the full complement of supplies been unloaded, they probably would have remained in Natal because of the absence of any means to get relief goods to the interior.[99]

Difficult terrain coupled with rudimentary means of transportation had plagued the region before the Great Drought, narrowing the range of commercializable goods.[100] The physical difficulties and dangers of traveling into the interior during the drought increased the carrying costs for relief. In some instances, the expense of transport might exceed the value of the goods.[101]

In June 1877, Paraíba abandoned any attempt to supply the *sertão*. Its provincial president advised all relief commissions to persuade *retirantes* to seek the littoral or the area of the capital where both work opportunities and relief supplies could be made available more easily.[102] That same month saw similar orders issued to interior relief commissions in Rio Grande do Norte.[103] Even Pernambuco, comparatively wealthy and with superior transportation infrastructure, had to acknowledge lack of success in supplying the interior. Poor road conditions and the "impossibility" of finding people willing to hazard the journey inland, especially to the high *sertão*, along with the concomitant high costs of transport, indicated the need for a new policy. On October 20, 1877, then, the Central Relief Commission in Recife issued a circular urging inhabitants of the interior to seek out places where both labor opportunities and relief supplies could be securely offered throughout the emergency.[104]

MIGRATION

These problems of supply, experienced throughout the provinces of the north, produced a shift in imperial policy. Relief efforts now focused on establishing food deposits, public works projects, and other labor opportunities, including the formation of agricultural colonies, in areas of easier access and more amenable climate. Although to some extent the movement of *retirantes* had already anticipated this new policy, its announcement magnified the flow. This translated into a vast migratory current to settlements either on, or with easy access to, the coast, and to areas bordering the São Francisco. It also saw state-sponsored shipping of *retirantes* to Maranhão, Pará, and Amazonas, northern provinces unaffected by the drought, and, in the latter two cases, hungry for labor because of their small populations and the accelerating rush for rubber. Many *retirantes*, again with the government paying their transportation, would travel completely out of the north to help fill labor needs in the south. In Ceará an "Emigration Commission" overseeing this process provided passage to some twenty thousand people in the months of April to October 1878. Passage for thousands more had been funded through the provincial president's office.[105] In another of the cruel ironies of the drought years, many ships that left Recife carrying slaves in the interprovincial trade to the south also carried *retirantes*.[106]

Even in the more favorable situation of journeying by ship rather than on foot, drought migrants did not always fare well. Overcrowding, the use of unseaworthy vessels, and the often difficult conditions of navigating coastal shoals all played a role in producing problems. In 1878, for example, a Portuguese brigantine bound for Pará with 241 *retirantes* from Ceará sank in the Japerico shallows. Officially blamed on "pilot error," this disaster claimed the lives of 132 *retirantes*.[107] The *Dantas*, carrying some fourteen hundred *retirantes* from Ceará, docked in Recife. Twenty-four of them had died en route, deaths a Recife newspaper intimated had been caused by unsanitary conditions produced by extreme overcrowding. *Retirantes* had traveled, virtually "piled one on top of another in the midst of a repugnant pig sty."[108]

Elite discourse often referred to *retirantes* wandering aimlessly, dazed by heat, hunger, and thirst. The initial migrations out of the dry *sertão*, however, followed trajectories well-established in *sertanejo* lore.[109]

Backlanders sought the *brejos*, river valleys and the coast. The subsequent multiple paths of *retirantes* in part resulted from the inability or unwillingness of smaller towns to provide for large numbers of backlanders. Local relief commissions and towns suddenly overrun with *retirantes* encouraged the departure of the drought migrants, passing them—and the problem—on to others. In Piauí, for example, the relief commission of Principe Imperial in November 1878 advised the provincial president that with food and other supplies absent, it had decided to send drought migrants to places in that province and in Ceará which could more easily receive shipments of government supplies. The commission complained, however, that despite the many *retirantes* it managed to move on, new ones seemed always to enter. The commission also noted that a relief commission in Icó, Ceará, had sent a group of *retirantes* to Principe Imperial, asking that they "be sent to a better locale." So, having arrived in Principe Imperial, these *retirantes* then were sent back to Ceará to the city of Sobral.[110] At that very moment, however, Sobral—which early on had been affected by the drought—was moving *retirantes* to Fortaleza and Aracatí.[111]

Official government policy, as we have seen, also took multiple paths. Initially, defying a reality obvious to the *sertanejos* themselves, despite reports of a failed "winter" in 1877 the government first denied the existence of drought, and then later minimized its seriousness.[112] The absence of any positive government action meant that survival depended on personal initiative. Given relatively similar economic circumstances and a culture in which tales of drought's devastation figured prominently, the multiple decisions of individual backlands families summed to a sizable out-migration that further spread the deleterious impact of drought. With drought once officially recognized, policy urged *sertanejos* to remain where they were and promised that supplies would reach them. When the government proved unable to fulfill that promise, it next had encouraged the move towards the coast.

That policy resulted in *retirantes* experiencing continued hardship. Many among them who successfully reached these supposedly "more favored" locales found themselves trapped in miserable circumstances. Others remained on the move, this time with an itinerary forced upon them by government officials. For example, Piranhas, along the São Francisco, became a prime refuge for *retirantes* from the backlands of Pernambuco and Paraíba. While its riverine location assured some availability of water and food, the town, according to the provincial president, was "an insignificant place without any resources," scarcely able to cope with "the extraordinary number of *retirantes*." He advised moving the *retirantes* to another locale. Three months later, continuing migration from the high *sertão* had swelled the *retirante* population in Piranhas to seven thousand. The president responded by moving the *retirantes* first to Penedo and then to Maceió. From there, he sent all the residents of Pernambuco back to that province.[113]

The example of Priajá further illustrates how the volume and fluctuations of migration complicated relief. Established by the Piauí relief commission in the middle of October 1878 as a congregating point for shipping *retirantes* to Maranhão and Ceará, Priajá began with about five hundred people. Ten weeks later, despite having embarked numerous drought refugees, "ever-growing streams of *retirantes*" had increased its population to some four thousand. Ironically, considering that Ceará had been a shipping destination, fully half of the *retirantes* in Priajá had come from that province![114]

Aracatí, a significant port and commercial center with a population of about seventeen thousand, certainly could not be equated with "an insignificant place" like Piranhas. But even so, how could it effectively house, feed, and clothe a *retirante* influx several times larger than its normal resident population? In April 1878, the head of the Aracatí relief commission, completely overwhelmed by the problems associated with so large a population of destitute people, requested authorization from the provincial president to "encourage emigration from the city, either voluntary or forced."[115] But emigration, though it did occur, proved no solution. Because of Aracatí's coastal location and the presence of relief supplies—however inadequate—drought migrants continued to stream in. Government policy encouraging *sertanejos* to seek the littoral certainly contributed to this movement. As a result, throughout the Great Drought the city's *retirante* population hovered between thirty and forty thousand. The ultimate reduction of the number of *retirantes* in Aracatí arose from deaths caused by disease and from the final twist in government policy that declared the drought at an end and ordered the cessation of relief.

HEALTH AND MORTALITY

As the example of Aracatí suggests, the drought radically altered the distribution of population in the provinces of the north, essentially emptying the high *sertão*, save for the few "drought resistant" areas, and producing exaggerated population densities in portions of the *agreste* and littoral. Overwhelmed, settlements in the *brejos* and *agreste* saw their resources depleted, and they soon became ridden with disease. The coastal towns and cities that became the major receiving centers for drought migrants replicated that experience on a larger scale.

Health facilities and general levels of sanitation, which left much to be desired even before the drought, proved totally inadequate to deal with the problems created by the drought-spawned migration. In Alagoas, the quarantine facility at Porto do Francez, 8 kilometers from the provincial capital, lacked sources for potable water, which, according to the provincial president, had to be brought in from "a place far away." Furthermore, no roads led to the hospital, so the sick were generally brought there by ship, which too often proved a difficult passage.[116] In Natal, the charity hospital had room for 80 beds, but owned only 63. Prior to the drought it typically held no more than 12 patients at one time. In June 1878, it struggled to accommodate 162 sick people, the majority of them *retirantes*. The hospital's chief reported that poor people made up almost the entirety of the city's population. Over a six-week period the hospital had admitted 321 people, and it had to set the sick to sleep on mats on the floor and feed them in shifts.[117] Reporting these problems to the minister of the empire, the province's president said that some sort of infirmary should be built, but pointed out that the necessary materials were not on hand, and could not be obtained as quickly as the urgency of the situation warranted. He further noted that in the nearby and ironically named settlement of Poço Limpo ("Clean Well"), some two hundred poor people suffered from fevers and anemia. Since Natal's two physicians were already overloaded with work, the best he could do was to send some medicine to a person in Poço Limpo who provided homeopathic cures.[118]

In Ceará, in February 1878 the relief commission of Fortaleza asserted that the behaviors of the city's ten thousand drought refugees, specifically their habit of urinating and defecating in the streets, posed the greatest hazard to health and sanitation. As a remedy, the commission suggested the importance of having guards to prevent this practice.[119] Two months later, the commission again remarked the negative consequences for public health caused by the large numbers of "dirty immigrants" in the city's streets and squares. Pointing to the existence of "pernicious fevers" and other diseases, it urged the provincial president to take measures to disinfect the streets.[120]

Not surprisingly, epidemic disease proved especially prevalent in the the immigrant lodging camps, where poverty, close-packed dwellings, and the absence of even rudimentary sanitary infrastructure proved a lethal combination. Even in death, *retirantes* posed a threat to public health. In Fortaleza, officials of the county council noted that cadavers were not being transported properly from the camps, located on the outskirts of the city, to the main cemetery, which was located in the central portion of the city. As a result, the smallpox epidemic, previously contained within the camps now had begun to spread within the city.[121]

44

THE DEATH TOLL

The combination of poverty, inadequate facilities, scarcity of health practitioners, problems of transportation, inadequate food, and overcrowding produced incredibly high mortality throughout the provinces of the north. Precisely how high remains unknown. Figures bandied about during the Great Drought usually had no empirical referent. Record keeping, never an exact practice even in larger towns and cities, became more slipshod under the pressures of the Great Drought. Numbers given for the *retirante* population in any particular locale varied widely, as might the number of deaths, depending on who was being asked and for what purpose. Since numbers usually translated into relief supplies and salaries, officials often cooked the books. Even without any such agendas, accurately tracking *retirantes*—often reported to be living in fields, clustered under trees, or crowded into *favela*-like dwellings, and forming a fluctuating, migratory population—proved impossible. Already weakened from hunger and with minimal supplies, many of those *sertanejos* who set out by foot on arduous journeys in search of relief perished along the way. Others, discouraged by the absence of any resources turned back, electing to die at home. Deteriorated conditions in cemeteries, as well as exploitation of *retirante* labor in agricultural colonies must also have resulted in unreported deaths.

The fragmentary data that do exist suggest that enormous numbers of *retirantes* died in the course of the Great Drought. Data from Piauí for the Emigrant Infirmary, established in May 1879, indicate that during the subsequent four-month period over a quarter of the 383 *retirantes* who entered the facility died. Statistics for that province's main infirmary for *retirantes* reveal a still more appalling situation. From May through July of that same year, of the 869 persons who entered, 362 died.[122]

Writing in April 1878, the County Council of the Ceará town of Sobral advised the provincial president that the city had suffered so high a death toll that the amount budgeted for grave diggers—which never had been fully expended in previous years—had already been entirely spent.[123] In 1879, the relief commission of the Ceará town of Crato advised the provincial president that a smallpox epidemic had produced an "excessive" death toll, but that did not include the "numerous and almost incalculable number of deaths" in the outskirts of the town. In about three months, 1,761 people had been buried in the quarantine hospital's cemetery.[124] During a six-month period in 1878, nearly 1,600 people were buried at public expense in a Recife cemetery.[125] In the capital of Paraíba in 1879, a variety of diseases, mostly all described as of an "epidemic nature," killed large numbers of *retirantes* and residents alike. Deaths increased from an average of about 10 per day in March to over 24 the following month. That already grim rate rose steadily over the next two months, peaking in July when the city daily witnessed 57 deaths! For the months from March through November, 9,318 deaths occurred.[126]

Describing conditions in 1878 Fortaleza, whose *retirante* population according to some estimates had reached 90,000, Rodolfo Theophilo suggests the horror that awaited drought migrants: "Bilious fever, beri-beri, dropsy, dysentery, and small pox had populated the cemeteries." The recorded total of 56,791 burials attested to the precarious living conditions. [127] Indeed, deaths recorded in Fortaleza during a six-month period from August 1878 to January, 1879 exceeded the total mortality for the previous thirty years.[128] One scholar of the history of Rio Grande do Norte writes that 35,000 people died in Mossoró between January 1878 and October 1879,[129] while another notes a conservative estimate for the entire province of 90,000 deaths.[130] Estimates for total deaths in the entire drought region range from 220,000 to as many as 500,000[131]

The hard evidence is exceedingly tenuous for any such estimates. Accurate mortality statistics even for those *retirantes* who managed to reach coastal refuges and became part of the official government relief system are not available. But if a precise total remains elusive, the existence of frightful drought-spawned mortality remains unquestionable. For, beyond any issues of fragmentary data, there lies the hard reality of a forced large-scale migration of poor people through a poor region, both beset with problems of supply and disease.

PUBLIC ORDER

Disruptions in the social fabric caused by the drought and its associated problems of hunger, privation, disease, crowding, and death produced insecurity and great public concern over the possibility or actuality of violence and crime. Persons self-described as having "something to lose" frequently expressed such fears. In December 1877 a petition to Ceará's president from merchants and property owners in Aracatí detailed an early morning assault on the city's public market by two thousand *retirantes*, who thus had taken "the first step on the road of crime and violence." As indicated by that phrase, the good citizens feared this initial act presaged further violence. Indeed, they reported that "the terror of the populace is such that the leading citizens will not leave their houses." They noted as well that the city had a *retirante* population of thirty thousand but only twenty to thirty troops.[132] When asked to provide "guarantees for their lives and goods," the president responded that he had no police at his disposal.[133] Two months later, the new provincial president warned the minister of the empire that Fortaleza's *retirantes* "who at first were peaceful, humble, and obedient already are becoming restless and demanding."[134] A November 1878 petition to provincial authorities in Rio Grande do Norte from twenty-two "merchants and property owners" in Mossoró affirmed that *retirantes* gathered there had generally obeyed the law and seemed "resigned to the sad circumstances of the calamity which afflicts us all." However, after hearing that relief might be cut off, they seemed "more like wild beasts than rational individuals."[135] Concluding that the *retirantes'* moral principles no longer were those of "humility" and "misfortune" brought on by hunger and suffering, but rather the product of idleness and its associated vices, the residents appealed for help from the provincial government. Failing that, they could either abandon their homes, or "by iron and fire defend their houses and families."[136] After all, as the county council of Sobral put it, "a rifle in the hands of a starving person is a danger to the well-to do."[137]

The connection between the drought and criminality seemed clear to provincial presidents. Pernambuco's president attributed the nearly 100 percent increase in crimes from 1876 to 1877 to the "abnormal state of the province."[138] Paraíba's president provided a more erudite discussion, citing the French statistician Maurice Block, who had demonstrated a relationship among the variables of emigration, food prices, and crime. The president observed that crime rose when conditions of life became more difficult.[139] Other provincial presidents explained rising violence and crime as the product of the interaction between drought-spawned conditions and the nature of the *sertanejos*. The president of Alagoas opined that people who lacked education more easily fell prey to hatred and passions. He also referred to the "bad instincts or poor habits" caused by idleness, "the origin of all vices and heinous acts."[140] A subsequent president of that province, summarizing the rise in thefts and homicides in 1877 and 1878 pointed to the role played by *retirantes*: "accustomed to the indolent existence of our backlands, impelled by the horrors of hunger and thirst, ignorant and without moral or religious education, they engage in crimes, for which many of them perhaps already had an affinity." [141]

From small towns to large cities, public officials declaimed the need for jails and a police or military force sufficient to maintain order. The county council of Santa Anna, a *municipio* of some thirteen thousand people, described desperate conditions in August of 1877, for the drought had destroyed the activities from which its inhabitants derived their livelihood. While pointing to their need for government relief, the council affirmed that "above anything else" they needed a jail.[142] That same month, the president of Ceará reported to the minister of the empire that officials in the interior continually asked for more police "to guard the

47

prisons which are full of recently captured criminals and to guarantee the right to life and property that is threatened by the hungry masses."[143]

Only capital cities had buildings that approached adequacy as jails. As a result, they often received prisoners from other locales. Those facilities, however, could not easily accommodate the rising number of inmates. For example, Rio Grande do Norte's police chief suggested the "urgent necessity" of transferring some prisoners from the capital to the national facility on the island of Fernando de Noronha. The Ministry of Justice responded that Fernando de Noronha itself was too crowded.[144] The following month, in June 1878, nineteen prisoners, "all murderers," escaped from the overcrowded jail in Natal.[145]

At times, public forces, whether police or soldiers, themselves disturbed public order. In one such case, Pernambuco had established a large food warehouse in the town of Piranhas to serve the nearby Pernambucan town of Tacaratí. Sending supplies to Tacaratí proved risky. In February 1878, the Pernambucan relief commission in Piranhas reported the theft of a large shipment of goods, and ascribed it to a Colonel Pedro Viera and other "potentates" of the towns of Matta Grande and Agua Branca. The commission claimed that some two hundred people took orders from the Colonel and his henchmen.[146]

The Tacaratí relief depot itself continued to be subject to threat. Rumors of an impending attack on the supplies led both Alagoas and Pernambuco to send in troops. Nonetheless, on April 21, 1878, a group numbering four hundred came across the border from Tacaratí and "by force and threats" made off with the foodstuffs. In the process, a "respected citizen" was killed. Pursuing those responsible, the Alagoan forces discovered that the assailant belonged to the police detachment from Pernambuco. Pernambuco abolished the warehouse, and withdrew its detachment, but that left Alagoas to deal with the twelve thousand or so *retirantes* who had come there because of the relief supplies.[147]

On October 12, 1878, Macau, in Rio Grande do Norte, suffered a day of terror. In response to various requests for troops to help maintain public order in the interior of Paraíba, the imperial government had sent a detachment of 148 troops with three officers aboard the steamer Jaguaribe. They disembarked in Macau to begin the overland journey to Paraíba at a time when rations were being distributed to *retirantes*. According to a police official in that city, the three officers disappeared, leaving the troops completely on their own. The soldiers began insulting the *retirantes*, then menaced the "regular" residents of the city, and, finally, ran amok through the streets.[148]

The presence of organized bands of outlaws or *cangaceiros* further contributed to insecurity in the provinces of the north. The president of Paraíba observed in 1879 that "the zone of the high *sertão* has for long been infested by groups of brigands." He ascribed this to the nature of the terrain, the pattern of scattered settlements, the ease with which bandits could move into neighboring provinces, the degree to which they had cowed the area's peaceful citizens, and the inadequate number of police. He added, too, that the impact of drought had further accelerated their activities.[149]

Bandit groups had become especially active in the provinces of the north since the early 1870s. Especially well-known as *cangaceiro* leaders were Jesuino Brilhante, Viriatos, and Meirelles.[150] Bandit gangs found the mountainous *brejos* areas attractive. Craggy slopes and high plains offered numerous hidden places for making camp, while the presence of fairs and active commerce provided opportunity for booty.[151] The drought had reduced normal commercial exchange, but it also introduced new targets: pack animals loaded with relief supplies and official government depositories or warehouses. At the same time, living under miserable conditions and maltreated by public officials, some *retirantes* joined the *cangaceiro* bands, while others participated when it came to making off with relief goods.

An ample scholarly literature has debated the genesis and nature of the *cangaceiro*. For some, the *cangaceiros* emerge as products of the institutional corruption and violence of the imperial system. Others stress the ties between bandits and local ranching and agricultural elites, an alliance that advanced the interests of both parties. Within Brazil, a strong tradition in popular culture—which also finds its way into scholarly literature—is the Robin Hood image, the *cangaceiro* as social bandit. Writing about Jesuino Brilhante, for example, Luís da Câmara Cascudo, long the foremost authority regarding history and customs in Rio Grande do Norte, observed: "Jesuino always went to Mossoró where he stayed with friends. Nobody except the legal system thought him a criminal."[152]

Whatever their role, there seems little doubt that during the Great Drought *cangaceiros* literally roamed the backlands at will, evincing little concern for local police authorities. Of course, in many cases, no such authorities existed, while in others, they were allied with these "outlaws." In 1878, a district judge in Rio Grande do Norte warned the minister of justice that the settlement of Luiz Gomes found itself threatened by "the celebrated criminals Meirelles and Viriatos." The authorities at Imperatriz had been asked to provide some troops, but the judge distrusted this recourse, because those in charge at Imperatriz had political alliances with a leading member of the Liberal Party, identified only as "Benjamin *de tal*" (Benjamin "so and so") who was Meirelles's brother-in-law. The provincial president reported receiving requests from authorities in several places that feared attacks, but he felt powerless to respond since the province's entire public force "did not exceed 250," the jails were full and needed guarding, and Jesuino Brilhante also was on the prowl.[153]

The threatened sacking of Luiz Gomes in fact took place on May 14, 1877. Reporting on the incident, the county judge of Pau de Ferros identified the two notorious bandits, and noted their company as including other people from "the lower class" who had joined with them because of the drought. At 10 in the morning, the band invaded the town, took foodstuffs, cattle, money—almost everything of value—then beat up several townspeople. The bandits also declared their intention to raid several other settlements. Concerned, the people requested help from the district's local police official, and he in turn requisitioned a detachment from the town of Porto Alegre. But that force numbered only six, whereas the bandit gang had over eighty members. The district judge in Apodi, one of the threatened settlements, advised the provincial president that the town could count on only two members of its public force, as the other four were escorting prisoners to the jail in Natal. According to the judge, those people in Apodi who "had something to lose" were especially concerned that "rude, low class people" would join with the bandits if offered a share of the loot. Disturbing as well was the presence of the very same Benjamin, who had come to town a short time ago from Cajazeiras. The judge believed that Benjamin, who actually belonged to the local police, was passing information to the bandits! [154] He urged the president to have the province's chief of police take direct charge of this problem. Meanwhile, the Ministry of War sent a supply of weapons to the provincial president to equip a volunteer force to help keep the peace. That ministry had already increased the number of line troops.[155]

Concerns regarding bandits dated back to at least March of 1877, when the Ministry of Justice received word of the threat posed by Meirelles and Viriatos, and urged cooperative efforts among the presidents of Rio Grande do Norte, Ceará, Pernambuco, and Paraíba. The four agreed to join forces, but with the absence of any effective public force and the ongoing struggle to transport relief supplies, conditions in Ceará remained unsettled.[156] In December, the president advised the minister of the empire that "groups of evildoers headed by celebrated criminals are infesting the backlands and invading settlements to rob the goods and possessions of the citizens living there." He noted as well that these criminals could act with impunity because of insufficient police resources. Fearful of growing disorder—if not the threat of anarchy—the president once more urgently requested a public force "sufficient for the needs of the province."[157]

The president's concern was well founded. Since the early days of the drought, those bandit gangs had preyed upon goods moving through trails in the Cariri valley. They had established a virtual tributary power over the districts of Crato and Jardim, extracting relief goods as the price

Map 3. The Drought Provinces

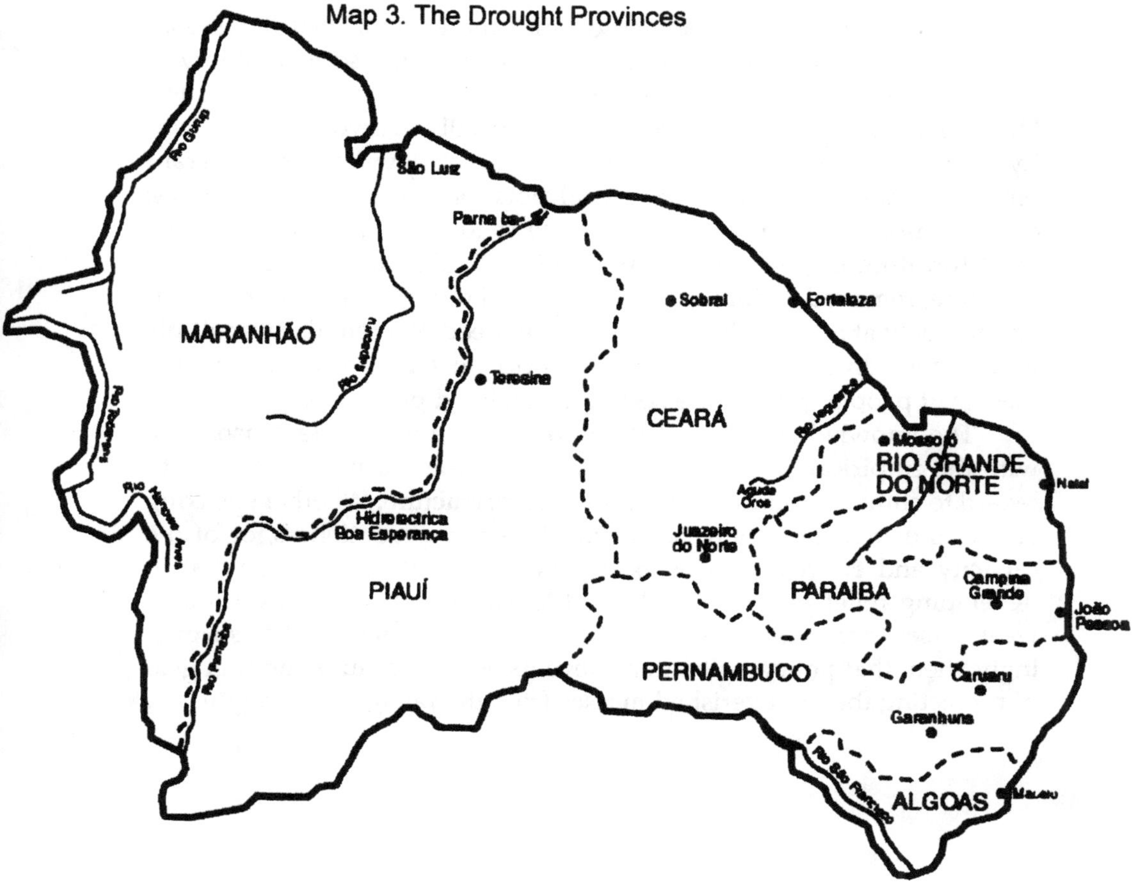

MARANHÃO

São Luiz

Parnaiba

Sobral

Fortaleza

CEARÁ

Teresina

Mossoró

RIO GRANDE
DO NORTE

Natal

Açude
Orós

Hidroelectrica
Boa Esperança

PIAUÍ

Juazeiro
do Norte

PARAIBA

Campina
Grande

João
Pessoa

PERNAMBUCO

Caruaru

Garanhuns

ALGOAS

Maceió

of peace. Their depredations came to end in 1878, but not as a result of any official police action. Canuto José de Aguiar, a seventy-five-year-old lieutenant colonel, sallied forth from Fortaleza into the *sertão* leading a group of forty-five men. His quarry: "three bands of brigands, each of 100-150 armed, disciplined men on horseback." The doughty Aguiar and his men proved more than a match, for these bandits, capturing fifty-three, and dispersing the remainder.[158]

Attacks on public markets or *feiras* proved particularly distressing. People living in Cajazeiras in Paraíba wrote to the provincial president that with resources absent because of the drought, begging and thefts had increased. Most alarming, though, "at the very *feira* of Santa Fe," groups of armed criminals invaded and carried off the small amount of numbers of people who depended on such markets for their livelihood. Towns themselves relied on markets for tax revenues, so their ability to fund services was affected.[160] Furthermore, *feiras* had social significance. "In the *sertão*," observes Robert Levine, "virtually everyone in the vicinity attended the *feira* at least briefly on market day: herders; itinerant repairmen able to mend shoes, metal pots, or harnesses and saddles; cowboys needing equipment; men riding to town to carouse and drink; used furniture dealers [and] horse traders."[161] Disruptions of markets, therefore, removed an important institutional pillar from backlands society precisely at a time when it was most in need of strength. In multiple ways, then, drought heightened insecurity in an environment where masses of people, even in the best of times, lived precariously.

The knowledge claims of the imperial elite bore little consonance with the empirical reality of the provinces of the north, especially with regard to climate, resources, and public infrastructure. Whether speaking of issues of transportation, health facilities and practitioners, or of the capacity and effectiveness of local government, it seems clear that in developing relief policy, elites had little awareness of the institutional weakensses that constrained its real world implementation. Not surprisingly, then, that policy failed to achieve its espoused humanitarian goal of protecting the impoverished masses from the ravages of drought.

CHAPTER 3

VIEWS FROM THE PROVINCES

The drought-spawned diaspora of a poor population in the difficult physical environment of the *sertão* presented a crisis that would have challenged any relief policy, no matter how well-intentioned or funded. In the case of the Great Drought, government policy in many respects actually magnified the suffering of *sertanejos*. Under the Conservatives, the government had questioned the very existence of drought. Its cautious policy during the early moments of the drought helped deepen the crisis. The Liberals, while more prone to acknowledge the actuality of drought, similarly minimized its dimensions. Measured against the daunting problems of transportation in the provinces of the north, the government's initial policy decision to send relief into the *sertão* certainly proved ill-advised, as did its suggestion that *retirante*s remain where they were and await the arrival of government supplies. Subsequent public policy continued to have little consonance with the day-to-day reality of the drought-afflicted region. And beyond its dubious assumptions, when brokered through the socio-political context of the provinces of the north, that policy in practice often exacerbated the difficulties confronting the *retirantes*.This chapter focuses more closely on relief policy in practice, from the moment that the government encouraged *retirantes* to seek out the towns and cities of the littoral to the declared end of drought and the return to the backlands. It examines the negative impacts associated with the various iterations of government policy, while also questioning some of the represented "truths" that justified those changes in the provision of relief. In turn, those "truths" further underscore the discursive unity of elite portrayals of *retirantes*, particularly with regard to the question of labor.

PROVINCIAL GOVERNMENT

Direct representatives of the national government, provincial presidents enjoyed a wide array of powers and considerable prestige. During the Great Drought, they oversaw the translation of imperial relief policy into actual programs, established and staffed relief commissions, opened special credits to defray expenses, and through numerous communications to the Ministry of the Empire interpreted their province's conditions and needs. In fulfilling these various functions, however, provincial presidents operated under a set of constraints that adversely affected the effectiveness and efficiency of relief policy.

From an imperial perspective, those presidents' most important role remained political: they functioned as key links in a system designed to deliver votes for the ministry.[1] Given both the primacy of this political function and the dependence of their appointments on the the government, provincial presidents remained loyal to the ministry and deferred to its wishes. This political role also resulted in a pattern of relatively brief tenure in any one province. The president of the Council of Ministers, "moved them from province to province, brought them to Rio de Janeiro to fill key positions, promoted them to Cabinet posts, or shoved them into minor sinecures when he found them lacking."[2] When the party in power at the national level fell, so too did all the presidents who had been appointed during its tenure. Moreover, even when a change in ministry did not involve a change in party, a new President of the Council of Ministers still needed to dispense favors to his own people. In March 1880, Liberal José Antonio Saraiva organized a ministry to replace the Liberal Sinimbu. Within four months time, new presidents had either been named or taken office in thirteen of the nation's twenty provinces.

In the three-year span of January 1877 to December 1880, the six drought provinces saw a total of twenty-six presidents take office. Even this does not fully capture the bewildering change at the apex of the provincial government. In the absence of a president, whether because of illness, service in the national legislature, or transfer, or resignation prior to a replacement's taking office, one of the six vice-presidents took over. An overview of the experience of Paraíba for the drought years indicates the revolving-door quality created by this system. Between January 1877, when the second vice-president assumed command of the province, and September 1880, that province experienced ten additional changes in its chief executive officer.[3] Even granting the best of intentions to all concerned, such instability made it difficult to maintain an orderly relief process. With pronounced partisanship and factionalism, the task became impossible.

In theory, Presidents could count on aid from the province's chief of police and his *"delegados* (commissioners) in each county [*municipio*] and *subdelegados* (deputy commissioners) in each parish."[4] The chief, a salaried official appointed by the minister of justice, made recommendations for the positions of *delegado* and *subdelegado*, and officially held supervisory authority over them. Their appointments, however, came from the provincial president. In practice, then, these lesser police positions became patronage posts filled by members of the local elite who shared the party affiliation of the sitting president. Given the political nature of the post, the impossibility of any close supervision by the chief of police, and the positions' lack of salary, *delegados* and *subdelegados* used their ample discretionary power to advance private interests.[5] As members of local relief commissions during the Great Drought, these officials naturally saw their positions in that same light.

Members of the judiciary always played a significant political role in the provinces, and they, too, typically served on relief commissions during the drought. The ranks of these officials included district and county judges (*juiz do direito; juiz municipal*), appointed by the minister of justice, and locally-elected justices of the peace (*juiz de paz*).[6] District and country judges remained creatures of the administration that had appointed them. Their primary goal was to represent the central government, but that became problematic when the administration changed hands.[7] Justices of the peace responded to those local powers who had secured their election. At all levels, then, the administration of justice remained highly politicized. Provincial presidents made interim judicial appointments and proposed candidates to fill open slots so as to have compliant allies. Powerful local actors might themselves become judges, then use that role to advance the interests of family and political faction. Judges who owed their appointments to a ministry no longer in power might scheme with local powers to frustrate the administration of a provincial president. The actions of both magistrates and police officials during the drought more often reflected partisan political and pecuniary considerations than those related to law and justice. Legal issues surrounding the distribution of relief received the same disposition.

LIFE AND LABOR IN THE LITTORAL

If the policy change that encouraged *retirantes* to seek the coast alleviated some of the problems of crowding and unrest in the *brejos* and *agreste*, it simply shifted them to the cities of the littoral. The initial urban response to the *retirante* influx centered around immediate needs for housing and health care. Central relief commissions already functioning in capital cities to coordinate the province-wide relief effort assumed direct responsibility, at times augmenting their ranks by establishing parish-based volunteer groups. Finding buildings that might be converted into mass dormitories or lodging houses and getting the seriously ill into hospitals or isolation facilities became an ongoing task, one again complicated by the sheer volume and episodic nature of the *retirante* influx. For example, on a single day in June 1878, two ships carrying 1,850 *retirantes* from ports in Rio Grande do Norte and Ceará arrived in Recife. Only a few days earlier, another ship had brought 1,400 drought migrants.[8]

Retirantes mostly traveled independently, their paths determined by their own health, the availability of jobs, food and shelter, the response of local relief commissions, and information gleaned from other backlanders. As a result, public officials at littoral locales could not easily anticipate needs. A commission might have dealt effectively with one day's arrivals, only to be presented with an even larger number the succeeding day. The repeated communications from towns of all sizes that described their *retirante* populations as "growing daily" bespeak this quality of the migration. Even diligent, well-intentioned relief officials had to scramble to meet needs as they arose.

Developing work opportunities quickly became a focal point for relief commissions. Both the general concepts and specific discourse regarding labor and relief expressed by the Rio de Janeiro elite resonated throughout the provinces. Provincial presidents, closely tied to that imperial elite (and in some cases already its members), all celebrated the positive moral advantages accruing to those who labored for their own sustenance rather than receiving a hand-out. Speaking of the importance of work relief, Ceará's José Julio de Albuquerque Barros cited no less an authority than Lord Salisbury, who had overseen British efforts to deal with a great 1877 drought in India. Salisbury favored large-scale projects as more efficient means of providing employment. He also saw them as "a more effective test of destitution than smaller local works," arguing that only the "truly needy" would leave their homes to seek out distant labor opportunities. José Julio adduced this as a strong argument favoring the inception of port works and railroads in Ceará.[9] Paraíba's president stressed the importance of having the *retirantes* engage in labor projects that would contribute to the public good. He reported that his efforts in this regard had suffered because of "the pronounced repugnance that the emigrants manifest toward labor." Indeed, provincial relief commissions had reported that *retirantes* "obstinately refuse" to work.[10]

Even those at more modest levels in the hierarchy saw the fiscal and moral advantages of work relief. A county judge in the small

Pernambucan town of Granito reminded the provincial president of the importance of assuring labor opportunities for the able-bodied so as to avoid idleness: ". . . as your excellency knows, idleness is the mother of all vices."[11] Recife's Central Relief Commission saw compensated labor through public works projects as "the most honorable [alternative] for the citizen and the most beneficial to the nation."[12] Provincial discourse also suggested that a drought-created struggle for existence might overcome the traditional unwillingness of the masses to engage in labor. As the Recife central relief commission put it, "In the present, as in no other time, will we find so many robust workers seeking work, nor so well disposed to overcome difficulties so as to save their own lives."[13] The drought therefore also presented an opportunity for moral uplift through labor, which "elevates and ennobles character." Productively employed *retirantes* would feel "happy and joyous because bags of sweat ran down their cheeks."[14]

The emphasis on creating structured, supervised work projects also responded to elite concerns with public order. Through slavery and other types of dependent labor relations, coercion, violence, and patronage, elites maintained as the primary feature of imperial Brazil the existence of an orderly, hierarchical society in which every one knew his or her proper place. Viewed from the perspective of that hierarchy, the drought had disorganized the society of the backlands, taking masses of lower-class people out of their normal existence, freeing them from the mechanisms, both formal and informal, that had maintained them in their properly controlled and deferential position. Ripped out from the constraints and controls of that social system, the masses of *retirantes* might lose their moral compass and engage in theft or use violent means to gain sustenance.[15] Conventional wisdom regarding the relationship between idleness and social problems provided a powerful rationale for putting the displaced *sertanejos* to work. This ideology of *vadiagem* gained further reinforcement from the strains on existing urban infrastructure caused by the drought-spawned population explosion. Logic and justice suggested that *retirantes* help meet the needs their presence had created.

Beyond needs generated by the presence of *retirantes*, every province had a lengthy wish list of material improvements that had been deferred, often for a long time, due to the absence of sufficient financial resources or because they had not yet received necessary authorization from the imperial government.[16] The existence of so many stalled projects once again undercuts assertions regarding the prosperity of the provinces of the north prior to the drought. Writing in January 1877, Caetano Estellita Cavalcanti Pessoa, president of Ceará, styled the province's finances as "precarious," and totally inadequate for any public works. He further remarked the province's recent history of decreasing budgets.[17] And, later that year, well before the worst of the drought, Estellita again spoke of the "weakness of provincial resources" and referred to Ceará as "a province where everything remains to be done."[18] If the supposedly flourishing Ceará confronted difficulties, what of a poor province like Rio Grande do Norte? Speaking to the provincial assembly in October 1876, President Passos Miranda noted multiple years of budget deficits and asserted the primacy of the "financial question" in causing "the ills afflicting the province," which included failure to pay numerous public employees, including provincial police and health officials.[19]

Relief money and *retirante* labor came as a welcome boon to the depressed provinces of the north, funding wish lists that included large-scale projects like roads, railroads, and port improvements, and numerous urban works like landfills, street paving, public markets, and administrative buildings. While the expressed needs of provincial capitals formed the majority of such urban works, at more modest levels similar projects were undertaken in the smaller cities and towns of the provinces of the north. For example, in Mamanguape, Paraíba, relief funds paid for street paving and road building, and in Campina Grande, repairs to the country council building.[20] In Pernambuco, jails were repaired in Tacaratu, Limoeiro and Ouricury, as were cemeteries in, among other places, Caruarú and Villa Bella.[21] The construction of *açudes* became widely carried out as did repairs on parish churches. *Retirantes* helped enlarge existing hospitals and constructed new ones. They expanded cemeteries and served as grave diggers, services needed to accommodate the ever-growing number of their fellow backlanders who succumbed to disease and privation. In many cases they provided for their own shelter by building barracks or squatter camps. They also formed the basic labor force for the newly-authorized railroad lines. The volume of *retirante* labor is suggested in an 1877 report by Ceará's president listing works on which they were employed which filled eight pages—this at a time when the worst of the drought lay ahead.[22]

The use of *retirante* labor in projects having little to do with drought relief also proved common, resulting, as we have seen, in critiques from the imperial bureaucracy as well as from the national legislative assembly that relief funds were being used to support grandiose constructions. But beyond those examples, it seems clear that *retirantes* were usually regarded as cheap labor, available for almost any purpose to anyone who enjoyed the right connections. So for example, two hundred *retirantes* were authorized to the man who held the street cleaning contract in Fortaleza.[23]

DECONGESTING THE LITTORAL

As we have noted, deepening drought and changing government policy accelerated the flow of *retirantes* to the littoral. Control of relief funds rested mainly with provincial presidents and central commissions in capital cities. Those larger urban places also enjoyed better infrastructure, more charity resources, and easier access to relief supplies. The capitals, therefore, generally wound up with the largest concentrations of *retirantes*. Both presidents and commissioners worried about the many problems associated with the presence of drought migrants. Once again public policy shifted. Mirroring the actions of the numerous *brejo* and *agreste* towns that had hurried *retirantes* off to other locations, provincial policy emphasized the need to decongest the capital cities and nearby littoral towns. Justified by an elite discourse that upheld the positive benefits accruing to those who worked, exploitation of *retirante* labor took new forms.

Alagoas's president authorized the placing of drought migrants on littoral sugar mills and plantations as a way to empty government lodging houses and make *retirantes* provide for their own support.[24] Rio Grande do Norte established a contract scheme whereby "hundreds" of *retirantes* would work at the mills, with the government providing foodstuffs in return.[25] Recife's Central Relief Commission saw that same measure as advantageous to both *retirantes* and the public coffers. *Retirantes* would provide needed labor for the mill owners, who in turn would provide them with plots on which they could erect dwellings and raise crops for their own sustenance.[26] Reporting on this initiative, the central commission stressed the concomitant reduction of Recife's *retirante* population by some thirteen thousand in a seven month span. It also acknowledged the largesse of planters and mill owners who without charge provided seeds, tools, materials for building a dwelling, and some clothing. *Retirantes* would work three days on their own plots, with the remaining time owed to the landowner.[27] That description omitted the added fillip for landowners, for in many cases public funds provided clothing and daily food rations for *retirantes*, sometimes in kind, other times in cash, until such time as they might become self-sustaining. Of course, control over these supplies rested with the landowner. In essence, then, under the guise of providing relief, in both Alagoas and Pernambuco displaced *sertanejos* were forced into the kinds of controlled, dependent labor systems preferred by the planter elite. Not surprisingly, this approach to relief also found favor in other of the drought provinces.

Piauí had tried a similar approach on a grander scale, establishing large numbers of *retirantes* in agricultural "*núcleos*" under contract with large land owners. Land owned by the Barão de Campo Maior held the largest contingent, two thousand *retirantes*, while other landowners, mostly bearing titles of colonel or captain, each had fifteen hundred. The provincial government used relief funds to pay the landowners 160 *réis* as a daily ration for each of the *retirantes*, with the expectation that at some point, able to support themselves, the backlanders would no longer require public assistance.[28]

As proved typical of such relief efforts, the anticipated self-sustaining stage never materialized.[29] In March 1878, the province's vice-president noted that little had come of the initiative to date due to the failure of winter rains: "the plantings have died, and there are no more seeds."[30] The committee he appointed to study the relief effort concluded that the *núcleos* still had not produced enough to become self-sustaining and urged their elimination. As a step toward this goal it also suggested modifying the contract so that the government no longer would have to provide food rations beyond the next few months.[31]

In 1879, the provincial president informed the minister of the empire that the contracting scheme had failed. He lodged all blame with the *retirantes*. Instead of clearing plots, they had simply idled about, content to consume the food rations provided by the contractor. Indeed, he noted, they even ate the seeds they were supposed to plant.[32]

To imperial elites, *retirante* indolence always seemed a plausible cause of failed relief initiatives. But upon closer scrutiny, the president's explanation seems unconvincing. The province paid each contractor largely in cash rather than with goods.[33] The 160 *reis* figure at best provided marginal survival possibilities for the *retirantes*. After all, meals for prisoners were generally calculated at 240 *reis* per day! It seems doubtful, then, that *retirantes* would have chosen to remain on near-starvation rations so as to avoid work. It seems doubtful as well that planters really would feed *retirantes* while getting absolutely no labor from them. To be sure, as has been noted, traditionally landowners did maintain large numbers of retainers—as captive voters, as a fighting force, and source of local prestige—whose purpose was as much, or more, political as financial. Yet even in those cases, the *agregados* largely saw to their own subsistence. Paiuí's economy more so than others of the northern provinces rested on cattle raising. The drought had decimated the herds. Those large landowners who remained no longer enjoyed the resources to support a large number of retainers, and they had much less need for their labor. Furthermore, the drought had interrupted the normal political calendar and caused the suspension of elections. Again, this would have reduced the attractiveness of having large numbers of *agregados*.

A more likely explanation for what occurred in Piauí, is that individuals of power and standing participated in a patronage opportunity precisely at a time when declining economic fortune made a large contract for relief especially attractive. Landowners, one suspects, took the government money and used it for their own purposes, providing little in the way of support for the *retirantes*. If *retirantes* did in fact consume the seeds they were supposed to plant, that suggests not their indolence but, rather, the extremity of their deprivation.

RESETTLEMENT COLONIES

The official rationale for creating agricultural colonies with *retirantes* drew strength from regional grievances—as counterparts to the state-supported settlements of European immigrants in the south—and from reformist attitudes stressing free labor and progress. Such colonies might serve as schools for practical agricultural education and perhaps develop into model farms. The scientists' critique also had suggested that rational productive agriculture would minimize much of the suffering caused by drought. A final argument for colonies, one invariably present in all such elite prescriptions for the masses, was that these settlements would transform lazy idlers into productive workers. And, of course, back in a controlled environment, those masses would cease to threaten public order.

Speaking of the inception of two such colonies in Paraíba, for example, that province's vice-president pointed out that public works projects had proved exceedingly costly. Moreover, they had taken *retirantes* away from their normal occupation as agriculturalists and, perhaps, inculcated new labor patterns. This he viewed as bad, in that agriculture stood as the base of Paraíba's economy. Establishing *retirantes* on agricultural colonies seemed much the better alternative. Cultivating their own land, the *sertanejos* would become self-sustaining, thereby increasing overall agricultural productivity while reducing the need for government funds. Furthermore, in the future, "one of the more advantageously located nuclei might serve as an applied agriculture school."[34]

The enthusiasm expressed for colonies vastly outran their performance as mechanisms for drought relief. Long before Alagoas's provincial president Soares Brandão exposed fraud at the São Francisco colony, other problems had occurred. In July 1878, Soares Brandão advised Sinimbu of supply problems. Vessels of both the Bahian and Pernambucan steamship companies arrived in Maceió with full holds, and could not take on any goods destined for Piranhas and the colony.[35] He again complained bitterly about this situation toward the close of the following month, noting that it had forced him to buy goods at higher prices in the river port Penedo, which was located nearer to the colony. He suggested that the Penedo merchants had deliberately created the problem so as to force the provincial government to buy from them. The merchants had vastly inflated their normal order of goods from Recife, so that fully loaded with goods for Penedo, the Pernambucan company's ships had no cargo space remaining to bring goods to Piranhas. At the same time, the larger order gave the Penedo merchants ample supplies to sell to the government.[36]

Having decided to shut down the *núcleo* following the revelation of fraud, Soares Brandão visited the site in November and found the entire colony "profoundly agitated," because of what he described as "open warfare" between the director and the vice-director, who was allied with another official whom Soares Brandão had dismissed fully two months ago as the person responsible for keeping dishonest records. He also expressed disappointment with the limited amount of planting that had taken place, and directly blamed this on the indolent *retirantes'* reluctance to labor. Finally, having dispersed a large number of the São Francisco's residents to sites of other provincial work opportunities, most notably on the Paulo Afonso railroad, he turned the colony over to the jurisdiction of the local *município*. Soares Brandão expressed doubt that the colony would survive, adding that he had "no faith in the county council's ability."[37] Then, shortly before Christmas, he sent a military officer and troops to close down the colony. The officer reported a sizable number of sick *retirantes*, including 152 orphaned children, and placed the daily death rate at 10-12 people.[38]

Eliseu de Sousa Martins, the president of Rio Grande do Norte, rather shamelessly named his proposed *retirante* agricultural settlement the Sinimbu colony, and suggested it as "a means of calling the people to work."[39] Beyond this announced objective, the colony enabled him to cashier conservative-appointed relief commissions and create patronage openings for *amigos*, while gaining a degree of independence from the province's two Liberal chiefs, Amaro Carneiro Bezerra Cavalcante and José Moreira Brandão Castelo Branco, both then serving as deputies in the National Legislative Assembly. To direct the colony, he chose Arsenio Celestino Pimental, a Portuguese whom he had known in Pernambuco who was beholden neither to Amaro nor Moreira Brandão. This caused a breach between Sousa Martins and the two Liberal chiefs, who subsequently declared formal opposition to their correligionist president. In August, Amaro sent telegrams criticizing Sousa Martins to a contact in Pernambuco, Luís Felippe de Sousa Leão, the nephew of the minister of foreign affairs, the Baron Vila Bela. He also sent telegrams to Vila Bela and Sinimbu decrying Sousa Martins's "betrayal" of the party.[40]

In July, 1878, after only some three months of existence, the colony became the scene of an armed conflict and the arrest of Pimental by a *subdelegado* of police from the nearby town of Estremoz, Lourenço

Fernandes Campos Café. In a confidential letter to the minister of justice, Sousa Martins explained this incident as resulting from the machinations of the *subdelegado*, who himself had coveted the colony's directorship. Sousa Martins pointed out that he had dismissed Café from the Estremoz relief commission, and had ultimately eliminated the commission itself. The jealous Café, had "intrigued with influential politicians" and conspired with area landowners.[41]

Soon thereafter, however, Sousa Martins entered into conflict with an inspector sent to Rio Grande do Norte by the finance minister, as well as with the new provincial police chief, who had become an ally of Amaro. As tensions rose, and letters both official and private flowed back and forth between Rio de Janeiro and Rio Grande do Norte, in October 1878, pleading ill health, Sousa Martins asked to be relieved of his post. Without even leaving a report for his successor, he set off to Rio de Janeiro. Protected by powerful friends in the capital, including the Baron Vila Bela, who described the fallen president's situation as a "real torment," Sousa Martins soon gained to the presidency of Espírito Santo.[42] Despite their far more profound torment, the *retirantes* of the Sinimbu colony had enjoyed no such protection.

Vice-president Manuel Januário Bezerra Montenegro, one of Amaro's followers, took over and sent an official, accompanied by a strong military detachment, to the Sinimbu colony to inventory its supplies. He found the storehouses mostly bare, for relief supplies had been taken by Arsenio Pimental's associates. He also reported that Pimental and his henchmen had used the colony's relief supplies to pay some of the costs of shipping the goods to the colony, thereby pocketing a goodly percentage of the funds allocated for that purpose. This was far from petty theft. From the colony's inception on June 1 1878 through October, transport costs had totaled nearly 8 *contos*.[43]

According to Montenegro's people, the Sinimbu colony presented a truly horrid spectacle. Some six thousand people crammed into twelve hundred hovels "each so small one would scarcely imagine that they were supposed to house human beings." Instead of carefully assigned lots, these dwellings, "surrounded by filth so bad that it takes great strength of will even to come close to them," formed "an intricate labyrinth where it becomes impossible to distinguish a street or a space that merits that name."[44]

The disarray and squalor of those conditions, however, paled before the tales of horror regarding Pimental's tenure as director. Disease had been rampant, especially from June through August, when an estimated 30-60 people died daily. While few records survived, one document indicated nearly 4,000 deaths, "a truly terrifying figure for a colony in existence only four months, and which never perhaps had as many as 10,000 people." Inattention extended even to death, as bodies were left for days to decompose, and then, often without a coffin, placed in shallow graves where dogs and birds could tear at the remains. When the colonists, without first asking permission, organized a funeral procession and marched behind an image of Saint Sebastian, Pimental ordered them to stop, threatened to shoot them, and said, "in this place I am Saint Sebastian!"

Despite detailing this fraud and misery, the official provincial report by Montenegro's fact-finding commission nonetheless found fault with the *retirantes*. Without direction and labor—because of Pimental's dereliction—the colonists became accustomed to a "reprehensible idleness." This had led to "exceedingly bad habits" that contributed to high rates of disease and mortality. In arguing for continuing the colony, provincial officials raised the specter of loosing on society "some 6,000 lost men...habituated to pillage" who doubtless would ravage the area.[45] The culpability of *retirantes* emerged in the official imperial report on the colony, which made no mention of Pimental's fraud or the various political machinations that had plagued the colony and caused its failure. Instead, it observed, "The condition of that colony was deplorable, because rather than engaging in labor its inhabitants immersed themselves in indolence and idleness waiting for relief supplies from the State."[46]

If culpability for the theft of the colony's relief goods remained a moot point, little doubt exists that the *retirantes* had never received appropriate support. If initially they had lazed about in the expectation of receiving supplies from the government, would they not soon have abandoned that notion when no such support materialized? Even were we to discount Montenegro's official report as largely fabricated to discredit his predecessor, the brief span of the colony's existence must be factored into any evaluation of the *retirantes'* responsibility for Sinimbu's failure. Granting the best of intentions to the colony's director and the most energetic action on the part of *retirantes*, with the colony beginning in the midst of the March rains, settling in, tracing streets and lots, and erecting dwellings would have been extremely difficult. Heavy rains would have interfered with preparation of gardens and would have washed away plantings. Once planted, of course, crops needed time to mature. Even the most hard-working of *retirantes* could not possibly become self-supporting prior to a harvest. Furthermore, Montenegro's report had detailed not only deprivation, but a high incidence of disease. Surely it was not reasonable to expect much work from a sick, malnourished *retirante*.

Pernambuco's Colônia Socorro proved the most successful of the colonies. Comparatively rich to begin with, Pernambuco also suffered much less of the direct climatic effect of drought. It had a better transportation network and its central relief commission, given its larger regional role, was in a good position to supply the colony with start-up resources. Located near Palmares, which had a railway link to Recife, Colônia Socorro seemingly should have had no problem securing supplies.[47]

Luiz José da Silva, an engineer, led an initial group of 385 *retirantes* to the site in April 1878. Writing to the provincial vice-president, da Silva acknowledged the wisdom of various suggestions that had been made by André Rebouças, including the importance of providing the displaced *sertanejos* with lands appropriate for agriculture and with adequate transportation whether by river or sea. In this fashion, drought relief would produce the maximum benefit for the *retirantes* for a minimal level of expenditure.[48] Further expressing the modernizing creed, da Silva referred to the vast fertile unused lands in the interior, and affirmed that their richness promised a hundred fold return for those who would work it.[49] By June 1878 the colony's population had risen to some 9,000 people.

But that rapid growth did not testify to the experiment's success. That same month, the district judge of Palmares, who served as head of that city's relief commission, had received a contingent of 241 *retirantes* from Recife and sent them on to the colony. The colony's director, a Capuchin priest, had sent them back to Palmares because the settlement's warehouse was completely out of supplies. This created difficulties in Palmares, as it struggled to cope with thousands of its own *retirantes*. The best it could manage for those returned from the colony was to house them in a brickyard located in a dank, low-lying area.[50] Explaining his refusal to admit those *retirantes*, the Capuchin father pointed to poor conditions among those already living in the colony. They had been getting by on half rations, and even with that expedient the larder remained bare. Heavy June rains had made roads virtually impassable, and no nearby settlement had the needed provisions.[51] Indeed, supplies that did reach the colony got there only when *retirantes* themselves did the transporting, carrying goods on their heads at a pay rate of one *milréis* per package.[52] Further complicating matters, as the vice-president later reported, relatively few backlanders had been permanently settled because the distribution of plots had not proceeded as quickly as planned.[53]

While early supply problems compounded by a large initial influx of *retirantes* in the first few months might seem a reasonable explanation for these difficulties, the colony continued to require enormous support throughout the year. The amount of dried beef sent to the colony almost equaled the total used for all other drought relief in Pernambuco, and the colony's share of *farinha* proved disproportionately high as well.[54]

Furthermore, despite the apparently good hygienic conditions of its phys-ical site, the colony soon witnessed massive epidemic outbreaks of fevers, boils, diarrhea, and measles. Over a six-month period, nearly 1,500 peo-ple died.[55] The formal cessation of relief spelled the end of Colônia Socorro. In April 1880, its director averred that conditions had improved to the point that the *retirantes* there no longer required relief supplies, However, without government subsidy, the settlement would not be able to "retain its organization and continue to provide practical instruction in agriculture."[56] Beyond continued financial support, he also suggested that an overseer would be needed to make sure that the "colonists did not ruin the land." He also worried about outsiders, who might menace the *reti-rantes* and usurp their lands. In true tutelary language, reminiscent of Jesuit reductions of the colonial era, he styled the colonists as "peaceful citizens from different places and provinces accustomed to the routine of the colony who could not deal with insults and threats."[57]

APPROPRIATE BEHAVIORS

The failure of Colônia Socorro suggests the difficulties of establish-ing such resettlement colonies even in a wealthy province where the director appeared to take his obligations seriously and where fraud seemed largely absent. Once again, elite optimism regarding both the prodigious fertility of the land and the ease of achieving change bore lit-tle consonance with quotidian reality. But such failures never called into question those fundamental articles of faith. In part, the reported corrup-tion of provincial relief officials provided elites with a ready explanation for failed initiatives. More important, however, were their paternalistic ethos and stock of "knowledge" regarding the *sertão* and the *sertanejo*, which predisposed them to apportion the greatest share of responsibility to the *retirantes* themselves. Despite having acknowledged the machina-tion of Penedo merchants and the fraudulent and irresponsible behavior of public officials, Soares Brandão nonetheless attributed the São Francisco colony's collapse largely to the propensity of *retirantes* to "flee from labor."[58] Public officials, as we have seen, used that same rationale to explain the failure of colonies in Piauí and Rio Grande do Norte.

To be sure, elites responded angrily to actions they defined as immoral exploitation of innocent *retirantes*. For example, the contractor overseeing the extension of the Recife-São Francisco Railroad told the Recife Central relief commission that he would take on *retirantes* as workers, guaranteeing a minimum daily pay rate of one *milréis*. The com-mission publicized this opportunity to other of Pernambuco's relief com-missions. However, it appeared that the *retirantes* received their wages monthly, and thus were forced in the interim to purchase food and other items on credit from the company store. Furthermore, they received pay in chits, redeemable only at that company store.

The Recife commission championed the cause of the *retirantes*. "Such exploitation" said the outraged commission, "in itself injurious to the poor classes, becomes intolerable . . . during a horrible crisis in which the Government, in order to save the poor has taken it upon itself to provide relief to these unfortunates."[59] The commission stopped promoting this labor opportunity pending a response from the contractor. It noted as well that it had advised him that in Pernambuco, it was customary to pay workers on a weekly basis.[60]

The commission's angry response and action evidenced its belief that the contractor had violated appropriate standards of behavior when it came to dealing with the virtuous, suffering poor. Roberto da Matta has pointed to "paradigmatic social characters or personages" that define "a certain way of being and belonging to Brazilian society."[61] The worthy poor formed an integral part of a paternalistic Catholic society. As Richard Graham observes, praise for charitable behavior toward the poor constituted a "celebration of patronal values."[62] The poor's existence allowed others to practice the virtue of charity, which, in such cases ennobled the giver but did not shame the receiver of alms. The "worthy" or "deserving" poor knew their place and behaved accordingly. They displayed the "virtues of honest poverty": humility, resignation, and gratitude for the assistance they received.

When *retirantes* appeared to step outside these prescribed ways of being and behaving, elites viewed them as unworthy, immoral, and threatening. Telling in this regard are the concerns expressed by Ceará President João José Ferreira de Aguiar regarding the large numbers of *retirantes* in Fortaleza, "All those people who at first were peaceful, humble, and obedient, already are becoming restless and demanding."[63] *Retirantes* regularly received censure for acting in bad faith, not only as malingerers but as dishonest individuals who connived to get more than their just share of relief goods. For example, in Pernambuco, the province's Public Health Inspector reported that some *retirantes* in Recife enrolled themselves in multiple government lodging houses so as to receive more relief goods. They then sold these extra rations to buy liquor or to gamble.[64] Alagoas's central relief commission opined that masses of *retirantes* had abused the relief system: "cloth exchanged for tobacco; meat for cigarettes; soap for impure honey."[65] A treasury official in Piauí justifying a request for funds to repair a building used to house *retirantes* explained that in a five-month period they had virtually destroyed the lodging. That destructive behavior occurred, said the offical, because they lacked both discipline and manners. To expect any other behavior from the *retirantes*, "one would have to be unfamilar with these people, their condition and customs, especially when gathered together in large numbers."[66]

Paraíba's president reported that *retirantes* used all sorts of stratagems to obtain extra rations, including securing multiple ration cards by having various members of their families register as heads of the household. To end such abuse and "regularize" the distribution of relief, he designated one central plaza as a gathering place for the capital's entire *retirante* population. All *retirantes* would have to appear at one specified time, so that officials could count their exact numbers. Relief supplies would be piled in six separate locations around the plaza, and, following a formal head count, the *retirantes* would be sent to one of them.[67] Picturing this scene—masses of hungry people pressing up against the doors that guarded the piles of relief goods—scarcely conveys an image of regularity or order. And what of those *retirantes* who, whether due to illness, a work situation, or problems with another family member, could not make it to the square at the appointed time? Clearly, then, imperatives of the social system allowed elites, with clear conscience, to subject *sertanejos* to treatment that an observer outside that system would see as dehumanizing.

Embedded in and emerging from a mental universe rooted in hierarchy and paternalism, elite judgments of appropriate *retirante* behavior provided the drought refugees little space for independent judgment or action. For example, the initial waves of *retirante* migration were seen as resulting from personal moral shortcomings. One Pernambucan, writing in December 1877, characterized arriving *retirantes* as "in the majority composed of murderers since up until the present, the moral and hardworking portion of the *sertão* still had not left.[68] The Capuchin prelate who oversaw Pernambuco's orphan colony refused admittance to those early *retirantes*, seeing in their migration proof of indolence and a failure to save for the future.[69] However, reporting on those who had waited longer to leave the backlands, the *Jornal do Comércio* scorned them as "improvident" and contrasted their lack of foresight with those "more prudent" inhabitants who had left in 1877.[70] Whether migrating early or late, then, backlanders received censure. Similarly, a refusal to passively suffer exploitative conditions became a "flight from labor." Furthermore, manipulating the system to secure advantage—a practice followed by all elites—was defined as immoral behavior when engaged in by *retirantes*.

THE HUMAN FACE OF DROUGHT

Throughout the years of the Great Drought, the displaced backlanders appeared in official discourse as *retirantes*, a generic term

that had the effect of homogenizing and, to a great extrent, dehumanizing those vast massses of people, children, women and men, old and
young, who had fled the ravages of drought. It becomes virtually impossible to give voice to these people through their own words for, invariably, they appear in documents produced by elite members of society.
Some of those, however, can suggest some of the human tragedy that lay
at the heart of the experience of drought.

In May 1877, *O Cearense* printed a report from Milagres about a family of *retirantes* who had spent the night sleeping in the bush. Setting off
the next day, they left behind two children. Later, some passers-by
encountered the children, one of whom lay dead, and the other dying.[71]
That same year, a county judge in Ceará wrote of a family in which four
people had already died from hunger and disease. Two more were being
buried that day, and the judge feared that the rest of the family would
soon be breathing their last.[72]

The *Jornal do Recife* in September 1878 wrote of a group of *retirantes*
found sleeping beneath a fig tree near one of the city's bridges. The
group included several young girls and four children, three women and
three men, all of whom appeared sallow and tattered. A member of the
city relief commission saw the group later that evening and sent the head
of one of the families along with his brother-in-law and three of the children to one of the city's *retirante* lodging houses; the women wound up
at a city hospital, while the remaining family group received some food
rations so they could go back to the interior.[73] Two months later, that
newspaper wrote about a family of *retirantes*, a mother and three small
children, homeless in the streets. Not only did they lack food and shelter;
they also had small pox. The paper observed that if help were not soon
forthcoming, the family would die in the street as though they were
dumb animals.[74]

Recife's health inspector went to a quarantine facility where 72 *retirantes* from Ceará had been sent. He reported that "the greater part of the
people are young children," and that they were in dire condition because
of lack of food and medical care.[75] Meanwhile, a Paraíba relief commission observed that, despite their best efforts, by May 1878 the situation in
their town had become wholly untenable. Hundreds of people "worthy
of a better fate" already had died. The local population was in too weakened a condition to migrate, while perhaps half of those who had left
previously had died.[76]

Though the various people in the above reports remain nameless,
each forms part of a massive tragedy: children dead and dying; families
sundered by migration, disease and death; many settlements throughout
the northeast abandoned; many others overwhelmed by streams of desperate refugees. And, even prior to the migration, these people already

had experienced growing anxiety as the winter rains failed. Then came the final, horrid realization that drought's grip left them no alternative but to abandon their homes. As one author has written, the *retirante* is one "who sees his crops reduced to powder, his cattle dead from hunger, and after walking in search of the last green branch of the juàzeiro, carving the last small hole in a the dry bed of a creek" finally leaves his home.[77] One of the most powerful evocations of drought and the plight of *retirantes* appeared in Graciliano Ramos's classic novel *Vidas Sêcas* ("Barren Lives").

> The jujube trees spread in two green stains across the reddish plain. The drought victims had been walking all day; they were tired and hungry. The foliage of the jujubes loomed in the distance. Slowly they dragged themselves in that direction. Vitória carried the younger boy astride her hip and the tin trunk on top of her head. Fabiano stumbled along gloomily . . . . The older boy and the dog straggled behind.
>
> The brushland stretched in every direction, its vaguely reddish hue broken only by white heaps of dry bones. Vultures flew in black circles over dying animals. They had left the road, full of thorns and stones, and for hours had been walking along the riverbed, whose dry, cracked mud scorched their feet. They had hunted in vain for roots to eat. The last of the manioc flour was gone . . . .[78]

Those deep scars of drought clearly emerge in the words of contemporary northeasterners. As Nancy Schepper-Hughes writes, "The people . . . approach each dry season with something akin to dread, as if it were an annual drought." And, she further notes, "the image of drought is formidable, capturing the imagination of people who are inclined to describe all that is bad in terms of dryness . . . ."[79]

The views from the provinces further delineate disparities between the real and imagined drought. The political culture of provincial government and politics magnified existing problems related to public sector infrastructure. Oriented toward patronage rather than toward public service, government officials pursued policies that rewarded friends and allies. At the same time, the conceptual unity of imperial elites, whether national or provincial, contributed toward the implementation of policies of work relief that exploited the very people that relief purported to serve. And when those various work schemes failed, thereby further victimizing the displaced backlanders, the defective character of the *retirantes* provided an easily accepted explanation.

REPRESENTATIONS AND REALITIES

Imperial policy pronouncements that limited and finally ended relief advanced a construction of reality that justified the government's position. Its central formulations hinged on assertions regarding the severity of drought, the necessity of continued relief, and the impact of public assistance on the *retirantes* as well as on Brazilian society and finances. The absence of rains had occasioned the emergency; improved weather conditions signaled its end. Drought had now become an artifice used to promote the self-interest of those who wrongfully profited from government largesse. Relief maintained large numbers of *retirantes* in idleness while the nation paid the bill. Accustomed to this support and having lost all habits of labor, these displaced *sertanejos* preferred a life on the dole in government-sponsored lodging houses and colonies. By forcing reluctant *retirantes* to return home, the government once more fulfilled its obligation to them and to the nation. Since the rains had returned and the immensely fertile land quickly recovered, the *retirantes* could easily resume their former existence. Through labor the *retirantes* would regain self-respect and dignity. And, if terminating the dole saved *retirantes* from a life of depravity, it also saved Brazil from the danger of becoming saddled with a permanent officially sanctioned class of paupers. Relief's end promised welcome respite from the financial sacrifice that had been borne willingly by all Brazilians, and the easing of a budgetary crisis that threatened the very future of the nation.

At various points in this discussion, I have noted the marked divergence between the representations embedded in official rhetoric and the reality of *retirante* exploitation, deprivation, and death. It seems appropriate, then, to again step outside that imperial perspective and evaluate several of the dominant representations that buttressed the elites' shared reality of drought, and to focus more closely on some of the political factors that affected the elaboration and implementation of relief policy.

RAINFALL BY DECREE

At first glance, climate seems one of those "hard" facts not susceptible to varying representations. On numerous occasions throughout the drought various officials suggested that conditions had improved to the point that relief might be either minimized or eliminated. When subjected to some scrutiny, however, many of those statments fly in the fact of empirical reality. Consider the words of a Paraíban vice president who saw an end to the drought because the capital and *brejos* had received abundant rains.[1] By definition, the *brejos* constituted the province's most drought-resistant areas—apart from the littoral where the capital was located. The worst droughts were the ones that ultimately affected even those favored areas. But even when afflicted with drought, the *brejos* and coast recovered first. The semi-arid *sertão*, by contrast, always experienced far more of the devastation of drought, and the interior certainly could remain dry, while the coast experienced some rain.

In July 1878, the commander of a government warship transporting *retirantes* from Pernambuco and Paraíba to Pará remarked that there was no more drought in Pernambuco because "it had been raining throughout the province for the entire month."[2] Assuming that his large ship simply plied the coastal waters from Recife to Pará, how could the commander have any direct knowledge about conditions in the interior? Yet such casual observations formed the basis of government pronouncements about weather conditions in the provinces of the north.

If elites accused *sertanejos* of fatalistically awaiting the onset of rains, government officials seemingly created it by decree. Recall that March and April witness the heaviest rainfall in the *agreste* and *sertão*, and June essentially concludes the "winter." In fact, in *sertanejo* tradition regarding drought, St. Joseph's Day—March 19—is the last day for rains to appear and produce a real "winter."[3] Consider, then, the timing of some of the imperial declarations regarding the declining severity of drought. In October 1878, citing improved weather, imperial officials had questioned the need for continuing relief. Rains again fell according to the emperor's *Fala* of October 30, 1879. Those pronouncements shared two critical characteristics: they were issued prior to the usual onset of "winter" in the *agreste* and *sertão*, and they had no data to support them. Furthermore, Finance Minister Afonso Celso de Assis Figueiredo's strongest push to shut down relief occurred in June and July of 1879, coinciding, therefore, with the onset of the dry season in the *sertão*.

The October 14, 1878 circular sent out by Minister of the Empire Leôncio de Carvalho had advised provincial presidents to have *retirantes* return to the interior. It had been motivated in part by September communications from the president of Alagoas, who had asserted that weather conditions had improved dramatically. While rains could fall along the coast in September and October, the interior rarely received any substantial rains at that time. Hence, the light rains known as the *chuvas de caju* fell in October on the coast, but in December in the interior. Furthermore, among the provinces of the north, Alagoas typically had a lesser incidence of drought, given its more southerly location and broad coastal plains.

Responses to the October circular from many of the provinces of the north reflected precious little optimism with regard to the possibility of ending relief, though all presidents assured the minister of the empire that they shared his concern and understood the importance of exercising fiscal restraint. Writing in November, Paraíba's president remarked that the province remained in bad shape, and that relief certainly could not be cut off prior to the arrival of winter. He noted as well that if returning *retirantes* were expected to plant anything, they would require seeds, as well as food and clothing for their journey home. He also expressed reservations about the possibility of getting the *retirantes* to return home, since conditions in the interior remained poor, and the current of migration out of the backlands had become well established.[4]

When the president of Piauí, Sancho de Barros Pimental, responded to the October circular, he immediately pointed out that if rains defined drought, then nothing had improved. After all, the onset of the rainy season still remained some months away. Assuring the minister that he had from the start always emphasized the need to have *retirantes* engaged in agriculture, the president also noted the "strict fiscal supervision" existing with regard to the province's colonies. Ground had been cleared, but planting awaited the first rains, which could not be expected until December. Pimental pointed to the prominence of women and children in the *retirante* population, saying that able-bodied men without families had emigrated to other provinces, and noted that harvest time in Piauí did not come until March.

Having justified his own administration by asserting its shared concern regarding the use of imperial funds, and defined the *retirantes* as deserving poor—women and children, workers, not idlers—he declared his willingness to follow the circular's directive to have the *retirantes* return to their homes. However, he also warned of probable resistance, diplomatically noting that conditions in Piauí did not match those said by the circular to obtain in Ceará.[5] When this response reached the ministry, officials remained unimpressed by the president's arguments.

Indeed, they essentially dismissed the nonconforming facts and emphasized that Pimental would be taking steps to meet the recommendations
of the circular.[6]

The Piauí president dutifully sent the circular to the province's several relief commissions. Their responses suggested even more com-
pellingly the discrepancy between the "facts" noted in the circular and
the "facts" of conditions in Piauí. That correspondence, furthermore,
mirrored in significant ways the communication between the president
and the empire. The relief commission of Campo Maior spoke of the
drought's decimation of herds of cattle and horses, and the absence of
grains for both *retirantes* and the town's resident population. The commission nonetheless assured him that they would do their part to carry
out the circular's instructions.[7] The commission of Paranagua pointed to
continuing migration from Ceará and Pernambuco, bringing people in
"a miserable state" to a locale where the "the poor class...that lives from
farming is dying of hunger and disease."[8] As a final example from Piauí,
a district judge and public prosecutor who headed the relief commission
of União wrote that the *municipio*, and indeed the entire province, was
going through the drought's worst period, with food and water both failing. Asserting that "death would infallibly result" if *retirantes* returned to
the interior, he pointed as well to a continuing flow of *retirantes* sent on
to União because of its location along the Parnahyba river. If these people were to be sent anywhere, it ought not be back to the *sertão*, he
advised, but to Maranhão and Pará.[9]

As is clear from such communications, conditions in Piauí did not
share the supposedly "improved" situation in Ceará. In point of fact, any
such improvement in Ceará also seems dubious. The president of Ceará
himself advised the Minister of the Empire that present circumstances—
including small pox raging in Fortaleza and a lack of foodstuffs in the
interior—did not permit any return to the *sertão*. The degree to which the
circular remained out of sync with climate patterns in the north again
became clear in the president's correspondence, for he told the minister
that when the winter rains fell in January and winter arrived, he would
immediately promote the *retirantes'* return home.[10] Those rains, of course,
never did fall, as the provinces of the north suffered through another horrid year of drought.

Responses to the ministry of the empire's June-July 1879 push to
end the drought recapitulated the October 1878 experience in that so
much of drought's devastation still gripped the land. Ceará President
José Julio de Albuquerque Barros advised provincial relief commissions
to "use all measures at their disposal to persuade the indigent to find
some useful work or occupation to support themselves." Further, should
they prove unable to secure such remunerated employment, they ought

to "seek the *serras*, banks of rivers and lakes, or other places" where they could engage in agriculture.[11] As in the case of the October 1878 circular, responses from relief commissions throughout Ceará noted the persistence of drought and consequent impossibility of implementing Barros's recommendations. The commission of Caixa flatly stated that no work opportunities existed in the immediate area of their dry *sertão*, save for one place already overrun with *retirantes*. It styled as "useless" the recommendation that *retirantes* be sent to places where they might engage in agriculture, saying that it had no idea where any such places might be. Furthermore, it lacked the means to provision *retirantes* for any such journey.[12] Authorities in Vila de Pereira expressed total bewilderment with Barros's circular. Gardens had been prepared and seeds planted, but then the rains ceased. When they again began to fall, the parched plantings already had died. As for potential employment, the commissioners could think of only two locales, one of which was in the littoral—the very area from which *retirantes* had been expelled. The other, in the Cariri Valley, was suffering from an epidemic of smallpox.[13]

Disheartening notices came from the very areas that *retirantes* had been advised to seek. Rich and fertile Baturité already had more people than it profitably could employ, so "innumerable" *retirantes* who had gone there, had left disappointed.[14] Telha had been spared the total drought experienced by the high *sertão*, but three years of sparse rain had reduced its productivity and resources. As for advising *retirantes* to seek other places, Telha's relief commission remarked that the *sertanejos* "already have traveled throughout the entire province and parts of Piauí, and found nothing."[15] Another of those supposedly favored locations, Granja, also offered little hope to *retirantes*. A physician working for the Sobral railroad reported that the absence of rains since late May had caused the nearby river to dry up into a series of small marshes, giving rise to the plague and assorted fevers that afflicted the city's residents. On top of that, smallpox had appeared.[16]

At precisely the time that *retirantes* left Fortaleza's lodging houses, there came news from União that the poor, "bereft of resources," were preparing to leave for Fortaleza.[17] Apparently, they were not alone. In July, several weeks after announcing the new relief policy, President Barros estimated the population of Fortaleza's lodging houses at twenty thousand. That figure, if accurate, represented a doubling of the *retirante* population over the previous few months. Meanwhile, waves of *retirantes* expelled from the littoral because of the end of relief journeyed back toward the sertão, and in the process overwhelmed settlements along their route. For example, Humaytá's relief commission pointed out that with five hundred *retirantes* already there, and the number "growing daily," it lacked all of the resources to which the president had referred:

"...after three years of drought, private charity does not exist, and there are no running rivers, mountains, or lakes."[18]

This latest shift in government policy resulted in crisscrossing waves of *retirantes* precisely because the conditions on which it was predicated had no basis in fact. Addressing the provincial legislature in July 1880, Barros noted that during the previous year, rains had fallen only in February, March, and May. Furthermore, February's rains had been sparse.[19] In Rio Grande do Norte the rains of 1879 had been "weak," adequate perhaps to provide pasturage for the cattle, but only because their numbers had dwindled drastically. [20] In the words of one well-regarded agriculturalist, a successful growing season required not just some rains, but a true "winter."[21] Given those conditions, the re-migration home doubtlessly proved a painful, if not deadly, experience.

Even had the rains of 1879 proved copious, sending *retirantes* back to the interior during June and July made little sense. Preparation of gardens and planting of food crops typically took place from March through the end of May. Normally, then, June and July were times for harvesting crops of beans and green maize. In fact, the corn harvest formed a key element in the backlands festivities honoring St. Anthony, St. John, and St. Peter during those months.[22]

The finance minister thus proposed to send *retirantes* into the *sertão* at a time no longer propitious for agriculture. Seeds could not be planted for at least six months, and then only for short-cycle crops, not the longer-maturing maize. Furthermore, successful plantings required a good rainy season. Nor could a few rains instantly restore the region's periodic rivers to their former volume, and fertile *vazantes* would not exist until those rivers, swollen with rain, overflowed their banks and submerged surrounding lands. The Great Drought's swath of dislocation, devastation, and death to a large extent reflected the absence of an effective infrastructure in the interior for capturing and storing water. The numerous discussions of the need to construct wells and dams and promote irrigation had remained largely in the realm of discourse. Returning *retirantes* would have had to rely on rains that remained several months distant.

The *brejos* had been overwhelmed by *retirantes* for much of the drought; encouraging more people to seek those locales would make matters worse. Furthermore, since government-funded projects provided one of the largest employment options in the region, ending those funds would throw still more people onto a virtually non-existent job market. After all, the drought had depressed economic activity throughout the region except in those "oasis" areas where normal rainfall patterns had not been interrupted. Aside from a few *brejos*, that left only the littoral, the very zone the government now urged the *retirantes* to leave.

THE RETURN HOME

While climate did not justify the policy pronouncements of the Sinimbu ministry, José Antonio Saraiva did speak accurately when he said that "abundant rains" had fallen in the "winter" of 1880. But did that mean that the displaced *sertanejos* provisioned with food, seeds, and clothing could now travel home and resume their former lives? Both the journey that *retirantes* presumably would make and the conditions awaiting them if they did in fact "return to their homes" merit some discussion.

Despite the elite's celebration of a compassionate national effort that avoided the "depopulation" of the provinces of the north, many *retirantes* never returned to their former homes. Both Pará and still more distant Amazonas had large resettlement colonies.[23] Similarly, *retirantes* had been shipped to ports in the south. How could any of these people easily return to their native provinces? Despite the discursive attention to formerly humble people now waxing wealthy, the drought years had not improved the *retirantes'* lot. In a pattern subsequently repeated in other extended droughts, many of the inhabitants of the provinces of the north remained permanently displaced, filling the labor needs of more dynamic regions, and swelling the "marginal" populations of major cities both within and outside the provinces of the north.[24]

In 1880, for example, Recife's major hospital, Pedro II, had 585 patients. According to an official associated with the local Santa Casa de Misericordia, occupancy was high because many *retirantes* had remained in Recife. He further opined that given their "irregular lives" and the climate difference between *sertão* and coast, they became more susceptible to disease.[25] The president of Pará reported in 1879 that the drought-spawned emigration to his province had increased, and many of those arriving had been sent on to Amazonas.[26]

Even those who had remained within the region faced a daunting journey. From a littoral perspective, the *alto sertão* remained isolated and remote. The new railroad lines—designed to haul freight, not passengers—did not extend very far into the interior.[27] Even within the small province of Rio Grande do Norte, journeys inland from a major refuge center like Mossoró involved difficult terrain and distances of up to 330 kilometers. Setting out on foot, carrying whatever supplies had been provided by coastal relief commissions, and, in many cases weakened by malnutrition and disease, *retirantes* could not necessarily count on finding assistance along the way. The years of drought had depleted the reserves of even the most favored communities. Assuming *retirantes* journeyed forth in May 1880 when the government officially ended relief, those *agreste* and *brejo* communities' main harvest remained several months in the future. After three years of drought, storehouses and interior markets certainly did not overflow with goods. Those migrating a bit later might find that the earlier waves of returnees already had depleted whatever resources these small settlements could offer. The original trek out from the *sertão* had proven arduous. But that migration had led the *sertanejos* out from drought while the present one delivered them into a land ravaged by its impact.

RESUMING "NORMAL" LIVES

What might have awaited those *retirantes* who reached their former homes? At the most basic level, we might question whether any of those homes still existed. Those who had migrated earliest were returning after an absence of some thirty months, and even the last to leave had been absent for at least a year. Throughout that time, neither their homes nor plots of land had been tended. The migration during the drought of many of the locally wealthy, those who owned the land and ranches, had further changed and depressed conditions. In some cases, lands formerly occupied by the returning *retirantes* had been sold to, or appropriated by another local landowner.[28] In any event, livestock had been liquidated because of the impossibility of maintaining herds in the absence of water and pasture, and corrals, barns, and the like had fallen into disrepair. And what of the need to reestablish *feiras* and commercial networks?

In her novel *O Quinze*, Rachel de Queiroz suggests some of the anguish felt by returning *retirantes* confronted by the devastation of ther land and homes. She writes of famished cattle, bruising their muzzles against the hard ground as they try to wrest some nourishment from the barely regenerated *mata*, and notes as well the absence of any stored supplies of grains and foodstuffs. This meant that the *retirantes* would still confront several hungry months. Writing of one of the returnees, she notes: "And upon seeing her house, the empty corral, the stockraising pen devastated and silent, life all dead despite the sheet of green that covered the ground, Dona Inácia cried bitterly, with that same hopeless affliction of one who has encountered the corpse of a person dearly loved who during one's absence had died." [29]

Even if successful returnees immediately set out to prepare their gardens, it was already late in the season to reap much immediate benefit. After all, an arrival home in June or July once again coincided with "winter's" end and the onset of the dry season. With no existing crops, and the possibility of regular rains nearly half a year away, the prospects for even bare survival, let alone prosperity, would seem minimal. If one measures that reality against the government's assistance to returning *retirantes*—some seeds and supplies for the journey home—neither compassion nor charity seem to characterize imperial policy.

Furthermore, resuming "normal" life required not only the resumption of normal weather, but of the institutions that bounded *sertanejo* existence. Critical among these were personal ties, those of household, family, kinship, and patron-client relationships. Traditionally, a high degree of mutuality characterized *sertanejo* existence, whether with regard to clearing land, constructing dwellings, or erecting corrals, and the household served as a vital economic unit and source of farm labor.[30] The tendency of *sertanejos* to migrate in family units reflected that traditional pattern. However, that massive outmigration and its associated death toll had decimated families, sundering the associational fabric of backlands life.

Ties to those of higher status and wealth provided backlanders with their only insurance against bad fortune.[31] However, many of the locally wealthy came back much later, only when it became certain that 1880 would indeed see a true "winter." For example, in June 1880, Sobral's county council wrote to the president of Ceará asking for a postponement in the scheduled elections for council members and justices of the peace. The council pointed to the three past years of drought and associated outmigration, and asserted that the lands of the *municipio* had been virtually deserted. Now, people were just beginning to return.[32] Paraíba's president made a similar request regarding the March 1880 meeting of the provincial assembly, asking that it be put off until October. He pointed out that "winter" was beginning, and that the members of the assembly needed to focus on rebuilding their holdings, "after a three-year drought that had ruined the province's agriculture and livestock."[33]

Many among the region's wealthier elements never did return, preferring instead to remain in the south or on the coast. In other cases the drought's devastation reduced those formerly well-off segments of backlands society to conditions in which they no longer could fulfill a seignorial role. For these varied reasons, then, the vertical links of pre-drought *sertão* and *agreste* could not automatically be restored.

An instantaneous recovery from other impacts of the drought similarly defies credibility. Consider, for example, the multiple implications of changed demographic patterns, including lower population concentrations in the *sertão* and higher densities in littoral settlements, as well as the veritable *retirante* diaspora. Indeed, it "helped establish a lasting pattern of seasonal migration."[34] Furthermore, the Great Drought had reversed a trend of rising salaries for agricultural workers, while at the same time raising food prices.[35] *Sertanejos*, therefore, would have a still more difficult time regaining pre-drought levels of existence, which, as we have seen, scarcely had been comfortable even in those so-called times of abundance.

Despite prevailing images of a rich and flourishing region that speedily resumed prosperity, the devastation and dislocation caused by the Great Drought would linger for years. While one decent winter might serve to produce both pasturage and foodstuffs, the drought had decimated most of the region's cattle. Rebuilding those herds of livestock would take some time. For example, in 1882, the county council of Caraúbas in Rio Grande do Norte reported that the local livestock industry—along with all other branches of the economy—was "taking giant steps toward an abyss."[36] It noted that poor people made up almost the entirety of its population, and attributed that to the great drought.[37] In fact, the Great Drought powerfully impacted on Brazil's exports of leather and hides, reducing them by some 50 percent.[38]

Nor would another staple, cotton, rebound so quickly. As Linda Lewin reminds us, "even the deeply rooted tree cottons of the backlands failed to survive the century's worst drought," and cotton trees need from five to seven years to mature.[39] While bush cotton would recover far more quickly, the steep drop in cotton exports caused by the drought suggests the ruination of many small planters.[40] Arguably, then, in 1880, the need for government assistance to both the provinces of the north and its people remained crucial even though the "winter" had appeared. That such rains quickly restored the proverbial healthfulness and prosperity of the provinces of the north—a "common sense" proposition to the elites of imperial Brazil—obscured that need, as did a discourse emphasizing the societal dangers of a life on the dole.

THE MYTH OF PERMANENCE

What of that elite image of *retirantes'* long-term residence in littoral refuges? Given the prevailing imprecision, or, in many cases, the absence of records, no sound empirical base supported that assertion. Our view of the actual workings of relief suggests transience as the more common pattern. The various twists and turns in government policy certainly set people moving in different directions, as did the multiple individual decisions of local relief commissions. As evidenced by the numerous work projects and shipping of *retirantes* from place to place, the displaced backlanders were treated as commodities and the exploitation of their labor remained a constant feature of the drought years. A pattern of migratory flux—rather than permanence—certainly characterized those *retirantes* in resettlement colonies and lodging houses. For example, data for the Jaraguá lodging house in Alagoas in April 1878 indicate that over a fifteen-day period 773 people entered, while 263 people left.[41] In August of that year, *retirantes* were shipped from Alagoas's capital to work on the Paulo Afonso railroad. When they arrived there, the engineer in charge said he needed only 50 of them, so the Penedo relief commission sent the remainder on to the São Francisco resettlement colony.[42] As we have seen, that colony failed and was shut down, so, assuming that they survived, the *retirantes* would again have relocated.

Political factionalism combined with alterations in provincial administrations to generate multiple new projects and schemes, all of which directly affected the living conditions of *retirantes*. When Rio Grande do Norte shut down the scandal-ridden Sinimbu colony, area property owners expressed fears regarding the hordes of *retirantes* who would be loosed upon the land. Vice-president Montenegro then authorized several public works projects to the benefit of his cronies, supported with *retirante* labor and government supplies. Similarly, he endorsed a contract scheme whereby "hundreds" of the former colonists would work at the sugar mills, with the government providing foodstuffs in return.[43]

At various points during the drought, furthermore, provincial presidents forced *retirantes* out of lodging houses. In both Alagoas and Pernambuco, we recall, presidential edicts authorized the expulsion of all "able-bodied" *retirantes*. The resulting lower numbers of *retirantes* in public facilities then became part of the "factual" basis for Minister of the Empire Leôncio de Carvalho's October 18, 1878 circular, which asserted that drought's impact had diminished and encouraged provincial presidents throughout the provinces of the north to take steps to reduce the number of people lodged at public expense. The diminished lodging house populations, however, truly reflected the presidential policy of forced expulsions. In other words, then, the "factual" basis for assertions of improved weather conditions was the product of policy rather than of rainfall.

Beyond this impact of government policy—and further undercutting the image of permanent residence in government lodging houses—it appears that *retirantes* themselves proved anxious to return home, often setting out from refuge points on little more than hearsay regarding the possibility of a "winter." When some rains fell in Ceará in May 1877 many *retirantes* abandoned public works projects and hastened home to see if their gardens might yet yield some harvest.[44] In January of the following year, Ceará's president noted that with the falling of rains in Fortaleza and its environs, many *retirantes* had requested help to journey back to the interior, and that some were already on the way. He urged them to be more cautious and await further evidence that a winter had indeed arrived.[45] The experience recounted by the vicar in

81

Teixeira provides another example of the strong pull of home. Recall that he noted the return of many former residents who, having encountered poor conditions in supposed refuge areas, preferred to return home, even if all it brought them was the opportunity to die in the familiar surroundings of their native land. At the same time, the Teixeira pattern of a migratory flux and reflux, one reported for many other locales, further undercuts the elite image of a unilinear movement of *retirantes* from *sertão* into littoral lodging places.

A LAZY LIFE ON THE DOLE

The living conditions that *retirantes* endured in the littoral belies another conceptual underpinning of public policy: the pampered existence enjoyed by those dole-dependent idlers, which had destroyed their work ethic and left them content to feed off the public trough. The term "lodging house" itself conveys an image rather at odds with reality. In some places, existing buildings, typically warehouses or abandoned military barracks, became *retirante* dormitories. In many cases, *retirantes* provided for their own shelter, putting up shacks on the outskirts of cities, essentially creating an outlying ring of squatter settlements.[46] Since *retirantes* overwhelmingly came from small towns or the lightly populated *sertão*, the densely packed close quarters of lodging houses and squatter settlements must have been still more oppressive.

Officials everywhere remarked the poor ambience of such lodgings, often blaming the *retirantes* for creating the foul conditions. According to one *cearense* sanitarian, *retirantes* remained ignorant of the most elementary principles of hygiene and used "substances noxious to their health."[47] Accurate at its face with regard to knowledge of the "elementary principles of hygiene," this statement could be applied more broadly to all classes in Brazilian society. In point of fact, whether speaking of conditions in county markets or of the adequacy of such public services as street sweeping, sewers, refuse collection, and the availability of potable water, levels of public sanitation in Brazilian cities remained extremely low during the nineteenth century, more so in the urban centers of the north. The condition of the masses reflected not only "ignorance" of hygiene, but the inadequacies of that public sector infrastructure and the harsh reality of poverty. Slum dwellings, whether inner-city *cortiços* or outlying shacks, already marked Brazil's urban experience at the time of the Great Drought. The influx of *retirantes*, then, occurred in a setting where the poor already suffered miserable, unhygienic living conditions. This strained modest service infrastructures well beyond their limits. In Fortaleza, for example, during most of the drought, the city's water company shut down entirely.[48] When combined with high population density, such conditions precluded any reasonable level of public sanitation and promoted the spread of disease. As late as April 1881, Recife's Pedro II hospital recorded an occupancy level some 50 percent higher than the average rate prior to 1877, largely due to the needs of displaced *sertanejos*.[49]

In discoursing on jammed lodging houses or other places where *retirantes* concentrated, and invoking the image of lazy idlers, authorities spoke of able-bodied males. Overwhelmingly, however, women and children formed the bulk of that *retirante* population. For example, when some 2,700 male *retirantes* went to Ceará to work on the Sobral railroad, their accompanying family members—women and children—exceeded 10,000.[50] Ceará's Meirelles resettlement encampment on the outskirts of Fortaleza had 11,435 people, of whom over 9,000 were women and children.[51] Among 400 people in a Rio Grande do Norte resettlement colony, only 52 were single males.[52] Public documents and newspaper accounts often acknowledged the presence of family groupings. When the vice-president of Pernambuco spoke of establishing a new hospital to accommodate sick *retirantes*, he mentioned the need to build provisional housing for members of their families. [53] A Recife newspaper noted that a group of *retirantes*, composed of three women, four children, and three men—all jaundiced and poorly dressed—had taken refuge by the footings of one of the city's bridges. Subsequent investigation showed the group represented two families.[54]

The absence of males, whether because of work opportunities or death, left families unprotected in a society that defined legitimacy and status in terms of male heads of household. The *Jornal do Recife* reported on a woman and her six children, afflicted with smallpox, who had been sleeping in a store front. Her husband supposedly had abandoned them.[55] In normal times, other male relatives would assume the function of protector, but the drought had disrupted, and in many cases destroyed, such kinship networks. Children certainly figured prominently in the *retirante* population. Death statistics from the Santa Casa in Pernambuco for a six-month period in 1878 indicate that children fifteen and under accounted for some 28 percent of public burials.[56] The very persons whom the normative values of Brazilian society said merited protection—"helpless women and children"—lost centrality in public policy as efforts to end drought relief accelerated. The discursive focus on idle, able-bodied males obscured the reality of thousands of dependent people for whom self-sustaining labor was not a reasonable alternative.

In 1880, Fortaleza still had 214 dependent children who had been orphaned by the drought. Since the city had no appropriate facility to house them, they slept in a lodging place formerly occupied by *retirantes*.[57] With aid no longer available from the imperial government, private charity stepped in. *Comendador* Luis Ribeiro da Cunha donated land along the Baturité railroad to found a colony, which soon housed some 200 orphans.[58] The president suggested that this colony might become the nucleus for a practical agricultural school.[59] News of the colony reached Rio Grande do Norte, whose president had been denied any further imperial support for drought-related expenditures, and he proposed sending some of the province's orphans there.[60]

As with the *retirante* resettlement colonies, the bright hopes for the Ceará colony never came to fruition. By October 1882, the colony's population had risen to the point where resources no longer sufficed, and it had become clear that its founders' goal of creating a permanent agricultural settlement was unattainable. By the following month, the settlement had been shut down, with its remaining orphans sent over to the Santa Casa de Misericordia.[61]

NO DROUGHT OF POLITICS

Elite representations of the drought also included righteous outrage at those avaricious individuals who had cynically exploited the emergency, identifying them largely as corrupt local officials and purveyors of relief goods. Here, there is no doubt that the nature of local politics adversely affected the day-to-day workings of relief. The lesser lights of the imperial elite, including police officials, the lower ranks of the magistracy, and a variety of provincial and county bureaucrats, remained enmeshed in webs of patronage. Accustomed to engaging in fierce competition to protect their local perquisites, they saw drought relief in terms of longstanding patterns of partisan rivalry and personal intrigue. Some sense of the Byzantine complexity that marked the operation of local relief emerges in an incident that occurred in Rio Grande do Norte and is recalled by local historians there as the "Hecatomb" in Mossoró.

As described in a letter from the local vicar, Antônio Joaquim Rodrigues, on the evening of January 26, 1879, in Areia Branca, a nearby small port town on the Mossoró river, a police commissioner attempted to arrest Francisco Moreira de Carvalho, a national guard lieutenant. Shots were fired, one of which killed the commissioner. Several members of Areia Branca's small public force were killed or injured. When the incident came to light on the following day, the person in charge of drought relief in Mossoró, João Avelino de Vasconcellos Lima, fled to Ceará. Henrique Câmara, who had been providing medical services to the *retirantes* and was a nephew of Rio Grande do Norte's dominant Conservative chief, accompanied him. The remaining people associated with relief operations in Mossoró shortly thereafter fled to Natal.[62]

Fearful of the situation, especially as the relief warehouse was nearly empty, several citizens met at the vicar's home and established a provisional committee to oversee the distribution of relief supplies. Stressing the perils of the situation, they urgently requested help from the provincial president. At that moment, however, the vice-president, Manuel Januario Montenegro, who headed the provincial government, was attempting to defend himself from charges that he had exceeded his authority by imprisoning a treasury agent sent by the Finance Ministry to check on fraudulent practices in provincial drought relief. Montenegro soon was forced out of office, and his two successors lasted only two weeks. In that state of instability, the presidency made no response.[63]

Lima had sent a telegram to Montenegro, saying that a "horrible massacre" had occurred, the work of the famed *cangaceiro* Jesuino Brilhante in cahoots with Moreira de Carvalho, who led a group of two thousand *retirantes*.[64] Dr. Câmara, however, told Ceará president José Julio de Albuquerque Barros that Moreira de Carvalho had acted alone. In typical bandit fashion, he had announced his intention to attack the city and take the relief supplies. He had also threatened Lima's life.[65]

On February 8, President Barros advised the presidency of Rio Grande do Norte that the arrival of a navy ship now enabled him to provide assistance to Mossoró, and that he was dispatching foodstuffs to see to the immediate needs of the people there. Along with those supplies, he sent a force of 40 men to restore public order.[66] Since Carvalho's attack and the flight of public officials had occurred on January 27, it would appear that for at least two weeks, Mossoró's *retirantes*, along with its citizenry, had been abandoned to cope as they might with their critical situation.

When those troops arrived, yet another vice-president, Vicente Inácio Pereira, headed the province. He sent the chief of police and a force of 100 men to Mossoró. The chief arrested Carvalho and brought him to Natal to stand trial. On November 14, 1879, the court absolved him of any wrong-doing.[67] In a communication to the Ministry of the Empire, Vicente Inácio Pereira reported that Mossoró for several days had fallen into a state of anarchy, but in accounting for that situation, he made no mention of Carvalho. Instead, he heaped the blame on his predecessor's policy, which left the distribution of relief to "the caprice and will" of a single person. Here, he was speaking of João Avelino de Vasconcelos Lima, whom he already had dismissed from that position.

The "Hecatomb" in Mossoró remains confusing in terms of both Carvalho's motivations and his relations with Lima, a confusion that suggests and reflects the complexities of local politics. At the time of his arrest, an anonymous letter in the *Jornal do Comércio* said that in Natal, and especially in Mossoró, public opinion seemed to favor Carvalho, and held him in esteem as "a worthy citizen." Thus, the moment he got word that the chief had come to arrest him, he had peacefully given himself up. According to this letter, the blame rested with João Avelino.[68] No less an authority than Luis da Câmara Cascudo also portrays Carvalho positively, and notes that he had accused the Mossoró commission of trafficking in relief goods. According to local tradition, says Câmara Cascudo, the "government troops had been ordered to fire on the people," and that rumor had it that Carvalho was at the point of leading "a true hunger march."[69]

Other facts, though admittedly sketchy, suggest a situation whose contours are not so clearly those of a morality play. Moreira de Carvalho's past history included an 1874 arrest for homicide and a recent dismissal from a local relief commission in the town of Páo dos Ferros.[70] Carvalho apparently had some sort of deal with Lima, the nature of which remains murky. Rio Grande do Norte Deputy Moreira Brandão suggested that the two men had extensive dealings with one another. Deputy Amaro Bezerra Cavalcante, Moreira Brandão's correligionist rival, minimized that relationship, asserting that Carvalho had responsibility only for a minor public works project in Areia Branca, and Lima therefore supplied him with foodstuffs for the *retirantes*.

Lima, who had served in several provincial posts that involved collecting revenues, had earned a reputation for both contentiousness and fraud. He had been appointed to his Mossoró position by Vice President Montenegro, another of Amaro's *amigos*. That appointment formed part of Montenegro's attempt to dismantle the patronage apparatus of departed President Eliseu de Sousa Martins. Politics also may have played a part in the seemingly public-spirited actions of Vicar Antônio Joaquim Rodrigues. A Conservative chief, he had long played a leading role in the affairs of Mossoró, and for a time had been a member of the Mossoró relief commission.[71] It seems possible as well that the interaction between Lima and Carvalho reflected antagonisms between the merchant communities of Mossoró and Areia Branca. In 1878, to the distress of Mossoro's merchants, the seat of one of the province's general revenue stations had been switched from Mossoró to Areia Branca.[72]

If causation and culpability for the "Hecatomb" remains unclear, there seems little doubt that the *retirantes* in Areia Branca had been ill-served. The report of the provincial police chief, who was an ally of Amaro's and, therefore, not disposed to give any comfort to Carvalho, noted that relief supplies had not been sent to Areia Branca, and referred to "hungry" *retirantes*. At the same time, the chief also indicated that the warehouse in Mossoró did have supplies.[73] If so, why had nothing been sent to Areia Branca? And how did the vicar and his group find it possible to purchase food locally, when Lima could not?[74] The term "Hecatomb" itself become highly evocative, for while it certainly would make an appropriate descriptor for the massive drought-spawned tragedy of *retirantes*, it seems rather overblown when applied to the few people who actually died in Areia Branca incident. One might reasonably suggest, then, that threats to the established order—especially when they involved lower-class participants—resonanted very powerfully among society's elite elements.[75]

Vicente Inácio Pereira closed the books on this celebrated incident, noting that order had been restored and that he had appointed a new Mossoró commission, "composed of leading local authorities and citizens of zeal and probity." He asked for payment of some bills for relief purchases, then remarked the need to substitute compensated labor for the dole. He concluded with a warning: "to deny these unfortunates some small means of subsistence, would be to condemn them to a certain death or to set them on the road to crime."[76]

DROUGHT RAILROADS

Transportation problems had gained in salience as a result of the frustrations attending attempts to provide relief to the interior. The scientists and modernizers had bestowed their blessing on railroads as "engines of progress." In the pages of the *Jornal do Comércio* and other newspapers there appeared letters stressing how helpful the presence of one or another railroad line would have been in the present emergency as an assured means of moving supplies and transporting *retirantes*. At the same time it could employ *retirantes* and avoid thereby the dangers spawned by idleness.[77] At the 1878 Recife Agricultural Congress, a spokesperson for Pernambuco's commercial association combined compassion and finances in arguing for railroads. If the various railroads on the books actually had been constructed in the provinces of the north, then during this time of terrible drought "many thousands of lives and *contos* of *réis* would have been saved."[78] One of the initial acts of the Sinimbu ministry was a request for funding railroads in Alagoas and Ceará. In a memorandum explaining this request, the ministry noted that the past experience with drought both of other countries and of the provinces of the north had clearly shown that railroads were the most efficient means of ameliorating the impact of that scourge. They would provide an effective means for shipping relief goods into the afflicted area, and, in extremis, allow a far easier emigration to the coast. The memo suggested as a further result of railroad construction that it would provide employment opportunities for idle masses, thereby strengthening their positive attachment to the idea of working.[79]

While couched in terms of progress, compassion, and public order, the granting of franchises and siting of railroad lines reflected multiple other factors, including political and commercial rivalries. In the case of Alagoas and the Paulo Afonso railroad, it is important to note that well before he became prime minister, Sinimbu had been interested in the agricultural and commercial development of his home province, and had supported this railroad project. By linking the upper and lower São Francisco River, Alagoas would become the entrepôt for much of the commerce that moved along the river.[80] Pernambuco and Bahia both had existing lines they wished to extend to the São Francisco River, which would have further cemented their regional commercial dominance and condemned Alagoas to remaining a minor, dependent province. As prime minister, then, he immediately pushed the project by securing the necessary imperial funding. He also instructed provincial president Francisco de Carvalho Soares Brandão to give it top priority. When Soares Brandão wrote of the need to establish a resettlement colony for the growing number of children orphaned by the drought, Sinimbu opined that the railroad had far more importance.[81] Work began on the line almost immediately, and its first section opened to traffic on February 25, 1881.

In Ceará, railroad politics presented a complex situation involving Fortaleza's desire to escape the domination of Recife and to become the chief commercial center for its own province where Sobral, Aracatí, and Crato also functioned as significant regional centers.[82] Aracatí, for example, absorbed the produce of the Jaguaribe River valley, but shipped it to Recife rather than to Fortaleza. Indeed, Aracatí and Fortaleza had been locked in combat for a long time. In 1851, Fortaleza merchants had successfully pressured the imperial government to remove the Aracatí customs house. This stratagem backfired. Much of the commerce that Aracatí lost now went instead to ports in Rio Grande do Norte, while Recife's attractiveness to the *cearense* south increased.[83] Furthermore, ships of the Pernambucan Steamship Company continued to make Aracatí a port of call, so the city maintained its position as a significant commercial center.

The original plans for creating a railroad network for Ceará included three lines from the coast into the interior: in the north, from Camocim or Acaraú to Sobral; in the center, from Fortaleza to Baturité; and for the south, from Aracatí to Icó, and then on to Crato in the Cariri Valley. In 1873, when the provincial legislature let the contract for the Aracatí line, the persons who won that concession were the leading stockholders in the Fortaleza to Baturité route. They had no interest in seeing the Aracatí line actually built. Coveting the potential offered by the rich produce of the Cariri, they planned to link that center to Fortaleza.[84]

The Baturité railroad had begun in 1870, backed by a group that included some of the province's leading political and mercantile figures, including Liberal senator Thomaz Pompeu de Sousa Brasil and Conservative leaders the barons Ibiapaba and Aquiraz.[85] Sinimbu's government authorized its extension to Baturité, but also took over that railroad. As it was a public rather than a private line, government revenues now would fund construction, with government guaranteed interest as the mechanism for attracting the necessary overhead capital. However, to generate decent revenue, the line would need the produce of the Cariri Valley. In essence, then, by taking over the Baturité line, the government allied itself with the Fortaleza interests, which naturally also put it in the position of opposing the request of Aracatí.[86]

Intra-provincial political rivalries added another dimension to the railroad question in Ceará. The proposed line from Camocim to Sobral enjoyed backing from a powerful faction of the Liberal party whose base was in Sobral. This included the ruling provincial president, José Julio de Albuquerque Barros—who had just been appointed by the Sinimbu ministry. Another strong advocate for that line was new imperial deputy, João Ernesto Viriato de Medeiros. Both those men were natives of Sobral and linked to its political and commercial elite.

Rhetorically a victory for the needs of *retirantes*, the Baturité line truly served the interests of Fortaleza merchants. The line from Camocim reflected the political clout of Sobral. Further, in both cases, the railroads served the political interests of Sinimbu by strengthening the Ceará Liberal faction loyal to his government. In other provinces as well, both during and after the drought, the "civilizing" railroads envisioned by the modernizers advanced into the interior along trajectories that reflected a complex calculus of economic and political advantage. The relatively minimal positive impact of these lines during the next large drought a decade later confirms the limited degree to which considerations of present and future drought relief figured in the development of the region's railroad network. So, for example, while the Camocim line reached Sobral by 1882, given the end of the drought and associated funding, the line essentially languished, and slowly deteriorated.[87]

A FRACTURED DROUGHT LOBBY

Representatives of the provinces of the north always saw the drought through the lens of politics. At all levels of government, the drought represented opportunity for Liberal politicians smarting from their long "exile" from power. Given the centralized nature of the imperial fiscal system, to capitalize on these opportunities provincial-based proponents of relief had to work through the national government while relying upon the strength of their representatives in the legislative assembly and links to the cabinet. So, for example, in the early days of the drought, Minister of Foreign Affairs Domingos Souza Leão, the Baron Vila Bela, advised his nephew, Luis Felipe, who functioned as his provincial lieutenant, that relief commissions would play an important role in the upcoming elections. His exasperation with Sinimbu's initially slow response to funding drought relief, therefore, proceeded not only from humanitarian considerations, but from a keen appreciation of the relationship between patronage power and electoral success.[88]

Relief funds represented a veritable bonanza to the politicos and potentates of the drought region, for their provinces, with the exception of Pernambuco, typically received little in the way of imperial funds. For example, prior to the drought, imperial expenditures in Rio Grande do Norte went almost exclusively to pay the salaries of various public officials. In March 1877, the Ministry of the Empire expended only four *contos* in Rio Grande do Norte, a figure that included some extra money to deal with an epidemic. By October of that year, the ministry's expenses for the province had risen tenfold.[89] And that was just the prelude to a pattern of presidents' opening extraordinary credits, and an expenditure by drought's end of nearly seven thousand *contos*.[90]

Throughout the drought provinces, shifting factions engaged in a feeding frenzy to control and profit from this imperial largesse. The highly partisan, factionalized nature of party politics at both the provincial and national level ultimately sundered the ties among those who lobbied for northern relief. And at both levels, those shut out from power and the associated opportunities for profit saw little point in maintaining a relief system that brought benefits to their opponents.

Ceará's Domingos Nogueira Jaguaribe, at first an impassioned supporter of relief who even criticized his coreligionist Conservative prime minister for paying insufficient attention to the needs of the north, became one of the harshest critics of the Sinimbu administration's relief policy. His numerous Senate speeches invariably centered on issues of fraud and the administration of Ceará president José Julio de Albuquerque Barros. Much of this attack turned on provincial politics. In 1863, allied with Joaquim da Cunha Freire, the Baron Ibiapaba, Jaguaribe had challenged the dominance of one of Ceará's leading families, the Fernandes Vieiras, and established a new Conservative faction.[91] Six years later, when Jaguaribe gained his Senate seat, he won out over Manoel Fernandes Vieira. At the time of the drought, Jaguaribe's faction was known as the *graúdos*. They opposed the *miúdos*, also called the Aquirazes after their leader, Gonçalo Batista Vieira, the Baron of Aquiraz.[92]

Ceará Liberals also had two wings, one oriented around Thomáz Pompeu de Sousa Brasil, who had represented Ceará in the Senate since 1864.[93] His cousin, Francisco de Paula Pessoa, patriarch of another of the province's leading families, headed the other faction. By the time of the Great Drought, the *municipio* of Sobral had long been the local power base for the Paula Pessoas. While Pompeu lived, animosities between the two wings remained muted. But he died in 1877, and Paula Pessoa died in July 1879. Antonio Pinto Nogueira Accioli, Pompeu's son-in-law, and José Liberato Barroso inherited one faction.[94] Paula Pessoa's son, Vicente Alves de Paula Pessoa, who had been directing his father's affairs in Ceará, wanted to unite both wings under his own leadership. His ally was none other than Ceará's president, José Julio de Albuquerque Barros. Though the formal split in the province's Liberal party occurred in 1880, tensions had been rising for some time.

The Paulas worked with the Aquiraz conservatives. The *acciolistas* had an understanding with Jagaribe's faction. Consequently, when Jaguaribe rose in the Senate to cite the existence of myriad problems in Ceará, he impugned Barros, a Liberal who was actively engaged in an attempt to alter the balance of provincial politics, and who had feelers out to the Senator's Conservative opponents. As the province's sole senator, then, Jaguaribe spoke against relief, largely because its continuation strengthened Barros's patronage power. At the same time, the factional split in Liberal ranks between *paulas* and *acciolistas* created disunity among Ceará's Deputies, so that the province's representatives no longer spoke with a single voice with regard to drought relief.

In the case of Rio Grande do Norte, the attitudes toward relief of its two Liberal deputies, Amaro Carneiro Bezerra Cavalcante and José Moreira Brandão Castelo Branco, depended on which one of them held the upper hand. Long rivals for power and influence within that province, the two men had managed to work together to oust Sousa Martins, since he threatened both their interests. That accomplished, however, they resumed their relentless jockeying for power. In May 1879, having completed an impassioned speech urging the necessity of continuing relief for the beleaguered provinces of the north, Moreira Brandão then turned his attention to refuting Amaro's accusations that the province's interim head—an ally of Moreira Brandão—had paid fraudulent relief bills submitted by his relatives. In their increasingly heated and bitter exchange, the two deputies summoned up many of the sorrier episodes that had earned their province a reputation for corruption, disorder, and fraud.[95] In fact, throughout the entire May session of the Chamber of Deputies, whenever Amaro or Moreira Brandão addressed the question of drought relief, it almost always took the form of accusations of impropriety. Still having at one another in September and hurling charges of political immorality and corruption, Moreira Brandão likened Amaro to Homer, saying he first made up the stories and then assigned names.[96] Neither man, then, made a credible advocate for continued relief.

Furthermore, Rio Grande do Norte's Liberal deputies regarded their province's Conservative Senator, Diogo Velho Cavalcanti de Albuquerque, as both an outsider and an enemy. Intimately connected to events in his native Paraíba, Diogo Velho fulminated against relief efforts there, since they remained largely in Liberal hands. He also used information brought to public attention by Amaro and Moreira Brandão as proof of the misguided policies followed by Sinimbu's ministry. In the October Senate session, he read from the official documents that had come out of investigations of the Sinimbu relief colony, including the sensational report of the fact that dogs and birds of prey feasted upon the corpses of *retirantes*, a revelation that brought forth exclamations of shock and horror from several senators.[97]

Pernambuco, the most politically powerful of the drought provinces, saw many of its leading lights locked in battle with one another. Vila Bela, who had resigned from his post as minister of foreign affairs in Sinimbu's administration, ostensibly because of disagreements over electoral reform, died on October 18, 1879. While at the imperial court as Minister of foreign affairs, Vila Bela had continued to function as an arbiter of provincial politics.[98] For example, he had used his ministerial clout to install his ally Adelino Antonio de Luna Freire as presiding vice president, and then to get his *amigo* Adolfo de Barros Cavalcante de Albuquerque Lacerda appointed as president. His death, therefore, precipitated still more intense conflict between the province's two main Liberal factions, the *Leões*, (followers of the Souza Leão family), and the *Cachorros*.[99] In September 1879, beleaguered president Adolfo Barros, disdained by both factions, had resigned. The *Leão* Adelino de Luna Freire took over, but soon clashed with the *Cachorro* chief of police, and "the province slid into administrative chaos."[100] Pernambucan politicians faced further complications when their province's longtime senator, Francisco de Paula Cavalcanti de Albuquerque, died in January 1880.[101] Furthermore, one of Pernambuco's most prominent senators, João Alfredo Correia de Oliveira, who consistently attacked the ministry's relief program, remained violently opposed to the rising power of the *Cachorros* because of personal antipathy for Recife power broker and imperial deputy José Mariano.[102] Thus locked in conflict and preoccupied with questions of local power, as in other drought provinces, Pernambuco's national representatives had difficulty making common cause to support any policy.

Itself subject to periodic droughts, Minas Gerais had lent its substantial voting block to the cause of imperial relief. However, the accession of Afonso Celso de Assis de Figueiredo to the post of finance minister, and his subsequent election to the Senate, altered that situation, for his concern with balancing the budget mandated an end to relief spending. His treasury agents had questioned invoices and held up payments in both Rio Grande do Norte and in Ceará. Furthermore, even the powerful Francisco de Figueiredo was finding the drought no longer profitable. The province of Paraíba owed him and his partners nearly three hundred *contos*, but had no funds to pay. The Budget Commission of the Chamber of Deputies refused to endorse Figueiredo's request that public money be used to make good the worthless paper.[103] In sum, if the initial success of the drought lobby had rested on mutual self-interest and the prospect of lucrative government spending and patronage opportunities, factional strife with regard to the control of that imperial largesse and the government's unwillingness to maintain such high expenditures ultimately pointed self-interest toward opposition to relief.

SENATORIAL POLITICS

As a result of the deaths of Pompeu, and, in August 1878, of Jeronimo Martiniano Figueira de Melo, Ceará had two vacant Senate seats. In December 1878, an election took place, providing the Emperor with a list of six names. He selected José Liberato Barroso and Viriato de Medeiros, even though neither man had been a leading vote getter. In this case, it appears that the emperor made these selections as an attempt to balance, and therefore appease, competing partisan interests. Barroso's Liberal faction was linked to Jaguaribe, while Medieros worked with the Sobral interests allied with provincial president José Julio de Albuquerque Barros.[104] This putative Solomonic decision failed. Ceara's Liberals remained divided. Meanwhile, Senate Conservatives had no desire to see the beleaguered council president gain any new allies. Furthermore, if the Sinimbu ministry did fall, a Conservative one might replace it, and a Conservative provincial president would preside over any elections.

Beyond the specific issue of Senate representation, given a political culture that focused more on the play of factional forces than on the specific matter at issue, Sinimbu's opponents—whether Liberal or Conservative—naturally saw an opportunity to frustrate, discredit, and weaken his ministry. The Ceará Senate seats, therefore, became a hostage of the Sinimbu opposition. On March 8, 1879, the Senate annulled the election.[105]

The ongoing drought provided the ostensible basis for this decision. Earlier, Jaguaribe had attempted to forestall all elections in Ceará, arguing that dislocations produced by the drought made it impossible to carry out that process. In response, the Senate and ministry had agreed that if conditions in that province worsened, the proposed postponement would take effect. The continued drought and that deal notwithstanding, the ministry had authorized Ceará to hold elections. The Senate's electoral committee, headed by Cotegipe, responded by recommending those results not be recognized and urged that no elections be held until the drought ended. In support of this position, Cotegipe pointedly raised the issue of relief expenditures in Ceará, styling them as the "thermometer of the state." Noting a vast increase in credits for the period of March-August 1878, Cotegipe proffered two possibilities—either conditions had gotten worse or fraud was rampant. He also noted Paula Pessoa's estimates that perhaps half of Ceará's population needed government assistance, and asked how the vote could have occurred so routinely with all the outmigration? Indeed, vote tallies from some parishes ranged from seven hundred to fourteen hundred when, said Cotegipe, such places perhaps no longer had "even a vicar or a sexton."[106]

An October 1879 Senate session witnessed attacks on elections in Paraíba, using the same logic that linked the continued flow of relief funds as evidence of conditions too unsettled to permit a legitimate process. Jaguaribe pointedly asserted this relationship: "Either the election ought be suspended, or the government ought tell the Senate: 'The province of Paraíba finds itself in normal conditions; there no longer are drought needs to be met.'"[107] Interestingly, Senate elections in the province of Espírito Santo also were overturned. However, new elections were soon held, and the results approved. Ceará, however, remained with Jaguaribe as its sole representative until after the drought had ended.

THE MINISTRY FALLS

Sinimbu's tenure had begun poorly; it remained difficult, and ended virtually in disgrace. In many respects, his government was doomed from the outset, in part because of the circumstances surrounding his very selection as prime minister, in part because of his self-proclaimed "mania" for electoral reform. Presidents of the Council most frequently came from the more populous provinces, ones with large delegations in the national legislature. Typically, too, they had gained recognition as party leaders.[108] Sinimbu fell short on both these measures. Two other Liberals, Nabuco de Araújo and José Antonio Saraiva, enjoyed more renown than Sinimbu and represented more powerful provinces.[109] Saraiva had largely inherited the mantle of leadership upon the death of Zacarias de Góes e Monteiro, the Liberal leader whose Ministry's 1868 fall ushered in a decade of Conservative power.[110] Some in the capital thought Sinimbu should have declined the prime minister's position, deferring to one of those Liberal chiefs, both of whom subsequently turned down invitations to join his ministry.[111] Other leading Liberals also rejected Sinimbu's overtures. When finally set, the cabinet lacked truly great names, save for the minister of war, the marquis of Erval, Manuel Luís Osório, a hero of the Paraguayan war.[112]

It also lacked experience. Among its members, only Sinimbu himself had previously filled a cabinet post; he also was the ministry's only senator.[113] Several of its relative newcomers aroused controversy. These included the aggressive Gaspar da Silveira Martins, a fiery orator and hard-ball-playing politico from Rio Grande do Sul, the finance minister, and the flamboyant and quixotic Lafayette Rodrigues Pereira—an avowed Republican—the minister of justice.[114] Silveira Martins was associated with the emotional issue of naturalization and religious reform. Coming from Rio Grande do Sul, which had a substantial and important non-Catholic immigrant population, he strongly advocated the need to promote their full citizenship. Minister of the Empire Leôncio de Carvalho, only thirty-one years old, had presented the reform Liberal program of 1875, which proposed abolishing life-tenure for senators.[115] Councilor of State and Senator J.J. Teixeira, Júnior remarked that while Sinimbu's "monarchical and constitutional precepts are well-known," he had surrounded himself with people "whose careers are associated with advocating extreme reform."[116] And Pedro Leão Veloso, a Liberal party stalwart from Bahia who would become a senator in the new legislature, similarly worried that some of these ministers were novices who represented some of the most "advanced" Liberal positions.

Surrounded by persons of such dubious orthodoxy, Sinimbu took an approach to electoral reform that further imperiled his tenure. Educated in England and an ardent admirer of the British parliamentary system, Sinimbu viewed electoral reform not as a procedural but as a behavioral issue. Speaking in the 1873 imperial Senate, Sinimbu frankly declared that this reform for him had become a "mania," an idea to which all others remained subordinate.[117] When in December 1878 Sinimbu first met the new legislature to present his ministry's program, he summarized it solely in terms of electoral reform. Further, he proposed constitutional amendment as the means by which it would be achieved.[118]

More radical Liberals, for example, those who championed the official Reform Liberal platform, resented the reductionist definition of the Liberal program as consisting of the single issue of direct elections. However, they welcomed the prospect of revising the constitution as a way of implementing a wide range of reforms. Other of their coreligionists recoiled from that possibility. More important than political philosophy were institutional or corporate concerns. Reform of the constitution would require dissolving the present legislature. Having just gained election after long years in exile, new deputies did not welcome the prospect of stepping down, and standing again for election in a new system whose rules could not promise the same result. To make matters worse, the ministry's proposed response to a possibile Senate rejection of its proposal was to call for the dissolution of the legislature. Deputy Martim Francisco—from the outset a leader of the Liberal dissidents—caught the irony of this approach. If the Chamber approved the proposal, it would be dissolved; if resistance occurred in the Senate, again, the Chamber of Deputies would be discharged. Commenting on this, he remarked, "we are damned if we do, and damned if we don't."[119]

The subsequent resignations of several cabinet members further complicated Sinimbu's efforts to carry out his mandate for electoral reform. Each time the increasingly beleagured President came before the National Legislative assembly to explain a minister's departure, his opponents used the occasion to heap scorn on his administration and question its viability. Commenting on the continuing cabinet changes, Deputy Saldanha Marinho likened Sinimbu's ministry to a flagless fleet that would soon be shipwrecked. Pushing this metaphor a bit further, he expressed hope that at least the crew might be saved, because the cargo—by which he meant the program of electoral reform—was surely lost, and along with it perhaps the Liberal party's governing position.[120] Another Senator simply remarked that the ministry seemed to be "falling piece by piece."[121]

In May 1879, Sinimbu finally shepherded his electoral reform bill through the Chamber of Deputies, despite a vocal opposition that included Silveira Martins and Nabuco de Araújo's son, the rising Liberal abolitionist Joaquim Nabuco, who scorned the bill as "a conservative reform, a reform that did not grant complete suffrage, a reform that we cannot accept without renouncing all our principles."[122]

After arousing such heated controversy and taking fully three months to pass through a uniformly Liberal chamber, the proposed election reform encountered intractable opposition in the Senate. For some time the Senate simply dragged its feet, refusing to bring the bill out of committee. When the regular legislative session expired, the emperor acceded to Sinimbu's request for an extraordinary session, giving the beleaguered prime minister one final opportunity to master the political situation and deliver on electoral reform. On October 14, 1879, the Senate's Constitutional and Legislative Committee had issued its opinion, which recommended against the bill. Most members of the committee had signed "with restrictions," but without indicating the nature of their concerns.[123] Then, on November 12, the full Senate flatly rejected the electoral proposal, offering no suggestions for modifications. Further deliberations of the extraordinary session were postponed until April 15, 1880.

The Senate thus mortally wounded an already weakened Sinimbu by rejecting electoral reform, for a ministry that failed to move its most important legislation through the National Legislative Assembly could not long survive. The event that proved its final undoing, however, occurred not in the halls of the National Legislative Assembly, but on the streets of Rio de Janeiro. In his attempt to raise revenues and balance the books, Finance Minister Afonso Celso de Assis Figueiredo had introduced a number of new taxes, including a levy of 10 percent on streetcar fares in the city of Rio de Janeiro.[124]

Beginning in December 1879, in response to the announced fare increase various protests occurred, including public assemblies and street demonstrations.[125] When the increase took effect on January 1, protest turned into what became known as the Vintém riot, with streetcars overturned, and heavy-handed action by the army and police, resulting, according to official reports, in three deaths and twenty-eight people injured.[126] Several legislators who formed part of the Liberal dissidence once again saw a compelling nexus of ideology and opportunity, and wound up issuing a manifesto published in the *Jornal do Comércio* that decried the excessive use of force: the military "had fired on unarmed people."[127] One of these was Joaquim Nabuco, who in the October legislative session had used the occasion of a memorial for the fallen Vila Bela to criticize the ministry's abandonment of Liberal principle.[128] Eduardo Silva suggests that Conservatives too "saw an opportunity in the general discontent to bring down the Liberal cabinet."[129] With Sinimbu's fall as with drought policy and its implementation, the imperatives of political factionalism and self-interest remained at the forefront.

THE DECLARED END OF DROUGHT

Since the represented reality of improved weather diverged markedly from empirical reality, large numbers of *retirantes* remained in the littoral. At the same time, however, pressure for ending expenditures increased, and the government proved unreceptive to requests for continued funding. *Retirantes*, therefore, had to be dispersed. In October 1879, numerous relief commissions in Ceará received communications from the provincial government advising them of the grave financial pressures confronting the nation, and the concomitant necessity of limiting public assistance to the drought migrants. The commission of Guayaba, for example, was notified that the government could no longer continue to send foodstuffs to all localities in the province. It suggested that all able-bodied *retirantes* could find employment on the Baturité railroad. Those in no condition to work—the women, children, aged and disabled—were to be sent to a town several kilometers distant, which still would receive some rations.[130]

In July 1879, Rio Grande do Norte's president, Lobato Marcondes Machado, remarked the critical situation confronting presidents in the drought provinces. On the one hand, they had to deal with thousands of hungry *retirantes*. On the other, the Senate opposition said that rains had fallen and pressured the government to stop spending. Machado asserted that nothing had changed. "This year's drought is just like that of the previous year."[131] Nonetheless, several months later he took personal charge of reducing the *retirante* population in the littoral. In November 1879, he informed the Ministry of the Empire that he was setting out for Mossoró to take steps to "dissolve the great agglomeration of poor people."[132] His twenty-three day stay in Mossoró proved miraculously successful in dispersing most of the estimated forty-thousand people living on government relief. Triumphing over both the reluctance of the *sertanejos* to leave and the machinations of profiteers, he reportedly managed to get "more than thirty thousand *retirantes* to return to the interior," providing them with food and clothing for the journey. To help achieve that result he also brought a force of one hundred soldiers.[133] If accurate, so forced and sudden a dispersal of 30,000 poor and generally sickly people into the parched *sertões* of Rio Grande do Norte and Paraíba surely condemned them to continued misery and privation, if not death.[134]

In January 1880, relief commissioners in Fortaleza received a still sterner message, instructing them to "take prompt measures" to get the *retirantes* back to the interior or to their home provinces. The able-bodied would be given eight days to find work. Whatever the success of that search, all assistance to them would terminate after that period. Those who left for the interior within that same eight-day span would receive some rations and seeds, as well as a document entitling them to some assistance when they reached their destination.[135]

With the imperial government's action, as political reality the drought no longer existed. With no drought, there could be no *retirantes*. Thus, all forms of government assistance ceased, save for those related to accelerating the population movement back into the interior. Given the conditions of that drought-scarred land and the impoverished state of the *retirantes*—who as we have seen surely did not wax fat and happy in the web of official relief—there seems little doubt that the cessation of relief resulted in further hardship for the backlanders. Once again, then, at drought's end, as throughout its course, political and discursive reality bore little consonance with empirical conditions in the provinces of the north.

CONCLUSION

Despite the outpouring of private charity, public relief and compassionate discourse, the Great Drought never held central importance for the elites of imperial Brazil. Absorbed into the nation's reigning political culture and associated hierarchical, paternalistic social structure, the empirical reality of drought—its broad swath of dislocation, suffering and death—lost salience. From local settings to the capital itself, the specific representations of drought bespoke political agendas and elite assumptions regarding the nature of the backlands and its people. Drought and relief, then, assumed multiple guises: "honest" local officials railed against profiteers; sober national political figures fretted over the profligate waste of resources; and scientists and reformers saw clear proof of the need for modern, progressive methods. Provincial presidents criticized the performance of relief commissions established by their predecessors and replaced them with supposedly more honorable, concerned citizens. Successor presidents and vice-presidents, however, found those replacements similarly wanting, and proceeded to stock commissions with their own allies.

By drought's end, official reality spoke with a single voice portraying a well-intentioned, charitable Brazilian government and people whose concern with the plight of the *retirantes* had led the nation to the brink of fiscal disaster. That effort, though marred by the despicable actions of some venal politicians and corrupt profiteers, had rescued the *sertanejos* from the drought-ravaged backlands and sustained them until the cruel scourge had ended.

AN ALTERNATIVE REPRESENTATION

Having suggested throughout this book the lack of consonance between discursive and empirical reality in elite representations of the Great Drought, it seems appropriate at this point to offer a representation of my own.

Trapped in exploitative relations of landholding and labor, and victimized by a political and judicial system that regarded them with contempt, the backlands masses perched on the margins of existence even during times of normal weather. During previous prolonged droughts, the harsh, unyielding environment of the provinces of the north had afforded the backlanders no option other than migration. At the inception of the Great Drought, government policy had tried to counter that pattern by sending relief supplies into the *sertão*. But the effort failed, forcing the government to adopt the *sertanejos'* traditional alternative as its own.

The existence of multiple migratory waves bespoke the determined effort of *retirantes* to survive adversity. Though some migration occurred in the early months of the drought, that movement accelerated when the drought deepened through the following years. The backlanders, then, abandoned their homes only in extremis, migrating when no other choice remained. Poorly provisioned, families set out on the long and arduous journey from *sertão* to coast. At almost every stop along the way, the charitable impulses so routinely celebrated in elite discourse seemed less in evidence than the fear and panic of local officials and property-holders in the *brejos* and *agreste*, who hurried the drought refugees off to some other location. Many fell along the way, their bodies left in shallow graves, or dessicating in the arid backlands. But others trudged on. The *sertão* had defeated the government, but, grimly determined, many thousands of *retirantes* reached the littoral.

They arrived at these government-sponsored refuges exhausted, ragged, and bereft of all possessions. Desperate for assistance, the unfortunate backlanders became enmeshed in the web of imperial relief and its attendant political and financial machinations. Forced into situations that denied them independence and opportunity, as in the *sertão*, they once again found their choices ruthlessly limited. Like the lower class masses throughout Brazil, *retirantes* confronted a brutal struggle for existence. Exploited for their labor or as a means to secure government funds, they experienced little of that compassion that figured so prominently in the self-congratulatory discourse of provincial and national elites. They were poorly housed and fed, and virtually traded as a commodity. Disease and death became constant companions. In such conditions, survival itself was accomplishment. Rather than living off relief, *retirantes* literally died on it, in all too many cases because of its deficiencies and inherently exploitative nature.

When the drought had outlived its political usefulness, and the charitable, paternalistic impulses of elites had been suffciently fulfilled, the government ended relief, even though the need for public assistance and a variety of development efforts remained urgent. Even worse, elites characterized the backlanders as slackers, dole-dependent-idlers, whose lack of ambition and energy had prolonged the crisis beyond all reason. The declared end of drought, then, represented one last cruel exploitation of the *retirantes*, for it sent them, forcibly, back into a ravaged land.

Far from providing a rich and flourishing environment, the physical geography of the provinces of the north posed numerous obstacles to establishing productive economic activities. The provinces of the north enjoyed but minimal fiscal resources and infrastructure, whether measured in terms of transportation, communication, water resources, or public facilities. In those circumstances, *sertanejos* seeking to reestablish their individual, family and community lives desperately needed continued public assistance. A supposedly compassionate nation, however, saw no justice to that claim.

Public officials all too often saw both the drought and the *retirantes* in terms of opportunity. Throughout the provinces of the north, when new presidents or vice presidents took over, they spoke of the suffering of *retirantes* and attacked those who wrongfully profited from relief—typically identifying them as allied with an opposition political faction or party. They upheld the honesty and fine reputation of their own new appointees and affirmed the importance of rigorously monitoring relief and achieving economies. Despite these pious pronouncements, many of these officials shamelessly fed at the trough of relief funds and used political power to benefit friends and crush rivals.

Emphasis on a compassionate government response celebrated elite values of charity and paternalism, while defining a very narrow range of appropriate behaviors for the nation's masses. *Retirantes*, dehumanized by that very term, remained a nameless, faceless mass, endowed with motivations and behaviors that reflected a reality congenial to the elite's axiomatic social class assumptions. Within that chummy, insular world of imperial elites, Senator Jaguaribe recoiled in horror at the prospect of a permanent pauper class supported by public funds, but he and his colleagues had no problem accepting and exploiting a class of permanently dependent *sertanejos*. Elites applauded a relief policy that placed *retirantes* and public monies at the disposal of planters and mill owners and praised those locally powerful individuals for their willingness to help. Enriching the already fortunate, then, received societal approval, while, again to use one of Jaguaribe's expressive images, enriching formerly "proletarian" elements qualified as corruption.

DROUGHT, DISCOURSE AND POLITICS

In exploring imperial policy during the Great Drought, a certain tension runs throughout this book with regard to the relative weight of such real world factors as partisan politics and outright avarice, versus the representational or imagic world communicated through discourse.

It becomes tempting, at times, to dismiss that representational world as nothing more than a a cynical use of pious platitudes to mask narrow self-interest. At the other extreme, as noted in the introduction, those wedded to what Roger Chartier called "the American lingusitic turn" might be impatient, if not annoyed, at the attention devoted to supposedly "real world" factors, seeing them at best as epiphenomenon. I see the interaction between the representational and the "real" as an appropriate and fruitful approach, one that provides a powerful perspective for understanding both the drought and imperial Brazil.

At one level, then, this study of the Great Drought highlights the degree to which protecting one's position, friends, and clients informed policy, both in its formulation and, especially, in its implementation. In some respects, in fact, government existed only to satisfy the demands of patronage. And given the extremely hierarchical nature of imperial Brazil, the masses could hold importance only as clients. Their needs and best interests, then, would be determined by those at the top.

The empire's leading lights themselves had cut their political teeth on provincial politics. They rose in the ranks precisely because they understood how to play the game. While they might see themselves as behaving more high-mindedly than local chiefs in dusty provincial towns, the corrupt nature of imperial politics remained systemic, cutting across all regions and levels of government. Indeed, to a large extent, politics in the provinces turned on the relationships that connected local actors with the elites of Rio de Janeiro. National elites might sneer when local magistrates allowed flagrant crimes of the locally powerful to go unpunished, but they engaged in that very same behavior, using their power to protect *amigos* and clients. So, despite his flawed tenure as president of Rio Grande do Norte, Eliseu de Sousa Martins gained the presidency of Espírito Santo, a far better post, given its proximity to Rio de Janeiro. Sousa Martins had disparaged the province's magistrates, citing their lack of honesty and concern for the public good—a criticism he himself surely merited. Sinimbu, a self-declared paragon of enlightened political morality, an admirer of England's parliamentary democracy, and an ardent advocate of honest politics, behaved quite like any traditional provincial politico when it came to the Paulo Afonso railroad, using his ministerial clout to push through that project. Baron Vila Bela viewed relief commissions as cogs in Pernambuco's electoral machinery, and his ministerial portfolio as a means of assuring the ascendency of his *Leão* Liberal faction.

After the initial—and ritual—outpouring of compassionate concern for the victims of drought, the political elite incorporated questions of relief into the ongoing game of power politics: advantaging *amigos*, punishing enemies, and dominating the distribution of spoils, both electoral and fiscal. In the provinces, this transformed the drought into opportunity. The drought lobby fractured in part because so many of the national politicos from the provinces of the north found it more palatable to have no imperially-funded projects than to see that largesse fall under the control of rivals. At the national level, the "real" drought yielded to a representation that suited Sinimbu's opponents; it became a vehicle to assail his ministry and frustrate electoral reform. In approaching the drought and issues of relief through the prism of partisan rivalry and personal advantage, members of the top echelon of the imperial political elite exploited the *retirantes* quite as ruthlessly as any local profiteering politico. They just did so in a less proximate fashion.

Scientists, too, saw opportunity in the drought. Definitely inferior in status to the *bacharéis*, they now had a chance to assert the importance of their expertise in terms of public policy. Engineers had an additional self-interested agenda. In proposing great hydraulic works or railroads, they in fact were advocating projects whose design and implementation would require their own participation. Furthermore, as chief or principal project engineers, they would enjoy significant patronage opportunities. Many of the members of the engineering commission sent to Ceará to work on enhancing Fortaleza's water supply urged the importance of railroads, and wound up working on the Sobral and Baturité lines themselves.[1] In this sense, engineers, too, behaved no differently than any small-time provincial politico. Clearly, then, self-interested and flagrantly corrupt behavior, including the demands of partisan rivalry and political factionalism, took precedence over the needs of *retirantes*, negatively impacting drought policy, and greatly complicating the *sertanejos'* struggle for survival.

At the same time, however, the conceptual world of Brazilian elites also exercised powerful influence, for policy emerged as well out of a stock of shared knowledge, "common sense" understandings regarding the nature of the *sertão* and its people. Predisposed to view the land as immensely rich and the backlanders as ignorant, lazy, and potentially dangerous, elites developed a policy reflecting those assumptions. Embracing the tenets of progress and modern science, they had few reservations regarding the value of the so-called "hydraulic" approach, and enthusiastically supported railroads as agents of civilization. Not only the nation's constitution, but their own understanding of appropriate behavior, mandated a compassionate, charitable response to the Great Drought. However, a reciprocal understanding of appropriate behaviors for those recipients of elite largesse dictated a harsh response toward *retirantes* who did not display the virtues of "honest poverty."

103

Whether referred to broadly as those classes "less favored by fortune," or more narrowly as *sertanejos* or *retirantes*, these conceptual categories dehumanized the very people whose interests were to be protected.

The declared end of drought and termination of relief also reflected the influence of representations. The discursive focus on the avarice and corruption of those connected with relief in the provinces of the north, along with the stock portrayal of *retirantes* as dole-dependent idlers, freed the imperial government from the demands of compassion and charity, enabling it to end relief without moral censure. Indeed, as we have seen, by drought's end the dominant representation had decentered thoroughly the hardship and suffering of the *sertanejos*, substituting for it the image of a nation imperiled by its own disingenuous generosity.

THE CREATION OF THE NORTHEAST

Despite numerous recorded instances of drought dating as far back as the 1500s, in the mid-nineteenth century cattle ranches and sugar plantations stood as the dominant symbolic representation of the provinces of the north. Drought remained simply an unfortunate fact of nature that affected various parts of the nation's vast interior. By the 1920s, however, the Northeast had emerged as a region, with drought as one of its widely-known characteristics.[2] This suggests one of the most powerful impacts of drought—its role in defining the northeast as a region.

During the Great Drought, as the relief effort wound down, much of the discourse in the National Legislative Assembly emphasized the endless sums of money "hurled into the abyss" on behalf of the northerners. The nation's collective financial sacrifice had been great not only because of the actual impact of drought itself, but because those provinces' backward inhabitants and corrupt politicians had exacerbated the problems caused by nature. Various senators even had suggested that profiteers and politicians had attempted to maintain an emergency situation long after it had ended. Domingos Nogueira's Jaguaribe had cautioned that in the future, people might be tempted to "invent" a drought so as to profit from relief. Together, such expressions might be seen as the seed of the popular notion of "drought industries."

As noted in the introduction, after the drought of 1906 the government created the first national agency officially designated to combat the problem of regional drought, the Superintendency of Studies and Works Against the Effects of Drought. Between 1919 and 1922 the funding of this agency increased enormously, a direct result of the ascension of Paraíba's Epitacio Pessoa to the nation's presidency.[3] Though it sponsored a variety of waterworks, including reservoirs and wells, yet another large-scale drought in 1930-32 produced the same devastating consequences. This apparent ineffectiveness of public expenditures strengthened the nascent association between drought, the northeast, and the "drought industries."

Coincident with those droughts came initial attempts to devise regional classifications for Brazil. André Rebouças produced one of the first of these, published in 1889 for M.F.J. de Santa-Ana Neri's famous book, *Le Brasil em 1889*. It divided the nation into ten zones, including a Zone of Paraíba do Norte, which embraced the present states of Rio Grande do Norte, Paraíba, Pernambuco, and Alagoas.[4] Four years later, a French geographer, Elisée Réclus grouped the northeastern states from Maranhão to Alagoas as the "Equatorial Coast." This unit reappeared in a 1905 regional scheme, but with the name "Brasil Norte-oriental," translatable as North-eastern Brazil, a designation that gained wide currency due to its replication in a 1913 work that became the standard text for geography instruction in Brazil.[5] In the course of the early decades of the twentieth century, then, it became increasingly common for Brazilians to conceptualize their nation in regional terms, and to associate those regions with specific characteristics. Given the decades of largely ineffective anti-drought expenditures, it became easy to associate the Northeast with drought, political corruption, and poverty.[6]

Northeasterners themselves helped to popularize these representations of regional reality. In 1926, in self-conscious opposition to the aggressive assertion of modernism that issued from Sâo Paulo's famous Modern Art Week, the northeast regionalist manifesto called for a cultural focus on authentic, traditional regional themes.[7] This found expression in the works of several talented authors, collectively known as the Northeastern Generation of 1930. Evocations of the harsh backlands and the tragedy of drought appeared as key themes in their literary production. Certainly, *Vidas Secas'* unforgettable characters helped sear images of drought, suffering *sertanejos*, venal politicians, corrupt local bosses, and cruel *fazendiros* into the consciousness of generations of Brazilians. Through the works of Graciliano Ramos, Rachel de Queiroz and other members of the Generation of 1930, drought became a powerful metaphor, representing the northeast as an afflicted region.[8]

Heightened regionalism witnessed more sharply drawn distinctions between a modern, progressive south and a retrograde northeast. Discursively, then, the old provinces of the north adopted the posture of a poor, suffering region, misunderstood and badly served by the national government, and, therefore, an area to which the nation owed a moral debt. Governments acknowledged this debt by funding a variety of institutionalized drought-fighting agencies. Falling further behind the south and southeastern portions of the nation, the "impoverished, drought-stricken northeast" complained of its "abandonment" by the national government, while residents of those richer areas expressed exasperation with the endless demands of a uniquely corrupt and backward region. In this regard, the Great Drought had also contributed toward the production of a peculiar discourse, a ritualized language for expressing the relationship between the provinces of the north and those of the south.

The conflating of drought, the northeast, and the *indústrias da sêca*, which continues to feed southern exasperation with the backward, tradition-bound north, parallels the discursive reality of the Great Drought, where elite discourse transformed the *sertanejos* from innocent victims of a natural disaster into shiftless architects of their own misfortune. The paradox of a rich land and a poor people continues to haunt the Brazilian imagination. And much of the nation's search for answers still proceeds along lines congenial to the assumptions of social class.

NOTES

INTRODUCTION

1. County Council of Telha to PP-CE, 15 Feb. 1877, AN-P, IJJ9/188.
2. PP-CE to ME, 7 Apr. 1877, AN-P, IJJ9/188. In this note he referred to the concerns he had raised in an earlier confidential memorandum.
3. Traditionally, *sertanejos* referred to the rainy season as "winter." It does not coincide directly with the actual calendar winter months.
4. *O Cearense*, 3 May 1877, p. 1. The editorial suggested that Alencar was confusing factual reality with his works of fiction. José de Alencar (1829-1877), an important figure in Brazil's literary movement of romanticism wrote numerous novels, including one in 1875 titled *O sertanejo: romance brasileiro*.
5. For examples of early columns by Carreira see *Jornal do Comércio*, 5 June, 2 July, 14 Aug., 9 Oct., and 4 Nov., 1877.
6. The term *retirante* comes from the verb *retirar*, to remove oneself from one location to another.
7. Gilberto Freyre observed that "when a Brazilian hears talk of drought . . . he immediately thinks of Ceará and of 1877. It is as though that place and those two sevens . . . have become the dramatic synthesis of the great droughts that Brazil has suffered." Freyre, Preface to Lôpes de Andrade, *Introdução à sociologia das sêcas* (Rio de Janeiro: Editora a Noite, 1948), 7. The only book-length study of the Great Drought in English is Roger L. Cunniff, "The Great Drought, 1877-1880" (Ph.D. diss., University of Texas, Austin, 1970), which deals mainly with Ceará. Rodolpho Theophilo provides valuable information in *História da secca do Ceará (1877 a 1880)* (Fortaleza: Typographia do Libertador, 1883). Joaquim Alves discusses multiple droughts, including that of 1877, in *História do Ceará. História das sêcas (séculos XVII a XIX)*(Fortaleza: Edições do "Instituto do Ceará, " 1953). Phelipe and Theophilo Guerra present chronologies of droughts in Rio Grande do Norte in *Seccas contra a secca*, 3rd ed., Coleção Mossoroense, 24 (1980). Gileno dé Carli, *Séculos de sêcas* (Recife: n. pub., 1984) sketches the ongoing northeastern drought experience.
8. Paulo de Brito Guerra, *A Civilização da Seca. O nordeste é uma história mal contada* (Fortaleza: Ministério do Interior, Departamento de Obras Contra as Secas, 1981), 24.
9. Friedrich W. Freise, "The Drought Region of Northeastern Brazil, " *Geographical Review*, 28 (1938), 367.
10. Rachel de Queiroz, *The Three Marias*, trans. Fred P. Ellison (Austin: University of Texas Press, 1963), xii. The quote comes from a *crônica*, and is cited in the introduction to suggest the importance of the *sertão* to the author.

11. For discussions of rainfall patterns see Manuel Correia de Andrade, *A terra e o homem no nordeste*, 4th ed., revised and updated (São Paulo: Livraria Editora Ciéncias Humanas Ltda., 1980). See also Stephen Hasenrath, *Climate Dynamics of the Tropics* (Dordrecht: Kulwer Academic Publishers, 1991), 302-09.

12. Guerra, *Civilização da seca*, 43-46. Known more commonly by its subsequent 1909 acronym, IFOCS (*Inspectoria Federal de Obras Contra as Sêcas*-Federal Inspectorate of Anti-Drought Works), this agency arose in response both to the large-scale drought of 1906 and to the legacy of the great droughts of 1877-80 and 1888-89. Other national agencies include DNOCS (*Departamento Nacional de Obras Contra as Sêcas* or National Department of Anti-Drought Works), which appeared in the 1930s and SUNDENE (*Superintêndcia do Desenvolvimento do Nordeste*, or Superintendency for Northeastern Development), established in 1959. See Anthony L. Hall, *Drought and Irrigation in North-East Brazil* (Cambridge, UK: Cambridge University Press, 1978), 6-7, 10-11. In 1936, a national law established the boundaries of what came to be known as the "drought polygon, " entitled to receive special assistance from the government in times of drought. Carli, *Séculos*, 152-53.

13. Nancy Schepper-Hughes, *Death Without Weeping: The Violence of Everyday Life in Brazil* (Berkeley: University of California Press, 1992), 68. She further observes, "The image of drought is formidable, capturing the imagination of people who are inclined to describe all that is bad in terms of dryness . . ." Ibid., 69.

14. On this issue see Antônio Callado, *Os industriais da sêca e os "Galileus" de Pernambuco. Aspectos da luta pela reforma agrária no Brasil* (Rio de Janeiro: Editôra Civilizaçao Brasileira, 1960); Jorge Coelho, *As secas do Nordeste e a indústria das secas* (Petrôpolis: Vozes, 1985); and Roger L. Cunniff, "The Birth of the Drought Industry: Imperial and Provincial Response to the Great Drought in Brazil's Northeast, 1877-1880, " *Revista de Ciencias Sociais* 6:1-2 (1975):65-82.

15. Max Fleiuss, *História administrativa do Brasil*, 2nd ed. (São Paulo, Cia. Melhoramentos, 1922), 343.

16. *Fala* on 3 May 1880, in Fleiuss, *História administrativa*, 346; BCN, *Anais da Camara dos Deputados* (hereafter Deputados, *Anais*), 1: 3 May 1880, 59.

17. Jonathan Potter and Margaret Wetherell, *Discourse and Social Psychology: Beyond Attitudes and Behavior* (London and Newbury Park, CA: Sage, 1987), 7.

18. Ibid., 6.

19. H. D. Harootunian, *Things Seen and Unseen: Discourse and Ideology in Tokugawa Nativism* (Chicago: University of Chicago Press, 1988), 10. For a first-rate example of a historical work using language and the construction of meaning as an approach, see D. S. Parker, *The Idea of the Middle Class, White Collar Workers and Peruvian Society, 1900-1950* (University Park: Penn State University Press, 1998).

20. Sheldon S. Wolin, "Hobbes and the Culture of Despotism, " in *Thomas Hobbes and Political Theory*, ed. Mary G. Dietz (Lawrence: The University Press of Kansas, 1990), 22. The quote comes from *De Homine*.

21. From a speech on 14 February 1923, noted in Robert H. MacDonald, *The Language of Empire. Myths and Metaphors of Popular Imperialism, 1880-1918* (Manchester, UK: Manchester University Press, 1994), xii.

22. David R. Shumway, *Michel Foucault* (Boston: Twayne Publishers, 1989), 24.

23. Roger Chartier, *On the Edge of the Cliff. History, Language, and Practices*, trans. Lydia G. Cochrane (Baltimore and London: The Johns Hopkins University Press, 1997), 4. Here he refers specifically to the "radical formulations of the American 'linguistic turn.'"

24. Ibid., 8. See also by Chartier, *Cultural History. Between Practices and Representations*, trans. Lydia G. Cochrane (Ithaca: Cornell University Press, 1988).

25. The term "common mental universe" comes from Jacques Le Goff, *Time, Work, and Culture in the Middle Ages*, trans. Arthur Goldhammer (Chicago: University of Chicago Press, 1980), 71.

26. Michel Foucault has remarked the link between power and knowledge, suggesting the importance of seeing knowledge as a product of power relations prevailing in a society. See Michel Foucault, *Power/Knowledge: Selected Interviews and Other Writings*, ed. Colin Gordon (New York: Pantheon, 1980). Nancy Leys Stepan, *"The Hour of Eugenics, " Race, Gender and Nation in Latin America* (Ithaca and London: Cornell University Press, 1991), 10-11, observes, "a corollary of the new constructivist history of science is that historians no longer conceptualize science as depicting 'reality' in any straightforward or transparent fashion but rather as *constructing* or *creating* the objects it studies and giving them their empirical weight and meaning." Ibid., 11, my italics. See also Stanley Aronowitz, *Science as Power, Discourse and Ideology in Modern Society* (Minneapolis: University of Minnesota Press, 1988). For an overview of the leading theoretical approaches on representations, see Jonathan Potter, *Representing Reality: Discourse, Rhetoric and Social Construction* (London: Sage Publications 1996).

27. Warren Dean, *The Industrialization of São Paulo 1880-1945* (Austin and London: University of Texas Press, 1969). Cooperation between coffee planters and factors in Rio de Janeiro is underscored by Joseph E. Sweigart, *Coffee Factorage and the Emergence of a Brazilian Capital Market, 1850-1888* (New York: Garland Press, 1987). For a specific example of this "marriage of trade and land, " see Richard Graham, "Brazil from the Middle of the Nineteenth Century to the Paraguayan War, " in *Cambridge History of Latin America*, ed. Leslie Bethell, 5 vols. (Cambridge, UK: Cambridge University Press, 1983-86), 3: 765.

28. June Hahner, *Poverty and Politics. The Urban Poor in Brazil, 1870-1920* (Albuquerque: University of New Mexico Press, 1986), 16-17, reminds us that "whether salaried or self-employed, the middle sectors aspired to gentility. Their economic and professional dependence on the governing elites reinforced the social and ideological bonds tying them to the upper classes."

29. See Roderick J. Barman and Jean Barman, "The Role of the Law Graduate in the Political Elite of Imperial Brazil, " *Journal of Inter-American Studies and World Affairs* 18:4 (Nov. 1976): 423-50 and "The Prosopography of the Brazilian Empire," *Latin American Research Review* 13:2 (1978): 78-97. See also Eul-Soo Pang and Ron L. Seckinger, "The Mandarins of Imperial Brazil, " *Comparative Studies in Society and History* 14:2 (March 1972): 215-44.

30. José Murilo de Carvalho, "Political Elites and State Building: The Case of Nineteenth- Century Brazil, " *Comparative Studies in Society and History* 24:3 (July 1982), 397. Roderick J. Barman uses the term "official world" or "official nation" to capture the difference between the governing elite and what he refers to as the "real Brazil." He too suggests that "the official world was, in short, defined as much by a shared outlook and culture as by the possession of any common racial, social, or economic standing." *Brazil: The Forging of a Nation, 1798-1852* (Stanford: Stanford University Press, 1988), 237.

31. For insightful discussions of the political culture of imperial Brazil see Emília Viotti da Costa, *The Brazilian Empire: Myths and Histories* (Chicago: University of Chicago Press, 1985), Richard Graham, *Patronage and Politics in Nineteenth-Century Brazil* (Stanford: Stanford University Press, 1990), and José Murilo de Carvalho, *Teatro de sombras: A política imperial* (São Paulo: Vértice, Editora Revista dos Tribunais, 1988). June Hahner, *Poverty and Politics*, 35, affirms that "the

political culture, formulated by the elites since colonial times, stressed conciliation, class harmony, and respect for hierarchy."

32. The 1824 constitution had established this power and granted it to the emperor to use for the "maintenance, equilibrium, and harmony of the remaining political powers." Quoted in Beatriz Westin de Cerqueira Leite, *O Senado nos finais do Império (1870-1889)* (Brasília: Senado Federal & Editôra Universidade Brasília, 1978), 24. The best discussion of the founding and early development of independent Brazil is Barman, *Forging of a Nation.*

33. Lydia Magalhães Nunes Garner, "In Pursuit of Order: A Study in Brazilian Centralization. The Section of Empire of the Council of State 1842-1889" (Ph.D. diss., The Johns Hopkins University, 1987), 40.

34. Viana, *O idealismo da Constituição* (São Paulo: Editora Nacional, 1939), 69, cited in Leite, *O Senado,* 92. Viana attributes this to José Antonio Saraiva. Barman remarks that given the reigning party's power over elections, "the parliamentary system of government which had emerged since 1826 would now have become an illusion were it not for the existence of the regulating power." *Forging of a Nation,* 227.

35. Costa, *The Brazilian Empire,* 75. She notes the inherent contradiction of Brazilian liberals, their desire "to conciliate order and progress, the status quo with modernization."

36. R. Graham, *Patronage,* 57. On the history of the Council prior to 1850 see Barman, *Forging of a Nation,* and afterward, R. Graham, *Patronage.* See also José Honório Rodrigues, *O Conselho do Estado. O quinto poder?* (Brasília: Senado Federal, 1978).

37. Leite, *O Senado,* 56. If *deputados* became ministers they had to stand for reelection. But since their party dominated the government (else they would not have been chosen) and a ministerial appointment enhanced their personal power, this requirment became meaningless. Since senators served life terms, they of course continued in power.

38. Carvalho, *Teatro de sombras,* 153.

39. In reference to the process Francisco Belisário Soares de Souza, *O sistema eleitoral no império (com apêndice contendo a legislação eleitoral no período 1821-1889* (Brasília: Senado Federal, 1979), 27, observed, "with the right qualification the election is almost decided." Quoted in Lydia Magalhães Nunes Garner, "In Pursuit of Order: A Study in Brazilian Centralization. The Section of Empire of the Council of State 1842-1889, " Ph. D. diss., The Johns Hopkins University, 1987, 322.

40. R. Graham, *Patronage,* 76. The law specified that electors would cast votes for only two-thirds of their province's allotment of Deputies. At least in theory, then, given appropriate discipline the smaller number of electors adhering to the party out of power would be able to secure sufficient votes to elect at least some of their candidates.

41. Francisco de Carvalho Soares Brandão to Sinimbu, May 2, 1878, AIHGB, L. 611, P. 2.

42. Ibid., 192.

43. See Evaldo Cabral de Melo, *O norte agrário e o Império, 1877-1889* (Rio de Janeiro: Editora Nova Fronteira, 1984), 13. To preserve the flavor of the discourse of the era, I use the regional vocabulary current at that time.

44. Due in part to new competition on the world market from cheaper Cuban sugar, rising United States production, and the development of beet sugar (which enjoyed a protected status in Europe), the nineteenth century saw the annual export growth of sugar fall below 1 percent. Warner Baer, *The Brazilian Economy: Its Growth and Development* (Columbus, OH: Grid Publishing, 1979), 23. Brazil's share of the world sugar market peaked at 10.3 percent during the years from

1846 to1850. At the time of the Great Drought, Brazil's market share stood at 5.3 percent. Moreover, "falling sugar prices, especially after 1860, reduced returns in the early 1870's to the level of the 1850's." It dropped to 4.4 percent for the period 1866-70, then gained slightly through the 1870s. See Peter L. Eisenberg, *The Sugar Industry in Pernambuco: Modernization Without Change, 1840-1910* (Berkeley: University of California Press, 1974), 14 and 20.

45. For data on the export trade in these products see Liberato de Castro Carreira, *História financeira e orçamentária do Império do Brasil*, 2nd ed., 2 vols. (Rio de Janeiro: Senado Federal, Fundação Casa de Rui Barbosa-MEC, 1980).

46. Brazilian cotton exports gained a greater market when the Civil War in the United States disorganized southern production. Nathaniel H. Leff, *Underdevelopment and Development in Brazil*, vol. 2, *Reassessing the Obstacles to Economic Development* (London: George Allen & Unwin, 1982), 9. Sugar's annual trend rate of growth expressed as a percentage was 2.3, while that of cotton was 4.1. For the period 1871-73, sugar accounted for 12.3 percent of Brazil's export receipts; cotton provided 16.6 percent. Ibid.

47. See Barbara Weinstein, *The Amazon Rubber Boom 1850-1920* (Stanford: Stanford University Press, 1983).

48. Toward the close of the empire, the rising economic power of Amazonas and Pará would contribute to defining a "new north" separate from the "old north." Melo, *O norte*, 12.

49. The proceedings of this conference may be found in a 1978 facsimile edition with an introduction by Gadiel Perruci, *Trabalhos do Congresso Agrícola do Recife, outubro de 1878* (Recife: Fundação Estadual de Planejamento Agrícola de Pernambuco, 1978). The originals are in *Trabalhos do Congresso Agrícola do Recife em outubro de 1878 comprehendendo os documentos relativos aos factos que o precederam* (Recife, 1879).

50. The term "satellite bloc" comes from Robert M. Levine, *Pernambuco in the Brazilian Federation, 1889-1937* (Stanford: Stanford University Press, 1978), 1.

51. Other provinces with but a single senator were Amazonas, Mato Grosso, Goiás, Pará, and Santa Catarina. Beatriz Westin de Cerqueira Leite, *O Senado nos finais do Império (1870-1889)* (Brasília: Senado Federal & Editora Universidade Brasília, 1978), 48. Provincial population totals are from the 1872 census, whose reliability, unfortunately, is suspect.

52. Afonso de Ecragnolle Taunay, *A Câmara dos Deputados sob o Império* (São Paulo: Imprensa Oficial do Estado, 1950), 47-48. The 122 total held from the eleventh through the eighteenth legislatures. Ibid., 48.

53. Leff, *Reassessing the Obstacles*, 9.

54. Melo, *O norte*, 14, says the years from 1871 to 1889 witnessed "fundamental modifications in the inter-regional equilibrium of Brazil."

55. Northerners headed the cabinets of 1866, 1871, 1878, and 1880. Also, the Bahian Cotegipe functioned as a sort of co-prime minister for the 1875 Caxias cabinet.

56. The speaker was Antônio Coelho Rodrigues, a leader of the 1878 Recife Agricultural Congress, and a member of the faculty of the Law School (*Faculdade de Direito*). *Trabalhos do Congresso*, 449.

57. For dates of railroads and information regarding costs, extent, and rolling stock, see Carreira, *História financeira* and Julian Smith Duncan, *Public and Private Operation of Railways in Brazil* (New York: Columbia University Press, 1932). Regional tensions also appeared with regard to slavery. Declining profits induced many northern sugar planters to sell slaves, whether to raise needed cash or because they had decided to liquidate their holding. The booming coffee areas of the south provided a natural market, especially after the cessation of Brazil's

participation in the Atlantic trade. As a result, a large-scale interprovincial slave trade developed. By 1874, among the six northern drought provinces, only three, Pernambuco, Piauí and Alagoas, had above 10 percent of their populations enslaved, with Pernambuco the highest at 12.4 percent. By contrast, the corresponding figure for the province of Rio de Janeiro was nearly 40 percent, while that for São Paulo stood at 20 percent. Sales accelerated during the Great Drought, further exacerbating this regional disparity. See Robert Conrad, *The Destruction of Brazilian Slavery 1850-1888* (Berkeley: University of California Press, 1972), 49; 54-55, and 284, table 2.

58. *Trabalhos do Congresso*, 359.

59. Sociedade Auxiliadora à Agricultura em Pernambuco, *Relatório Anual*, 53.

60. *O Cearense*, 26 July 1877, p. 1.

61. *Jornal do Comércio*, 15 May 1877, p. 1. The editorial singled out two Liberal deputies who would successively serve as finance minister in Sinimbu's administration: Rio Grande do Sul deputy Gaspar da Silveira Martins, who it termed "the elastic man, " for the ease with which he modified his position so as to frustrate the Conservatives; and Afonso Celso de Assis Figueiredo from Minas Gerais, whom it scorned for his unwillingness to release "a few hundred *contos*" for relief. In the Brazilian monetary system, one *conto* equaled 1, 000 *milréis*. For the period 1874-89, with the average values of the *milréis* at 46.27 cents, one *conto* was worth about $462. See Duncan, *Public and Private Operations of Railways*, 43.

62. R. Graham, *Patronage*, 272.

63. ME, *Relatório*, Dec., 1878, 117.

64. PP-CE to ME, 28 July 1877, AN-P, IJJ9/188.

65. Optimistically and imprecisely calculated, laws setting imperial budgets underestimated expenditures while overestimating revenues so as to produce—at least on paper—a balance or surplus. For the 1876-77 fiscal year, with the total budget deficit having climbed to some twenty-three thousand *contos*, the legislature in a small nod to reality approved a budget law authorizing a nine hundred *conto* deficit. By the conclusion of the fiscal year, the Ministry of Agriculture had spent nearly double its allotted amount and the deficit climbed to nearly thirty-five thousand *contos*. The best source for imperial finances is Carreira, *História financeira*. See also by Carreira, *O orçamento do Imperio desde sua fundação* (Rio de Janeiro: Typographia Nacional, 1883). In addition to problems generated by the decline in export agriculture, the phenomenal costs of the 1865-70 war with Paraguay—Brazil's per capita government debt doubled during that conflict—followed by the ambitious railroad-building and other infrastructure improvements of the Rio Branco years (José Maria da Silva Paranhos, the Baron, and later Viscount, Rio Branco, headed the Council of Ministers from March 1871 to June 1875) had shaken the nation's finances. The western world depression that began in 1873 further exacerbated matters, as did the 1875 crisis in commercial banking.

66. Carreira, *História fianceira*, 520-23.

67. For these discussions, see José Honório Rodrigues, org. *Atas do Conselho de Estado. Obra comemorativa do sesquicentenário da instituição parlamentar*, 10, Terceiro Conselho de Estado, 1875-1880 (Brasília: Senado Federal, 1973), 121-36. On the Council itself, see Rodrigues, *O Conselho de Estado: O quinto poder?* (Brasília: Senado Federal, 1978). Wedded to classical nineteenth-century orthodoxy in monetary matters, Brazil normally shied away from emissions of non-convertible paper money. One of the councilors referred to these as "abnormal, " and spoke of the "gravity and dangers" of such measures. Rodrigues, *Atas*, 96.

68. Carli, *Séculos de sêcas*, 89.

69. Taunay, *A Câmara*, 203.
70. Fleiuss, *História administrativa*, 336.
71. Carreira, *História financeira*, 522.
72. Brazil, Ministerio da Fazenda (hereafter Fazenda), *Relatório*, 1880, Table 5, "Demonstração de todas as despezas . . . com a secca . . . ."
73. ME, *Relatório*, Dec. 1878, 119.
74. In all, six lines in the provinces of the north received authorization for studies, saw construction begin, or were provided with imperial support during the drought. These lines were in Ceará, Pernambuco, Paraíba and Rio Grande do Norte. See Carreira, *História Financeira*, 780-833 for data on Brazilian railroads. I discuss some of the politics of railroads in Chapter 4.
75. The government declared that henceforth presidents ought to authorize only those expenditures having "the most intimate link with the drought." ME, *Relatório*, Dec. 1878, 119.
76. Sinimbu to Soares Brandão, 10 Mar. 1878, AIHGB, L. 611, P. 1.
77. Ibid., 10 Oct. 1878.
78. ME, *Relatório*, Dec. 1878, 120.
79. For example, in 1871 Bahia and Pernambuco had extracted approval for railroad lines in their provinces as a condition for supporting the government's railroad program for the south.
80. Blake, *Diccionario*, 2: 446; Ridings, *Business Interest Groups*, 61.
81. Sinimbu to Saraiva, 23 Feb. 1880, AIHGB-CCS, L. 270, D. 38. Saying that he had been treated "ignominiously" by both Conservatives and Liberals, Sinimbu noted that electoral reform was being held up because of that personal hostility, and suggested that Saraiva would stand a better chance of shepherding the reform through the legislature.
82. Cunniff, "Great Drought, " 271. The Baron Homem de Mello was Francisco Ignacio Marcondes Homem de Mello.
83. Deputados, *Anais* 1: 3 May 1880, 59.
84. Ibid., 2: 25 June 1880, 439-459.

CHAPTER 1
THE IMAGINED DROUGHT

1. Joaquim Alves, *História do Ceará*, 203.
2. Rohan, who belonged to several other national learned societies, including the Brazilian Historical and Geographic Institute (*Instituto Histórico e Geográfico Brasileiro, IHGB*), later became a member of the Council of State. See Blake, *Diccionario*, 3: 213 and Fernando de Azevedo, *As ciencias no Brasil*, 2 vols. (São Paulo: Edições Melhoramentos, 1956), 1: 340.
3. Medeiros had previously served in that Chamber from 1866 to 67; Buarque de Macedo would go on to become minister of agriculture in Saraiva's cabinet; he later became a senator.
4. Cunniff, "Great Drought, " 69; Blake, *Diccionario*, 3: 199. Capanema had been invited to participate in the Polytechnical gathering, but illness prevented him from attending. His letter formed part of the proceedings of the session of 18 Oct. 1877.
5. Lilia Moritz Schwarcz, *O espetáculo das raças: cientistas, instituições e questão racial no Brasil, 1870-1930* (São Paulo: Companhia das Letras, 1993), 102.

6. According to Simon Schwartzman, "The apogee of imperial science was marked by the active presence of Pedro II himself in all matters dealing with science, technology, and education. Playing the role of a Brazilian Maecenas, the Emperor's attraction to the sciences led him to seek the company of scientists both within Brazil and abroad and to participate in all of Brazil's more significant cultural and scientific events." *A Space for Science, The Development of the Scientific Community in Brazil* (University Park, PA: The Pennsylvania State University, 1991), 55.

7. As Simon Schwartzman, ibid., 68, observes with regard to such technically-oriented institutions as the Polytechnic School and the School of Mines, "What gave meaning [to them] . . . was mostly their role in the creation of a new breed of elite intellectuals who could challenge the established wisdom of priests and lawyers in the name of modern science."

8. Deputados, *Anais*, 3: 10 Aug. 1877, 75-76.

9. Ibid.

10. Ibid., 77.

11. Carreira long had been involved with railroads and banking, and he later became an imperial senator. Studart, *Dicionario*, 2: 250-55; Taunay, *O Senado*, 198.

12. *Jornal do Comércio*, 4 Nov. 1877, p. 2.

13. *O Cearense*, 22 July 1877, p. 1.

14. Jaguaribe, who had held the post of Minister of War from 1871-72, had served Ceará as a provincial legislator and as a deputy. He also had founded the province's official Conservative newspaper, Dom Pedro II. Leonardo Leite Neto, *Catálogo biográfico dos Senadores brasileiro de 1826 a 1896* , 4 vols. (Brasília: Senado Federal, Centro Gráfico, 1986), 2: 655.

15. Ibid. For information on Jaguaribe's Ceará base see Maria Arair Pinto Paiva, *A elite política do Ceará provincial* (Rio de Janeiro: Tempo Brasileiro, 1979), especially 56-57.

16. Quoted ibid., 153.

17. He became a senator on April 17 1880. Taunay, *A Câmara*, 208.

18. Deputados, *Anais*, 2: 21 Jan. 1879, 59.

19. Ibid.

20. Ibid., 62.

21. Ibid., 2: 12 Feb. 1879, 469.

22. Ibid., 1: 21 May 1879, 320.

23. Ibid., 242.

24. Ibid., 116.

25. Ibid., 117.

26. BCN, *Anais do Senado do Império do Brasil* (hereafter Senado, *Anais*) 6: 23 Oct. 1879, 302.

27. Ibid., 1: 26 June 1877, 236.

28. Ibid., 243.

29. Deputados, *Anais*, 2: 14 Feb. 1879, 538. Francisco de Paula Pessoa Júnior was the son of long-time Ceará senator and provincial Liberal party leader Francisco Alves de Paula Pessoa, who headed one of the province's most powerful family oligarchies.

30. Ibid., 12 Feb. 1879, 463.

31. Senado, Anais, 3: 7 July 1879, 85.

32. ME, *Relatório*, Dec. 1878, 119.

33. Ibid., 121.

34. Congreso Agrícola, *Colleção*, 67.

35. Ibid., 400. The initial draft of the official response had called for laws forcing workers to reside in a specific location.
36. *Trabalhos do Congresso*, 290-91.
37. The *Ventre Livre* included clauses requiring freed slaves to labor, and effectively maintained them under the control of their masters until the age of twenty-one. The law is reproduced in E. Bradford Burns, *A Documentary History of Brazil* (New York: Knopf, 1966), 257-58. See also George Reid Andrews, *Blacks and Whites in São Paulo Brazil, 1888-1988* (Madison: The University of Wisconsin Press, 1991), 49. On abolition, see Conrad, *The Destruction*.
38. Lucio Kowarick, *Trabalho e vadiagem. A origem do trabalho livre no Brasil* (São Paulo: Editora Brasilense, 1987), 69.
39. Andrews, *Blacks and Whites in São Paulo*, 48. He also refers to the elite's "own autochthonous *ideologia da vadiagem*, a firm and unshakable belief in the innate laziness and irresponsibility of the black and racially mixed Brazilian masses." Ibid.
40. *Trabalhos do Congresso*, 291.
41. Report of Central RC of Alagoas for 1-15 Aug. 1878, printed in *O Liberal*, 26 Aug. 1878, AN, Presidentes, IJJ9/294.
42. Martins, *Inteligência*, 3: 321, citing Antonio Soares Amora, refers to this belief in Brazilian abundance as one of "the eight great national myths arising during the romantic period." The roots of this belief date to the colonial period. Such books as Ambrósio Fernandes Brandão's *Diálogos das grandezas do Brasil* (Dialogues of the Great Things of Brazil) and Andre João Antonil's *Cultura e opulencia do Brasil* (Culture and Opulence of Brazil) gave currency to this idea, as did the sugar boom, the discovery of gold and diamonds, and, of course, the sheer vastness of the land. Brandão, a planter in Paraíba, wrote the *Diálogos* in 1618, but his work did not enjoy much circulation until the eighteenth century. See José Antonio Gonsalves's forward to *Dialogues of the Great Things of Brazil (Diálogos dos grandezas do Brazil)* Attributed to Ambrosio Fernandes Brandão, trans. and annot. Frederick Holden Hall, William F. Harrison, and Dorothy Welkner (Albuquerque: University of New Mexico Press, 1987), vii-ix. Antonil's book was published in Lisbon in 1711. See E. Bradford Burns, *Nationalism in Brazil, A Historical Survey* (New York: Praeger, 1968), 20. See also Demétrio Magnoli, *O corpo da patria: imaginação geográfica e política externa no Brasil, 1808-1912* (São Paulo: Editora Moderna, 1997).
43. *O Auxiliador da Indústria Nacional: Periódico da Sociedade Auxiliadora da Indústria Nacional*, Rio de Janeiro, 45 (Mar. 1877), 109.
44. *Revista Agrícola do Imperial Instituto Fluminense de Agricultura*, 9:1 (Mar. 1878), 15.
45. Deputados, *Anais*, 1: 25 June 1877, 252.
46. Henrique A. Milet, *Auxilio à lavoura* (Recife: Typographia do Jornal do Recife, 1876), 32. An agriculturalist at the Rio de Janeiro Congress affirmed that rather than work, the masses preferred a life of idleness where they "stay in their little corner and take a bit of coffee and *rapadura*." Congresso Agrícola, *Colleção*, 155.
47. *Trabalhos do Congresso*, 149.
48. Antonio Marco de Macedo, *Observações sobre as seccas do Ceará e os meios de augmentar o volume das aguas nas correntes do Cariry* (Rio de Janeiro: Typographia Nacional, 1878), 50.
49. Senado, *Anais*, I, 27 June 1877, 254.
50. For Capanema's comment, see *Jornal do Comércio*, 23 Oct. 1877. For Medeiros, see Viriato de Medeiros, *Ponderações sôbre a memoria do dr. André Rebouças, A secca nas provincias do Norte* (Rio de Janeiro: Typographia Acadêmica, 1877), 25.
51. ME, *Relatório*, Dec. 1878, 121.
52. This quote comes from *Exposição*, Paris, 1867, 68.

53. ME, *Relatório*, Dec. 1878, 121

54. André Rebouças, *A secca nas provincias do norte. Propaganda no Jornal do Commercio, no Instituto Polytechnico, na Associação Brazileira de Acclimação e na Sociedade Auxiliadora da Indústria Nacional* (Rio de Janeiro: Typ. de G. Leuzinger & Filhos, 1877), 75.

55. Rebouças, *A secca*, 78. Under the pseudonym *"Sertanejo,"* Oliveira, a *bacharel* in math and a military engineer, wrote a series of newspaper articles on the drought that appeared in *O Globo*, in January and February 1878. Studart, *Diccionario*, 1: 36. He also participated in the Polytechnical meetings.

56. ME, *Relatório*, 18 Dec. 1878, 118-19.

57. In 1856, the IHGB had proposed the formation of a commission to explore the interior of several Brazilian provinces. Three years later, with support from the imperial government, the commission set to work, broadly charged to explore, collect, and catalogue. Alves, *Historia do Ceará*, 150. See also Simon Schwartzman, *Formação da comunidade científica no Brasil* (São Paulo: Editora Nacional, 1979), 373.

58. Giacomo Raja Gabaglia, *Ensaios sobre alguns melhoramentos tendentes à prosperidade da provincia do Ceará* (Rio de Janeiro: Typ. Nacional: 1877).

59. Ibid., 4.

60. Ibid. Cunniff, "Great Drought," 70, notes Gabaglia's stress on the personal culpability of the *sertanejos*, and affirms that Gabaglia's opinions "eventually were to carry the most weight." Ibid., 69.

61. Medeiros, *Ponderações*, 25.

62. Rebouças, *A secca*, 67.

63. *Jornal do Comércio*, 23 Oct. 1877, p. 2.

64. Rebouças, *A secca*, 22. André Rebouças, who became a leading abolitionist, was "strongly committed to a radical reorientation of Brazilian society." Conrad, *Destruction of Brazilian Slavery*, 145.

65. This discussion occurred at an 1877 meeting of the national acclimatization society. While one of those present cautioned that such trees "generally do not produce water," others remained more enthusiastic. One, in fact, identified this tree with a Latin name, and said it existed in Peru. Rebouças, *A secca*, 102.

66. Medeiros, *Ponderações*, 23-24.

67. Rebouças, *A secca*, 86.

68. Ibid., 85.

69. Senado, *Anais*, 6: 23 Oct. 1879, 304.

70. Barros, *A ilustração*, 9-10. Focusing more on political issues, Emília Viotti da Costa characterizes this period as an "age of reform." See "Brazil: The Age of Reform, 1870-1889," in *The Cambridge History of Latin America*, ed. Leslie Bethell, 5 vols. (Cambridge, UK: University Press, 1985-86), 5, "c. 1870 to 1930."

71. Ibid., 168.

72. Schwarcz, *O espetáculo*, 51-52. See also Jeffrey Needell, *A Tropical Belle-Epoque. Elite Culture and Society in turn-of-the-century Rio de Janeiro* (New York: Cambridge University Press, 1987), 1-22. João Cruz Costa, *A History of Ideas in Brazil. The Development of Philosophy in Brazil and the Evolution of National History*, trans. Suzette Macedo (Berkeley and Los Angeles: Univ. of California Press, 1964), 76-77, sees 1870 as the inception of "a new period. . . in the history of Brazilian thought," and notes that "positivism, naturalism, evolutionism, in short, all the modalities of European thought of the nineteenth century, now found expression in Brazil. . . ."

73. José Americo dos Santos, *Secca no Norte do Brazil, Março de 1878* (Rio de Janeiro: Typographia e Lithographia de Machado & Companhia, 1883), 14-15. This volume includes articles originally written in March 1878 that were published in *Illustração do Brasil*. After making those remarks about the masses, Americo dos Santos observed that he would say no more on the subject, because it had been dealt with more fully by Raja Gabaglia.The derogatory term *"matutos"* derives from the word *"mata"* or forest.

74. Ibid.

75. Gabaglia, *Ensaios*, 17.

76. Santos, *Secca no Norte*, 33.

77. ME, *Relatório*, Dec. 1878, 120.

78. Ibid.

79. This remark does not appear in the *Anais*, apparently because Leôncio did not turn in the text of his speech. However, as will be noted, both deputies and senators often referred to it.

80. Deputados, *Anais*, 2: 21 Jan. 1879, 459.

81. Ibid.

82. Ibid.

83. Ibid.: 12 Feb. 1879, 461.

84. Ibid., 463.

85. PP-RN to MJ, 10 July 1879, AN, Ministerio da Justiça, Ofícios dos Presidentes, IJ1/299; *Jornal do Comércio*, 4 Aug. 1879, p. 2.

86. Theophilo, *História da secca*, 292-94, and 309-10.

87. Ibid., 1: 19 May 1879, 241. He referred to various public buildings and parish churches.

88. Ibid.

89. Ibid., 242.

90. Ibid., 26 May 1879, 374.

91. Senado, *Anais*, 8 July 1879.

92. Senado, *Anais* 6: 13 Oct. 1879, 104.

93. Ibid., 106.

94. Ibid., 111.

95. Ibid., 112.

96. Ibid.

97. Ibid., 23 Oct. 1879, 293.

98. Ibid., 295.

99. Ibid., 297.

100. Ibid., 301.

101. Ibid. Correia also made that charge. Ibid., 293.

102. Ibid., 298.

103. Ibid., 16 Oct. 1879, 190.

104. Ibid., 191. The other senator was Jeronimo Fernandes da Cunha of Bahia.

105. Ibid., 6: *Anexo*, 23 Oct. 1879, 17.

106. Ibid., 6: 23 Oct. 1879, 303.

107. Ibid., 302.

108. Ibid., 16 Oct. 1879, 185.

109. Ibid., 23 Oct. 1879, 303.

110. Ibid., *Anexo*, 23 Oct. 1879, 15.

111. Deputados, *Anais*, 1:19 May 1879, 242.

112. Senado, *Anais*, 2: 7 Feb. 1879, 65.

113. Ibid., 6: *Anexo*, 23 Oct. 1879, 16. Cruz Machado made this observation in relation to Ceará.

CHAPTER 2
ANOTHER NORTHEAST

1. Here a point raised by Joaquim Alves in regard to the various scientific discussions of the drought deserves mention: those who opined so knowingly on the drought were often unfamiliar with northern reality. *História do Ceará*, 203.
2. Azevedo, *As ciencias*, 1: 216-217.
3. These rivers simply swelled during the rainy season, then dried completely with its end. Henrique de Beaurepaire Rohan, *Relatório final da Commissão Geral do Imperio apresentado ao Ministerio da Agricultura, Commércio e Obras Públicas pelo Marechal do Campo Henrique de Beaurepaire Rohan* (Rio de Janeiro: Typographia Nacional, 1878), 7-8. He acknowledged the many shortcomings of his own official general map of Brazil, particularly with regard to its indications of mountains and rivers. Given orography's "notable backwardness, " said Rohan, it was hard to be sure of the existence of some mountains indicated on maps, let alone accurate measures of their elevations. Ibid., 7.
4. Cândido Mendes, *Atlas do Império do Brasil comprehendo as respectivas divisões administrativas, ecclesiasticas, eleitoraes e judiciarias dedicado a sua magestade o Imperador O Senhor D. Pedro II, destinado à instrucção pública no Imperio com especialidade à dos alunos do Imperial Collegio de Pedro II organisado por Cândido Mendes de Almeida* (Rio de Janeiro: Lithographia do Instituto Philomathica, 1868), 8.
5. For a list of these estimates see IHGB, *Diccionario histórico, geográphico e ethnográphico do Brasil (commemorativo do primeiro centenario de independencia)*, 2 vols. (Rio de Janeiro, Imprensa Nacional, 1922), 1 *Introdução*, 2. The problem of accuracy became still worse when it came to the area of individual provinces.
6. Ibid., 3.
7. Alves, *História do Ceará*, 164.
8. Based largely on its mix of economic activities, it gained definition as a separate region toward the close of the nineteenth century.
9. The differing extent of *sertão* finds expression in contemporary boundaries of the official drought polygon, which, for example, includes nearly 98 percent of Rio Grande do Norte, but only 44 percent of Alagoas. See Manoel Correia de Andrade, *The Land and People of Northeast Brazil*, trans. Dennis V. Johnson (Albuquerque, NM: University of New Mexico Press, 1980), 22.
10. Kempton E. Webb, *The Changing Face of Northeast Brazil* (New York: Columbia University Press, 1974), 24. The broad Borborema plateau extends through both *agreste* and *sertão*. Webb notes that it "varies from 100 to 200 kilometers in width from east to west, and is about 250 kilometers from north to south." Ibid.
11. Phillip Vaugn-Williams, *Brasil. A Concise Thematic Geography* (London: Dell & Hyman, Ltd., 1986), 162.
12. Andrade, *Land and People*, 16. However, higher elevations produce lower average temperatures.
13. Not all high elevations enjoy good rainfall. While the eastern or windward slope of the Borborema is an area of *brejos*, the leeward slope becomes dry *sertão*. For discussion of variability in rainfall patterns see Andrade, *Land and People*, 16-30.

14. Fred Hartt, *Geology and Physical Geography of Brazil* (Boston: Fields, Osgood & Co., 1870), 474.
15. Manuel Correia de Andrade, the leading authority on the contemporary northeast, notes that the São Francisco's discharge varies seasonally along its middle and upper course by a factor of eleven. Andrade, *Land and People*, 28.
16. Harry Robinson, *Latin America. A Geographical Survey*, rev. ed. (New York: Praeger, 1967), 374.
17. Ibid., 23.
18. The following section draws extensively on Andrade, *Land and People*, especially chapter 2, "The Northeast, Region of Contrast." For this reason, I will note only direct quotes and material from other sources.
19. There it covers "almost all of the area between the Borborema Plateau and the Atlantic Ocean." Andrade, *Land and People*, 10.
20. Ibid., 16.
21. Ibid.
22. Andrade points to the counties of Bom Jardim and Orobó in Pernambuco that once, covered with forest, belonged to the *zona da mata*, but that now "are considered part of the Agreste, more because of human occupance and land use than environmental conditions." *Land and People*, 16.
23. Ibid., 17.
24. Ibid., 22.
25. Theophilo, *História da Secca*, quoted in Andrade, *Land and People*, 22.
26. Andrade, *Land and People*, 25.
27. Ibid., 144.
28. João Capistrano de Abreu, wrote of the "age of leather" in ch. 9 of his 1907 work, *Capítulos de historia colonial: 1500-1800*. See also Djacir Menezes, *O outro Nordeste, ensaio sobre a evolução social e política do Nordeste da "civilização do couro" e suas implicações históricas nos problemas gerais*, 2nd ed., rev. and enlarged (Rio de Janeiro: Editora Artenova, 1970).
29. Session of 7 Oct. 1878, reported in *Jornal do Recife*, 31 Dec. 1878, p. 2. The speaker was Henrique Milet.
30. Webb, *Changing Face*, 4-5. He explains, "the original caatinga can be thought of as a dense xerophytic mata composed of shrubs and trees, with small, shriveled, thorny leaves." Ibid., 55.
31. Andrade, *Land and People*, 151.
32. Vaugn-Williams, *Brasil*, 16.
33. Webb, *Changing Face*, 63.
34. Ibid., 150.
35. Low-lying soils often are less fertile than top soils, further reducing the benefits from plowing. Ibid.
36. Webb, *Changing Face*, 81. He also remarks, "The productivity of ranching was low, considering the great areas devoted to it, because forage was scarce." Ibid.
37. According to Robert M. Levine, "in the mid-nineteenth century, certainly less than 5 percent and probably less than 1 percent of the rural population owned land." *Vale of Tears. Revisiting the Canudos Massacre in Northeastern Brazil, 1893-1897* (Berkeley: University of California Press, 1992), 43.
38. Robert M. Levine sees *agregado* and *morador* as interchangeable—a "renter who lives by favor on another's land." A *rendeiro* is "a sharecropper who, lives on another's land and pays rent in cash or produce, " and a *foreiro* is "a renter." A *meiro* works "a marginal piece of land in exchange for corvée labor performed for

the landowner, usually during harvest and planting seasons." See *Vale of Tears*, glossary, 327-35, for these and other terms pertaining to the northeast.

39. Luís da Câmara Cascudo, *Historia do Rio Grande do Norte* (Rio de Janeiro: Ministerio de Educação e Cultura, Serviço de Documentação, 1955), 184.

40. Linda Lewin, *Politics and Parentela in Paraíba. A Case Study of Family-Based Oligarchy in Brazil* (Princeton: Princeton University Press, 1987), 74.

41. Meznar, "Deference and Dependence, " 135.

42. Ibid., 71.

43. Levine, *Vale of Tears*, 79, in reference to the *sertão* of Ceará, Rio Grande do Norte, and Pernambuco.

44. As an example of incomplete data, the review of health conditions in the empire attached to the 1878 report of the Ministry of the Empire had no information for São Paulo, Goiás, Rio Grande do Sul, and Pará because the chief health officials of those provinces had not submitted anything. *Relatório da Junta Central de Higiene Pública*, 16, appended to Império, *Relatório*, 1878.

45. See Diane Kennedy, "The Perils of the Midday Sun: Climate Anxieties in the Colonial Tropics, " in *Imperialism and the Natural World*, ed. John M. Mackenzie (Manchester: Manchester University Press, 1990): 118-43.

46. Nancy Leys Stepan, *Beginnings of Brazilian Science. Oswaldo Cruz, Medical Research and Policy, 1890-1920* (New York: Science History Publications, 1976), 49.

47. Sidney Chalhoub, "The Politics of Disease Control: Yellow Fever and Race in Nineteenth Century Rio de Janeiro, " *Journal of Latin American Studies* 25:3 (Oct. 1993), 442. Yellow fever remained a periodic scourge in the ensuing years, further strengthening the association between the presence of disease and coastal heat and humidity. Cholera, the other great epidemic disease of the nineteenth century, first appeared in Brazil in the mid-1850s, returning again in 1866. Ibid.

48. Stepan, *Beginnings of Brazilian Science*, 49. Headrick, *Tools of Empire*, 64 notes, "Early nineteenth-century European medical opinion, influenced by the age-old association of malaria with swamps, blamed humid air and putrid smells for the disease; hence the French word *plaudisme* (from the Latin word for swamp) and the Italian *mal'aria*, or bad air.

49. Webb, *Changing Face*, 113, notes the prevalence of dried animal manure, which can be burned as fuel, but not used for agriculture.

50. Kenneth F. Kiple, "The Nutritional Link with Slave Infant and Child Mortality in Brazil, " *HAHR* 69:4 (Nov. 1989), 680.

51. Kiple suggests that the high incidence of infant deaths ascribed to gastrointestinal problems misdiagnosed the impact of beriberi, and that adult deaths from beriberi "represented only the most severe cases of thiamine deficiency—cases which generally became manifest during that time of the year when supplemental foods were in shortest supply." In support of this observation Kiple notes a thesis presented to the Faculty of Medicine of Bahia in 1887 ("História da alimentação") by Hernani da Silva Pereira that suggested a far greater reliance on manioc flour in the northeast than in other regions of Brazil. Ibid., 679-80.

52. Ibid., 687, 689.

53. On the health of *sertanejos* see Levine, *Vale of Tears*, 81.

54. The central government's tax revenues were 4.5 times those of the provinces. Leff, *Reassessing the Obstacles*, 105.

55. For data on regional income see Mircea Buescu, "Regional Inequalities in Brazil during the Second Half of the Nineteenth Century, " 352, in *Disparities in Economic Development Since the Industrial Revolution*, ed. Paul Bairoch and Maurice Levy-Leboyer (New York: St. Martin's, 1981): 349-58. By monopolizing the main

sources of provincial income, the national government became the chief patron for the entire country, and the provinces were transformed into clients. Melo, *O norte*, 249, says the government took the role of the "magnanimous father . . . smiling on its prodigal sons."

56. The president of Rio Grande do Norte, writing in 1880, remarked that the tax on cattle (*dizimos de gado*), which he characterized as one of the province's most lucrative taxes, had virtually disappeared throughout the years of drought. RN, *Relatório*, 1980.

57. Provincial law 1.291.30, September 1878.

58. *Jornal do Recife*, 9 June 1877.

59. According to Joan Meznar, *municipios* in the *agreste* derived almost all their revenues from these *feiras*. Joan E. Meznar, "Deference and Dependence: The World of Small Farmers in a Northeastern Brazilian Community, 1850-1900" (Ph.D. diss., University of Texas at Austin, 1983), 20.

60. *Jornal do Recife*, 24 Aug. 1877, p. 1.

61. District judge to the president of Pernambuco, 31 Aug. 1877, printed in *Jornal do Recife*, 21 Sept. 1877, p. 1.

62. Hartt, *Geology and Physical Geography*, 398-99.

63. Ibid., 398. Hartt had accompanied the 1865-66 Thayer expedition to the Amazon led by Louis Agassiz. He returned to Brazil in 1870 as head of the Morgan expedition. See Stepan, *Beginnings of Brazilian Science*, 25-27. An extensive listing of foreign scientific expeditions to Brazil is in Schwartzman, *Formação*, in an appendix, "Cronologia da Ciencia Brasileira (1500-1945), " compiled by Tjerk Guus Franken.

64. Penedo RC to PP-AL, 20 Jan.1878, AN-P, IJJ9/234.

65. Ibid.

66. Paulo Afonso RC to PP-AL, 18 Aug. 1877, AN-P, IJJ9/293.

67. Andrade, *Land and People*, 116.

68. Ibid., 26.

69. Central RC of PE to PP, 1 Sept. 1877, APEP Da 33.

70. PP-PI, 19 July 1877, AN-P, IJJ9/162.

71. CE, *Fala*, 17 Nov. 1878, 20.

72. County judge of São Matheus to PP-CE, 14 Nov. 1877, AN- P, IJJ/188.

73. County council of Villa da Palma to PP-CE, 28 Feb. 1878, APEC, CM 59.

74. CE, *Relatório*, 22 Feb. 1878, 12.

75. Noted in Hartt, *Geology and Physical Geography*, 463.

76. Quoted ibid., 465.

77. Henry Koster, *Travels in Brazil*, ed. and intro. by C. Harvey Gardiner (Carbondale, IL: Southern Illinois University Press, 1966), 26-28.

78. Andrade, *Land and People*, 113.

79. County Council of Russas to PP-CE, 19 Apr. 1877, AN- P, IJJ9/188.

80. Interim district judge of Villa Bella to the president of Pernambuco, 7 September 1877. Printed in *Jornal do Recife*, 26 Sept. 1877, p. 1.

81. Billy Jaynes Chandler, *The Feitosas and the Sertão das Inhamuns* (Gainesville: University of Florida Press, 1972), 162.

82. *Relatório Teixeira*, AN-P, IJJ9/233.

83. PP-CE to ME, 20 Jan. 1878, AN-P, IJJ9, 162.

84. CE, *Fala*, 17 Nov. 1878, 56.

85. Companhia Pernambucana to PP-PE, 19 Oct. 1877, APEP, CPN 3, 1876-82.

86. Hartt, *Geology and Physical Geography*, 435.

87. Ibid., 442.

88. Arthur Indio do Brazil e Silva, *Portos principaes do Brazil* (Rio de Janeiro: Typ. Nacional, 1882), 15.
89. Ibid., 8.
90. Daniel R. Hedrick, *The Tentacles of Progress. Technology Transfer in the Age of Imperialism, 1850-1940* (New York: Oxford University Press, 1988), 33. Headrick's description of the requirements for truly modern ports of the day provides a further sense of the inadequacy of northeastern shipping infrastructure: "All the world's first-class harbors, where the largest ocean-going ships could safely dock, had to have certain features: lights, buoys, and breakwaters; a minimum depth at dockside of 9.75 meters; dry docks and repair shops; cranes and warehouses; and supplies of food, water, and naval stores." Ibid.
91. CE, *Fala*, 17 Nov. 1878, 17.
92. A. Silva, *Portos*, 9.
93. Ibid., 9-10.
94. Studies of the port at Fortaleza included those by Bernardo José Gomes Jardim, 1858; Giacomo Raja Gabaglia, 1860; Zosimo Barroso, 1864; and Sir John Hawkshaw, 1874. Ceará, *Fala*, 17 Nov. 1878, 18.
95. A. Silva, *Portos*, 11-12; Hartt, *Geology and Physical Geography*, 454.
96. Ibid., 22.
97. RN, *Fala*, 18 Oct. 1877, 40.
98. PP-RN to ME, 22 May 1877, AN-P, IJJ9/566.
99. Ibid.
100. See, for example, *Trabalhos do congresso*, 165.
101. PP-CE to ME, 29 May 1877, AN-P, IJJ9/188.
102. PP-PB to ME, 20 June 1877, AN-P, IJJ9/233.
103. RN, *Fala*, 18 Oct. 1877, 49. The president averred that relief supplies had been getting through to the interior, but he knew that after October it would be "absolutely impossible" for pack animals to make the journey. Ibid.
104. PE, Central RC, 20 Oct. 1877, APEP, Da 33.
105. CE, *Fala*, 17 Nov. 1878, 55.
106. For example, the *Jornal do Recife*, 7 July 1878, noted the docking of a packet ship carrying 476 slaves and 150 *retirantes*. All but 17 of the *retirantes* continued on to the south.
107. CE, *Fala*, 17 Nov. 1878, 55.
108. *Jornal do Recife*, 4 June 1878.
109. For a discussion of traditional backlands traditions regarding the probability of drought or rains see José Magalhães, "Previsões Folclóricos das Sêcas e dos Invernos no Nordeste Brasileiro." *Revista do Instituto do Ceará*, 1952: 253-68.
110. Principe Imperial RC to PP-PI, 21 Nov. 1878, AN- P, IJJ9/162.
111. CE, *Fala*, 2 July 1877.
112. Marginal notes by Ministry of the Empire officials on a December, 1877 message from the vice president of Piauí suggested that the vice president's assertions regarding the province's difficulties were "vague" and that conditions there must be improving because rains had been falling. VP-PI to ME, 28 Dec. 1877, AN-P, IJJ9/162.
113. PP-AL to ME, 20 Mar. 1878; 2 May 1878, AN-P, IJJ9/294. Hartt, *Geology and Physical Geography*, 412, similarly described Piranhas as "a miserable little village."
114. PI Central RC to VC, 29 Dec. 1878, AN- P, IJJ9/162.
115. Theophilo, *História da secca*, 255.
116. PP-AL to ME, 21 Feb. 1879, AN-P, IJJ9/295.

117. Physician of the Natal Charity Hospital to PP-RN, 14 June 1878, AN-P, IJJ9/566.
118. PP-RN to ME, 25 May 1878, AN-P, IJJ9/566.
119. Fortaleza RC to PP-CE, 8 Feb. 1878, APEC, CM, 37.
120. Ibid., 8 Apr. 1878.
121. Fortaleza CC to PP-CE, 16 Nov. 1878, APEC, CM 37. The Council urged that cadavers be buried only on the outskirts of the city.
122. PI, *Relatório*, 11 Dec. 1879, np.
123. Sobral, CC to PP-CE, 11 April 1878, APEC-CM, 64.
124. Crato RC to PP-CE, 8 July 1879, AN-P, IJJ9/189. This document itself indicates problems in accurate counting. It includes burials through 9 July, the day *after* it was written.
125. Empreza Funeraria, *Relação dos retirantes fallecidos e conduzidos em carros funebres para o cemeterio público.* . . . APEP, Santa Casa, 16.
126. PB, *Relatório*, 1 Jan. 1879, 21. The diseases included various bronchial infections, beriberi, malaria, dropsy, pernicious fever, and smallpox. Hospital data for a seven-month period in 1878 in the provincial capital show entry of 3, 669 people and a death total of 1, 202. *Relatório do Presidente da Junta de Higiene. . .*, 1878, 24, annexed to Império, *Relatório*, 1879.
127. Theophilo, *História da secca*, 253.
128. This review estimated total mortality in the capital reached 60,000, including *retirantes* and residents. Junta Central de Hygiene, *Relatório*, 24 Apr. 1879, 25-26, annexed to Império, *Relatório*, 1879.
129. Luís da Câmara Cascudo, *Historia do Rio Grande do Norte* (Rio de Janeiro: Ministerio de Educação e Cultura, Serviço de Documentação, 1955), 184.
130. José Francisco da Rocha Pombo, *Historia do Estado do Rio Grande do Norte, edição commemorativa do centenario da independencia do Brasil (1822-1922)* (Rio de Janeiro: Editores Anuario do Brasil, 1922), 367.
131. Cunniff, "Great Drought, " 283; Webb, *Changing Face*, 30. The 500,000 figure appeared in Eloy de Souza's book, *O Calvário das sêcas* (Natal: Imprensa Oficial, 1938).
132. Fifteen merchants and property owners in Aracatí to PP- CE, 8 Dec. 1877, AN-P, IJJ9/188.
133. PP-CE to ME, 13 Dec. 1877, AN-P, IJJ9/188.
134. PP-CE to ME, 11 Feb. 1878, AN-P, IJJ9/189.
135. Petition to VP-RN, 4 Nov. 1878, AN- P, IJJ9/212.
136. Ibid.
137. County Council of Sobral to PP-CE, APEC, CM, 64.
138. PE, *Relatório*, 1877, 6.
139. PB, *Relatório*, 1 Jan. 1879, 9. He cited Block's work, *Traité théorique et pratique de statistique*, and referred as well to a German statistician, Georg von Mayr, as having established the relationship between rising food prices and rising crime.
140. AL, *Fala*, 13 Apr. 1877, 4.
141. Ibid., 30 Apr. 1879, 49.
142. County Council of Santa Anna to PP-CE, 1 Aug. 1877, AN-P, IJJ9/188.
143. PP-CE to ME, 22 Aug. 1877, AN-P, IJJ9/188.
144. PP-RN to MJ, 3 May 1878, AN-JOP, IJ1/299.
145. Ibid., 28 June, 1878.
146. Telegram from Piranhas RC to PP-PE, 9 Feb. 1878, AN-P, IJJ9/234. The commission noted that it had received more than five hundred letters from Viera demanding they turn over relief goods.

147. PP-AL, *Fala*, 1878, annexed to PP-AL to ME, 2 May 1878, AN-P, IJJ9/294.

148. Acting *Delegado* of Police of Macau to PP-RN, 13 Oct. 1878, AN-JOP, IJ1/299. The vice-president then in charge of the province reported this to the minister of justice, who sent it on to the minister of war.

149. PB, *Relatório*, 1 Jan. 1879, 7. The actual term *"cangaceiro"* came into usage later. At that time, bandits usually were referred to as *"malfeitores"* (evil-doers), or *"desordeiros"* (disorderly people). I am indebted to Linda Lewin for this observation.

150. For a listing of bandits with years and areas in which they were active, see Hamilton de Mattos Monteiro, *Crise agrária e luta de classes (O Nordeste brasileiro entre 1850 e 1880)* (Brasília: Horizonte Editora Limitada, 1980). A classic source on the genesis and nature of northeastern banditry is Rui Facó, *Cangaceiros e fanáticos* (Rio de Janeiro: Civilização Brasileira, 1963). See also Abelardo F. Montenegro, *Fanáticos e cangaceiros* (Fortaleza: H. Galeno, 1973).

151. On the long-standing attractiveness to bandits of the area around Teixeira, see Linda Lewin, "Oral Tradition and Elite Myth: The Legend of Antônio Silvino in Brazilian Popular Culture, " *Journal of Latin American Lore* 5. 2 (1979), 169.

152. Luís da Câmara Cascudo, *O Livro das Velhas Figuras*, 6 vols., (Natal, RN: Instituto Histórico e Geográfico do Rio Grande do Norte, 1978) 4: 57.

153. MJ, 3rd Section, 16 July 1878. AN-JOP, IJ1/299.

154. Both *delegados* and *subdelegados* remained enmeshed in local politics and its various factional conflicts. At the same time, however, that was also true of judges. This receives some discussion in the next chapter.

155. Ibid.

156. PP-CE to ME, 2 Dec. 1877, AN-P, IJJ9/188.

157. Ibid., 13 Dec. 1877, AN-P, IJJ9/188.

158. CE, Fala, 5, AN, Presidentes, IJJ9/190; PP-CE to minister of justice, 27 Feb. 1879, AN, JOP, IJ1/283.

159. Inhabitants of the District of Cajazeiras to PP- PB (nd., probably Apr. 1877), AN-P, IJJ9/283. The signatures on this petition filled an entire page. For a similar complaint, see county judge of the *termo* of Souza, 13 Apr. 1877, Ibid.

160. Meznar, "Deference and Dependence, " 4; 160-61. She suggests that by the mid-nineteenth century, *feiras* provided almost all public revenues of *agreste* market towns. Ibid., 20.

161. Levine, *Vale of Tears*, 87. He remarks that "feira-connected activities may have accounted for half or more of the employed labor force of the region."

CHAPTER 3
VIEWS FROM THE PROVINCES

1. Their "chief function, " says Richard Graham, *Patronage*, 58, "was to produce electoral returns favorable to the Cabinet, and they used patronage as the principal tool in accomplishing that task. To the same end the Cabinet relied heavily on the presidents for political information and sound judgements in the appointment of loyal supporters."

2. Ibid., 59. Presidents could be simultaneously members of the national legislature and remain absent from their provinces throughout the sessions of the national legislative assembly.

3. Compiled from runs of provincial *falas* and *relatórios*.

4. Graham, *Patronage*, 59.

5. The 1841 reform of the Code of Criminal Procedures, which "reestablished in the hands of the central government total control over the administrative and judicial structure of the empire" gave *delegados* and *subdelegados* most of the judicial and police powers that had formerly been vested with the *juizes de paz* (justices of the peace), who now became the only judges selected by election. Leslie Bethell and José Murilo de Carvalho, "Brazil from Independence to the middle of the nineteenth century, " in *Cambridge History of Latin America*, 3: 714. Thomas Flory refers to the reformed Procedural Code as "the true political constitution of the empire." *Judge and Jury in Imperial Brazil, 1808-1871. Social Control and Political Stability in the New State*, Latin American Monographs, no. 53 (Austin: University of Texas Press, 1981), 181.

6. The magistracy also included the post of *desembargador* or high court judge.

7. Flory, *Judge and Jury*, 184; Leite, *O Senado*, 101.

8. *Jornal do Recife*, 8 June 1878, p. 1.

9. CE, *17 Fala*, Nov. 1878, 44.

10. PP-PB to ME, 20 Nov. 1877, AN-P, IJJ9/233.

11. County judge of Granito to PP-PE, 6 Aug. 1877, printed in *Jornal do Recife*, 24 Aug. 1877, p. 1.

12. PE Central RC to PP-PE, 16 Jan. 1878, AN-P, IJJ9/270.

13. Ibid., 16 Aug. 1877, AN-P, IJJ9/269.

14. County Council of Natal to VP-RN, 18 Nov. 1878, printed in *Jornal do Recife*, 19 Dec. 1878.

15. Sidney Chalhoub speaks to the issue of elite concerns with the "dangerous classes" in the first decade of the twentieth century. See *Trabalho, lar e botequim: o cotidiano dos trabalhadores no Rio de Janeiro da Belle Epoque* (São Paulo: Brasiliense, 1986), 35-58. He notes the conflating of poverty, laziness, and criminality as attributes of the masses, accounting for it as a constructed reality that justified the domination of the elites. Ibid., 51.

16. Roger L. Cunniff points out that provincial elites saw "an opportunity to finish major projects started in the prosperous sixties and now stagnating in the depressed seventies." "The Birth of the Drought Industry: Imperial and Provincial Response to the Great Drought in Brazil's Northeast, 1877-1880," *Revista de Ciencias Sociais*, Fortaleza, 6:1-2 (1975), 70.

17. CE, *Relatório*, 10 Jan. 1877, 3.

18. CE, *Fala*, July, 1877, 22.

19. RN, *Fala*, 17 Oct. 1876., 1-2; 18; 24.

20. PB, Treasury, *Demonstração de Despezas*, 1877-1881, AN-P, IJJ9/234.

21. *Relatório do Presidente da Junta de Hygiene*, annexed to Império, *Relatório*, 1880, 83-84.

22. CE, *Relatório*, 25 Nov. 1877, 22-30.

23. County Council of Fortaleza to PP-CE, 24 Dec. 1878, APEC, CM, 37.

24. AL, *Relatório*, 26 Nov. 1878, 9.

25. RN, *Relatório*, 4 Dec. 1878, 17.

26. PE Central RC to VP-PE, 1 May 1878, APEP Da 35, 1878, v.2.

27. PE-Central RC, *Relatório*, APEP, ms., 4.

28. PI Central RC to First VP, 29 Dec. 1878, AN-P, IJJ9/162.

29. Commission studying relief issues in Paiuí to VP-PI, 15 May 1878, AN-P, IJJ9/163.

30. Second VP-PI to ME, 30 Mar. 1878, AN-P, IJJ9/162.

31. Ibid.

32. PP-PI to ME, 20 May 1879, AN-P, IJJ9/163.

33. Of the estimated thirty-six *contos* expended per month, twenty-three were in cash. Commission studying relief issues in Paiuí to VP-PI, 15 May 1878, AN-P, IJJ9/163.

34. Ibid. He also pointed out that a colony would reduce the masses of *retirantes* who had swollen the capital.

35. Soares Brandão to Sinimbu, 3 July 1878, AIHGB, L. 611, P. 2.

36. Ibid., 21 Aug. 1878.

37. Ibid., 6 Nov. 1878.

38. AL, *Relatório*, 28 Dec. 1878, 13.

39. First Directory of the Imperial Tesouro da Fazenda, 18 July 1878, AN-P, IJJ9/566.

40. Deputados, *Anais*, 1: 1 May 1879, 788-89; 791-92.

41. Sousa Martins to MJ, 31 July 1878, AN-JOP, IJ1/299.

42. Domingos de Sousa Leão to Luís Felipe de Sousa Leão, 15 Sept. 1878, AIHGB, CSL, L. 456, P. 31. In hopes of arranging another political appointment for Eliseu, Vila Bela spoke to both Silveira Martins and Sinimbu. Ibid. Writing in the *Jornal do Comércio* (3 Jan. 1879, p. 5) Amaro Carneiro Bezerra Cavalcante sarcastically observed of Eliseu's appointment, "having thus *regenerated* Rio Grande do Norte, he now will bring success to Espírito Santo!"

43. Antonio Cypriano de Araujo Silva to VP-RN, 7 Oct. 1878; Contadora da Thezouraria de Fazenda do RN, 23 Oct. 1878, AN- P, IJJ9/212.

44. Colônia Sinimbu, *Relatório*, AN-P, IJJ9/212.

45. Ibid.

46. Interior, *Relatório*, May, 1879, 41.

47. Carreira, *Historia financeira*, 786. In 1876, the imperial government authorized an extension of this Estrada de Ferro Recife a São Francisco, from Palmares to Garanhuns on the Pirangy River, a distance of some 94 kilometers. Duncan, *Public and Private Operation of Railways*, 32-33.

48. Adelino Antonio de Luna Freire, "Colônia Socorro, " *Revista do Instituto Arqueológico e Geográfico Pernambucano* 49 (1896), 37.

49. Ibid., 40.

50. District judge of Palmares to PP-PE, 17 June 1878, APEP, Da 35, 1878, vol.2.

51. Director of Colônia Socorro to the district judge of Palmares, 17 June 1878, APEP, Da 35, 1878, vol. 2.

52. A. Freire, "Colônia Socorro, " 43.

53. PE, *Relatório*, 1878, 12. Almost half the *retirantes* were Pernambucans. The next largest group came from Paraíba.

54. In 1878, Pernambuco's central relief commission listed some 265 kilos of dried beef as going to Palmares and the colony, with all other locations totaling about 303, 000 kilos. In the case of *farinha*, not counting the allotment to Recife, the colony and Palmares received about 4,000 more sacks than that expended on relief throughout the rest of the province. PE Central RC, *Relatório*, 1878. APEP, ms.

55. A. Freire, "Colônia Socorro, " 44.

56. Director of Colônia Socorro to PP-PE, 24 Apr. 1880, AN-P, IJJ9/272.

57. Ibid., 24 May 1880, AN-P, IJJ9/272.

58. Soares Brandão to Sinimbu, 6 Nov. 1878, AIHGB, L. 611, P.2.

59. PE Central RC to PP-PE, 25 May 1877, APEP, Da 33.

60. Ibid., 1 Sept. 1877, APEP, Da 33.

61. *Carnivals, Rogues, and Heroes—An Interpretation of the Brazilian Dilemma*, trans. John Druty (Notre Dame, IN: University of Notre Dame Press, 1991), 239.

62. Graham, *Patronage*, 25. He adds, "Generosity toward the poor received constant praise because the propertied in general recognized that such acts validated the

implied exchange and preserved the proper structure of society. Whether the rich actually dispensed such generosity is not so important as the insistence on it as a principal virtue." Ibid.

63. Aguiar to ME, 11 Feb. 1878, AN-P, IJJ9/189. Andrews, *Blacks and Whites in São Paulo*, 46, notes this same type of concern in the exaggerated fear in regard to slave uprisings, which "flourished more in the imagination of the time than in reality."

64. Dr. Pedro d'Attahyde Lobo Moscoso to PP-PE, 12 July 1878, APEP, Saúde Pública, 4.

65. *O Liberal*, Maceió, 15 Oct. 1878.

66. Provincial treasury inspector to PP-PI, 28 June 1878, AN-P, IJJ9/162.

67. PB, *Relatório*, 1 Jan. 1879, 51.

68. Antonio Machado dos Santos, resident of Altinho to the president and chief of police of Pernambuco, 27 Dec. 1877, printed in *Jornal do Recife*, 7 Jan. 1878, p. 2. As another example, the *Jornal do Recife* (9 Nov. 1877) warned that Pernambuco was becoming "the receptacle for the inert and vicious population of our neighboring provinces."

69. Director of Colônia Orphanológica Isabel to PP-PE, 31 Jan. 1878, appended to PE, *Relatório* (Pernambuco, 1878), 20.

70. *Jornal do Comércio*, 13 Jan. 1879.

71. *O Cearense*, Fortaleza, 27 May 1877, p. 3.

72. County judge of São Mateus to PP-CE, 14 Nov. 1877, AN-P, IJJ9/188.

73. *Jornal do Recife*, 28 Sept. 1878, p. 2.

74. Ibid., 23 Nov., 1878, p. 1.

75. Health Inspector of PE to PP-PE, 10 Jan. 1878, APEP, SP4, 1878-87.

76. *Relatorio Teixeira*, AN-P, IJJ9/233.

77. Ernani Silva Bruno, ed., *O sertão, o boi e a sêca, Maranhão, Piauí, Ceará e Rio Grande do Norte*, 2nd ed. (São Paulo: Editôra Cultrix, 1959).

78. Graciliano Ramos, *Barren Lives (Vidas Sêcas)*, trans. and intro. Ralph Edward Dimmick (Austin: University of Texas Press, 1965), 3-6.

79. Schepper-Hughes, *Death Without Weeping*, 68-69.

CHAPTER 4
REPRESENTATION AND REALITIES

1. VP-PB to ME, 4 Apr. 1879, AN-P, IJJ9/233.

2. Commander of the war ship Purúa to PP-PA, 8 July 1878, AN, IJJ4/63.

3. Itamar de Souza and João Medeiros Filho, *Os Degredados filhos da seca. Uma análise sócio-política das secas do Nordeste* (Petrópolis: Editora Vozes, 1983), 43.

4. PP-PB to ME, 3 Nov. 1878, AN-P, IJJ9/233. At the same time, he acknowledged that the government was "overburdened" with expenditures and could not continue providing relief for very long.

5. PP-PI to ME, 19 Nov. 1878, AN-P, IJJ9/162.

6. Ibid. The ministry's response is in marginal notes made by several officials.

7. Campo Maior RC to PP- PI, 4 Dec. 1878, AN-P, IJJ9/162. The commission also advised the president that "misery, hunger, and nakedness is the lot of almost all the inhabitants of these devastated sertões." Ibid., 17 Dec. 1878.

8. Oeiras RC to PP-PI, 17 Dec. 1877, AN-P, IJJ9/162.

9. União RC to PP-PI, 22 Nov. 1878, AN-P, IJJ9/162.

10. To assure the minister of his seriousness about this, he informed him that he had recommended that relief commissions place priority on the preparation of *roças* and repairing fences and *açudes*, so that all would be ready to take advantage of the winter rains. PP-CE to ME, 14 Nov. 1878, AN-P, IJJ9/189.

11. See Theophilo, *História da secca*, 304-05.

12. Caixa RC to PP-CE, 25 July 1879, AN-P, IJJ9/189.

13. Vila de Pereira RC to PP-CE, 1 July 1879, AN-P, IJJ9/189.

14. Ibid.

15. Arrayal da Telha da Serra da Mattos to PP-CE, 15 June 1879, AN-P, IJJ9/189.

16. Henrique da Câmara to PP-CE, 31 July 1879, AN-P, IJJ9/189.

17. União RC to PP-CE, 8 July 1879, AN-P, IJJ9/189.

18. Humaytá RC to PP-CE, 20 July 1879, AN-P, IJJ9/189.

19. CE, *Fala*, 1 July 1880, 66.

20. Guerra and Guerra, *Seccas*, 40.

21. PP-RN to ME, 11 July 1879, AN-P, IJJ9/212.

22. Meznar, "Deference and Dependence, " 59, noted to Beatriz Maria Alasia de Heredia, *A morada da vida: trabalho familiar de pequenos produtores no nordeste do Brasil* (Rio de Janeiro: Paz e Terra, 1979), 54.

23. For a discussion of the exploitative environment of the colonization in the Amazon, see Moacir Facury Ferreira da Silva, *A emigração nordestina para a Amazônia em 1877: Uma tentativa de colonização pela administração provincial* (Rio Branco: Acre, 1977).

24. In August 1880 the *Jornal do Comércio* reported that a police official had found a group of *retirantes* from Ceará, including 11 men, 17 women, and 25 children, "abandoned" in Rio de Janeiro. Deputados, *Anais*, 5: 9 Sept. 1880, 48. The Ceará Deputy who pointed this out urged the government to return them to Ceará, since "abundance reigns there."

25. Recife, PE, Santa Casa, *Relatório*, 1882, 8.

26. PP-PA to ME, 7 May 1879, AN, IJJ9/122.

27. In Ceará, for example, the railroad did not reach Baturité until February 1882. At that time, then, the railroad's trackage totaled almost 110 kilometers. Carreira, *História financeira*, 782-83.

28. See Luiz Luna and Nelson Barbalho, *Coronel dono do mundo. (Síntese histórica do coronelismo no Brasil)* (Rio de Janeiro: Livraria Editora Cátedra em convênio com o Instituto Nacional do Livro, Fundação Nacional Pró-Memória, Brasília, 1983), 208.

29. Rachel de Queiroz, *O quinze* (São Paulo: Siciliano, 1993), 144-45. My translation.

30. With regard to the farms of Paribá's *agreste* Meznar, "Deference and Dependence," 29, remarks, "Family members provided almost all farm labor; only a select few owned slaves."

31. Small farmers in the *agreste* also valued such ties. Ibid., x.

32. County Council of Sobral to PP-CE, 3 June 1880, APEC, CM, 64.

33. PP-PB to MI, 24 Feb. 1880, AN-P, IJJ9/234.

34. B. J. Barickman, "Persistence and Decline, Slave Labour and Sugar Production in the Bahian Recôncavo, 1850-1888," *Journal of Latin American Studies* 28:3 (Oct. 1996), 615.

35. João Luís Fregoso, "Economia brasileira no século XIX: Mais do que um plantation escravista-exportadora, " in Maria Yedda Linhares, et al., *História geral do Brasil* (Rio Comprido, RJ: Editora Campus, 1990), 158.

36. RN, *Relatório*, 16 Mar. 1882, p. 37.

37. Ibid.

38. Laura Randall, *A Comparative Economic History of Latin America*, 1500-1914, 4 vols. (Ann Arbor: University Microfilms International, 1977), 3 (*Brazil*): 150.

39. Lewin, *Politics and Parentela*, 69.

40. For example, in Paraíba, exports fell from a 1876 level of 341, 000 *arrôbas* to 87, 750 the following year. It then dropped to 67, 988 in 1978, and rose the next year to 109, 057. See Meznar, "Orphans and the Transition from Slave to Free Labor in Northeast Brazil: The Case of Campina Grande, 1850-1888," *Journal of Social History* 27. 3 (Spring 1994), 503. An *arrôba* equals 15 kilograms. Only in 1916 did a drought resistant long-fiber cotton get introduced in Ceará. Ana Cristina Leite, *O algodão no Ceará. Estrutura fundiária e capital comercial (1850/1880)* (Fortlaeza: Secretaria da Cultura e Desporto do Estado do Ceará, 1994), 49.

41. AL Central RC, *Relatório*, 1878, AN-P, IJJ9/294.

42. PP-AL to MI, 5 Aug. 1878, AN-P, IJJ9/294.

43. *O Liberal*, Natal, 9 Nov. 1878; RGN, *Relatório*, 4 Dec. 1878, 17.

44. *O Cearense*, 6 May 1877.

45. PP-CE to ME, 15 May 1878, AN-P, IJJ9/163.

46. Theophilo, *História da sêca*, 160-61, discusses this practice in Fortaleza and reproduces the official document.

47. CE, presidente da Junta de Hygiene, annexed to ME, *Relatório*, 1879, 25.

48. County Council of Fortaleza, 4 Apr. 1879, APEC, CM, 37.

49. Recife, Santa Casa, *Relatório*, 1882, 8.

50. Ministerio dos Negócios de Agricultura, Comércio, e Obras Públicas, *Relatório*, May 1879, 182.

51. CE, *Fala*, 17 Nov. 1878, 52. Data from various other of the encampments showed this same pattern.

52. *Folhos de socorros aos indigentes . . . da colonia 'Custodia, '* 28 Feb. 1880, Instituto Histórico do Rio Grande do Norte, pasta 60.

53. PE, *Relatório* [Adelino Antonio de Luna Freire, to the new provincial president, undated]. A 17 July report in the *Jornal do Recife* noted a shack housing "forty persons from the *sertão*, among them men, women, and children."

54. *Jornal do Recife*, 28 Sept. and 30 Sept.1878.

55. Ibid., 22 Aug. 1878, p. 1.

56. Empreza Funerária, *Relação dos retirantes fallecidos e conduzidos em carros funebres . . .*, APEP, Santa Casa, 1878, 16.

57. PP-CE to ME, 11 July 1880, AN-P, IJJ9/190.

58. Ibid., 18 Mar. 1881, AN-P, IJJ9/190. The president suggested that the *comendador* ought to receive the title of baron. For a discussion of the place of orphans in Brazilian society at that time see Joan Meznar, "Orphans and the Transition from Slave to Free Labor in Northeast Brazil. The Case of Campina Grande, 1850-1880," *Journal of Social History* 27. 3 (Spring 1994): 499-515.

59. Ibid.

60. PP-RN to ME, 28 Oct. 1880, AN-P, IJJ9/273.

61. Santos Barros Pimental to Board of the Colonia Christina, 10 and 12 Oct. 1882, APEC, Colonia Christina, Ofícios Diversos, 1882, 1329.

62. Souza, *Mossoró*, 19.

63. Antonio Joaquim Rodrigues and four citizens of Mossoró to PP-RN, 30 Jan. 1879, AN IJJ9/212.

64. João Avelino to the provincial president, 31 Jan. 1879, AN, Justiça, IJJ1/299.

65. PP-CE to PP-RN, 8 Feb. 1879, AN, Presidentes, IJJ9/212.

66. Ibid.

67. Souza, *Mossoró*, 20.

68. *Jornal do Comércio*, 6 Apr. 1879, 2. *Riograndense* historian Francisco Fausto de Souza subsequently offered a similarly favorable appraisal of Carvalho, saying he enjoyed strong support among *retirantes* in Mossoró. According to Souza, Carvalho had differed with the commission on the distribution of relief supplies. The commission, fearful of his influence, tried to have him arrested. Tipped off, Carvalho, accompanied by a large number of *retirantes*, went to one of the commissioners "to intercede on behalf of the hungry people." *Mossoró*, 103-04.

69. Cascudo, *Mossoró*, 16.

70. Regarding the homicide, see RN, *Fala*, 13 July 1874, 12. Eliseu de Souza Martins had dismissed him from that commission. *Jornal do Comércio*, 19 Aug. 1878, 2.

71. According to Francisco Fausto de Souza, speaking of provincial legislation that affected the city, "every political or administrative act that was made regarding Mossoró in the period from 1850 to 1879 was either at the initiative or with the approval of Father Antonio Joaquim." Souza, *Mossoró*, 124.

72. Ibid., 271.

73. Costa Miranda to Lobato, 17 Mar. 1879, annexed to Lobato Marcondes Machado to the Minister of Justice, 18 Apr. 1879, AN, Justiça, IJJ1/299.

74. Raimundo Nonato [da Silva], *Figuras e tradições do nordeste* (Rio de Janeiro: Pongetti, 1958), 50, observes that *retirantes* went hungry because "inexplicably" the warehoused *farinha* had never been distributed.

75. I am indebted to Linda Lewin for pointing to the curious use of the term "hecatomb."

76. Vicente Inácio Pereira, first vice-president of Rio Grande do Norte to the minister of the empire, 22 Feb. 1879, AN, Presidentes IJJ9/212.

77. For an example, see *Jornal do Comércio*, 7 Mar. 1879, p. 3.

78. *Trabalhos do Congresso*, 274.

79. Sinimbu Ministry to the emperor, 1 Jan. 1878, reproduced in André Frota Oliveira, *A Estrada de Ferro de Sobral* (Fortaleza, 1994), 35-37.

80. João Craveiro Costa, *O Visconde de Sinimbu; Sua vida e sua atuação na política nacional (1840-1889)* (São Paulo: Companhia Editora Nacional, 1937), 332. A decree on 19 June 1878 authorized studies for the railroad, which were carried out on 7 August of that year. Carreira, *História financeira*, 791.

81. Sinimbu to Soares Brandão, 2 June 1878, AIHGB, L. 611, P. 1.

82. Evaldo Cabral de Melo remarks that Ceará's "regions existed almost autonomously." *O norte*, 222.

83. Ibid., 223.

84. Ibid., 224.

85. Oliveira, *Estrada de Sobral*, 37.

86. Ibid., 225.

87. Ibid., 122-23.

88. Domingos de Sousa Leão to Luís Felippe de Sousa Leão, 26 May 1878, AIHGB, CSL, L. 456, P. 22.

89. Contadoria da Tesouraria da Fazenda, Rio Grande do Norte, 9 Mar. 1877; Ibid., 17 April 1877, AN, Presidentes, IJJ9/389.

90. RN, *Relatório*, 1880, 12. Establishing precise total expenditures remains impossible since many officials failed to keep records and, in some circumstances, records disappeared.

91. Abelardo F. Montengro, *História dos partidos políticos cearenses* (Fortaleza: author's ed., 1965), 19. Their newspaper, *O Constituição*, opposed the existing *Dom Pedro II*. Ibid.

92. Gonçalo became head of the Ceará Conservative party in 1862 upon the death of his cousin, Senator Miguel Fernandes Vieira. He broke with the party over the Law of the Free Womb, and formed the *miúdos*. Studart, *Diccionario*, 1: 344-45.

93. Azevedo, *As ciencias*, 1: 358.

94. Paiva, *A elite política do Ceará provincial*, 56, 109.

95. Deputados, *Anais*, 1: 21 May 1879, 319-24.

96. Deputados, *Anais*, 3 Sept. 1879, 10. Their running battle appears on pages 6-16.

97. Senado, *Anais*, 13 Oct. 1879, 109-11.

98. For a discussion of the Liberal party in Pernambuco, see Marc Jay Hoffnagel, "From Monarchy to Republic in Northeast Brazil: The Case of Pernambuco, 1868-1895" (Ph.D. diss., Indiana University, 1975). He notes that "throughout the intra-party struggle in Pernambuco the fate of each of the Liberal factions ultimately rested with the central government." Ibid., 38-39.

99. Vila Bela's ascension to the cabinet had led to fears among some of Pernambuco's Liberals that he would use that position of power to dominate the party totally. This resulted in the formation of the *cachorros*, led by Antônio Epaminondas de Melo and José Mariano. Vila Bela had derisively dubbed this faction *"cachorros,"* or dogs. For a detailed discussion of the split, see Hoffnagel, "From Monarchy, " 32-63.

100. Ibid., 41. Needing peace in the provinces, Sinimbu urged unity, and did not empower either faction. See João Lustosa da Cunha Paranaguá [then, minister of war] to Luís Felipe de Sousa Leão, 5 Nov. 1879, AIHGB, CSL, L. 456, Doc. 182. In December, however, a staunch *Cachorro*, Lourenço Albuquerque de Melo, who was the nephew of Sinimbu's friend, Deputy Sousa Carvalho, took over. Hoffnagel, "From Monarchy, " 42.

101. He had represented Pernambuco since 1839.

102. Hoffnagel, "From Monarchy, " 464.

103. Deputados, *Anais*, 22 July 1879, 272.

104. On Ceará politics see Paiva, *A elite política*. Both Barroso and Medeiros had been vocal in newspaper articles with regard to the drought.

105. The provincial election had taken place in December 1878. Taunay, *O Senado*, 198-99.

106. Senado, *Anais*, 3: 5 March 1879, 69-71. To no avail, Senate Liberals voted to postpone consideration of the electoral committee's report and recommendation. Ibid., 8 March 1879, 138.

107. Ibid., 14 Oct. 1879, 6.

108. A. Tavares de Lyra, *Os ministros de estado da independência à republica* (Rio de Janeiro: Imprensa Nacional, 1949), 97-98. Of the twenty-three Council Presidents, nine came from Bahia and four from Minas Gerais.

109. Joaquim Raymundo de Lamare, who also had refused a ministry post, remarked in a letter to Saraiva that as "one of the most distinguished chiefs" of the Liberal party, he should have had the office of president of the council. Lamare to Saraiva, 17 Jan. 1878, AIHGB L. 273, D. 8. The reorganized Liberal party of 1869 originated in a meeting at Nabuco de Araújo's home. Joaquim Nabuco, *Um estadista do império*, Nabuco de Araújo. Complete works of Joaquim Nabuco, vols. 3-6 (São Paulo: Instituto Progresso Editorial, 1949), 3: 137.

110. Afonso Arinos de Melo Franco, *The Chamber of Deputies of Brazil: Historical Synthesis* (Brasília: Câmara dos Deputados, 1977), 68. For a brief account of the fall of the Zacarias ministry see José Maria Bello, *A History of Modern Brazil, 1889-1964*, trans. James L. Taylor (Stanford: Stanford University Press, 1966), 34-35.

111. J. Costa, *Sinimbu*, 217-18.

112. Those who refused Sinimbu's overtures included José Bonifácio de Andrada e Silva, a *deputado* from São Paulo and heir to one of the most distinguished names among Brazilian Liberals, and Francisco Otaviano de Almeida Rosa, a powerful senator from Rio de Janeiro and member of the national Liberal Directory. José Bonifácio, was referred to as "the younger, " to distinguish him from the "patriarch" who held the post of minister of the kingdom in the first cabinet of Pedro I, and was instrumental in pushing for a declaration of Brazil's independence from Portugal. The younger José Bonifácio was born in France during the exile of the Andradas, and was the son of Martim Francisco de Andrada e Silva. He had served as minister of the navy in the 1862 Zacarias cabinet, and, again with Zacarias, in 1864 as minister of the empire. In 1878, he became a senator. Lyra, *Os ministros*, 65.

113. J. Costa, *Sinimbu*, 221, points to the inexperience of Sinimbu's cabinet.

114. Edmundo da Luz Pinto, *Principais estadistas do Segundo Reinado* (Rio de Janeiro: Livraria José Olympio, 1938), 117, observes that "his career always was sensational, provoking enthusiastic admirers and implacable enemies."

115. Ibid., 291; Barros, *Ilustração*, 292.

116. Senado, *Anais*, 1: 19 Dec. 1878, 21. Teixeira pointed specifically to Lafayette and Leôncio, and asked whether the ministry's program would reflect traditional Liberal ideas, or the more "advanced" notions of those ministers. Ibid., 20.

117. J. Costa, *Sinimbu*, 239. He went perhaps even further in 1879. Speaking before the Chamber of Deputies, he declared that electoral reform had become his personal equivalent of "Carthage must be destroyed." Deputados, *Anais*, 2: 29 Jan.1879, 292.

118. Ibid., 194.

119. Ibid., 21 Jan. 1879, 69.

120. Ibid., 5: 11 Oct. 1879, 337.

121. Senado, *Anais*, 2: 10 Feb. 1879, 78. The senator was Silveira de Mota.

122. C. Nabuco, *Life of Joaquim Nabuco*, 43, quoted from a speech in the Chamber of Deputies, 21 Feb. 1879. As Graham, *Patronage*, 194, explains, "the bill proposed that Deputies to the next Parliament be charged with altering the nation's basic charter so as to institute direct elections and limit suffrage to those whose income equaled that already required of electors. The bill implied that this amount would be set only as a lower limit, and could later be raised by law. Furthermore, illiterates would not be allowed to vote (nor would Protestants), regardless of income."

123. J. Costa, *Sinimbu*, 256-59.

124. Eduardo Silva, *Prince of the People. The Life and Times of a Brazilian Free Man of Colour*, trans. Moyra Ashford (London: Verso, 1993), 8.

125. For a discussion of the Vintém affair see Sandra Lauderdale Graham, "The Vintem Riot and Political Culture: Rio de Janeiro, 1880, " *HAHR* 60. 3 (Aug. 1980): 431-49. Silva, *Prince of the People*, 68, notes the role of pro-abolition and pro-republican journalists in fanning the flames.

126. Silva, *Prince of the People*, 69.

127. *Jornal do Comércio*, 4 Jan. 1880, p. 1, quoted in S. Graham, "Vintem Riot, " 440. Graham, ibid., 439, identifies these eight legislators: José Ignácio Silveira da Mota (whose home served as the meeting place), Francisco Otaviano de Almeida Rosa, Antonio Marcellino Nunes Gonçalves, Carlos Leôncio de Carvalho, José da Costa Azevedo, Joaquim Baptista Pereira, Joaquim Nabuco, and Joaquim Saldanha Marinho. In addition to the motives adduced by Graham sfor this gathering, traditional partisan/factional politics certainly provided reasons for the presence of some of these people, especially the deposed minis-

ter of the empire, Leôncio de Carvalho, and such Sinimbu critics as Joaquim Nabuco and Saldanha Marinho, as well as Otaviano de Almeida Rosa, who had refused to join Sinimbu's ministry.

128. He suggested that Vila Bela had resigned so as not to sacrifice principles important to Pernambuco's Liberal party, while also remarking that the national party had suffered because of Sinimbu's ministry. Deputados, *Anais*, 5: 20 Oct. 1879, 358-60.

129. Silva, *Prince of the People*, 69.

130. Presidency of CE to Guayuba RC, 22 Oct. 1879, APEC, I-76-B. See also ibid., a similar message to Bebedouro, 17 Dec. 1879.

131. PP-RN to ME, 11 July 1879, AN-P, IJJ9/212.

132. Lobato Marcondes Machado to ME, 8 Nov.1879, AN Presidentes IJJ9/212.

133. Ibid., 13 Dec. 1879, AN-P, IJJ9/212.

134. By May 1880, only some three thousand *retirantes* remained in Mossoró.

135. Presidency of CE to relief commissioners of Fortaleza, 10 (?) Jan. 1880. *Poder Executivo, Circulares*, 1877-80.

CONCLUSION

1. CE, *Fala*, 1878, 58.

2. It was rare to encounter the term "northeast" prior to 1930, and the area's people were usually referred to as *"nortistas,"* and "rarely as *nordestinos."* Gadiel Perruci, *A república das usinas. Um estudo de história social e econômica do nordeste: 1889-1930* (Rio de Janeiro: Paz e Terra, 1977), 92.

3. Hall, *Drought and Irrigation*, 6.

4. Fábio de Macedo Soares Guimarães, *Divisão regional do Brasil* (Rio de Janeiro: Instituto Brasileiro de Geografia e Estatística, 1942).

5. Ibid., 23-27.

6. Perruci, *A república*, 16, remarks that when he began his study of the region, sugar cane and drought "comprised the only phenomenon worthy of attention . . . ."

7. See Gilberto Freyre, *Manifesto regionalista de 1926* (Recife: Edições Região, 1952).

8. Graciliano Ramos, *Vidas seccas: romance* (Rio de Janeiro: Livraria José Olympio, 1988). For a quick overview of northeastern literature, see Gilza Saldanha da Gama, *Presença do nordeste na literatura braisleira* (Rio de Janeiro: Arte Final, 1995). Discussions of the association of drought and the northeast in literature appear in Ernani Silva Bruno, comp., *O sertão, o boi e a sêca; Maranhão, Piauí, Ceará e Rio Grande do Norte* (São Paulo: Cultrix, 1959), and Teoberto Landim, *Sêca, a estação do inferno: uma análise dos romances que tematizam a sêca na perspectiva do narrador* (Fortaleza:Universidade Federal de Ceará, Casa de José de Alencar, 1992).

BIBLIOGRAPHY

ARCHIVES

Arquivo do Instituto Histórico e Geográfico Brasileiro, Rio de Janeiro.
    Coleção Conselheiro Saraiva.
    Coleção Cotegipe.
    Coleção Senador Nabuco.
    Coleção Sousa Leão.
Arquivo Nacional, Rio de Janeiro.
    Conselho do Estado, Consultas.
    Ministerio do Império, Presidentes, Correspondencia do Presidente da Provincia.
    Ministerio da Justiça, Ofícios dos Presidentes.
Arquivo Público do Estado de Ceará.
Arquivo Público do Estado de Pernambuco.
Arquivo do Instituto Histórico e Geográfico do Estado de Rio Grande do Norte, Natal.

GOVERNMENT DOCUMENTS

Alagoas, Presidente da Provincia.*Falas* and *Relatórios*, 1875-82.
Brazil. Congresso Nacional, *Anais do Senado do Império do Brasil*, 1877-81.
    Congresso Nacional, *Anais da Câmara dos Deputados do Império do Brasil*, 1877-81.
    Directoria Geral de Estatística. *Recenseamento da população do Imperio do Brasil a que se procedeu no dia 1 de agosto de 1872.* Rio de Janeiro, 1873-76.
    Ministerio de Agricultura, Comércio, e Obras Públlicas, *Relatórios*, 1876-80.
    Ministerio da Fazenda. *Relatórios*, 1877-81.
    Ministerio do Império. *Relatórios*, 1877-81.
Ceará, Presidente da Provincia. *Falas* and *Relatórios*, 1875-82.
Paraíba, Presidente da Provincia. *Falas* and *Relatórios*, 1875-82.
Pernambuco, Presidente da Provincia. *Falas* and *Relatórios*, 1875-82.
Piauí, Presidente da Provincia. *Falas* and *Relatórios*, 1875-82.
Rio Grande do Norte, Presidente da Provincia. *Falas* and *Relatórios*, 1875-82.

CONTEMPORARY JOURNALS AND NEWSPAPERS

O Auxiliador da Indústria Nacional: Periódico da Sociedade Auxiliadora da Indústria Nacional, Rio de Janeiro, 1875-80.

O Cearense, Fortaleza, CE 1877-80.
Correio do Natal, Natal, RN 1880-81.
Jornal do Agricultor, Principios Práticos da Economia Rural, Rio de Janeiro, 1879.
Jornal do Comércio, Rio de Janeiro, RJ 1877-81.
Jornal do Recife, Recife, PE 1877-81.
Revista Agrícola do Imperial Instituto Fluminense de Agricultura, Rio de Janeiro, 1877-80.

BOOKS, ARTICLES, AND UNPUBLISHED THESES

Alves, Joaquim. *História do Ceará. História das sêcas (séculos XVII a XIX)*. Fortaleza: Edições do "Instituto do Ceará," 1953.

Andrade, Lopes de. *Introdução à sociologia das sêcas*. Preface by Gilberto Freyre. Rio de Janeiro: Editora a Noite, 1948.

Andrade, Manuel Correia de. *The Land and People of Northeast Brazil*. Trans. Dennis V. Johnson. Albuquerque, NM: University of New Mexico Press, 1980.

_____. *A produção do espaço Norte-Rio-Grandense*. Seca: Coleção Especializada, Série C, 1, 2nd, ed. Natal: UFRN-Pró-Reitoria de Pesquisa e Pós Graduação, 1984.

Andrews, George Reid. *Blacks and Whites in São Paulo Brazil, 1888-1988*. Madison: The University of Wisconsin Press, 1991.

Aronowitz, Stanley. *Science as Power, Discourse and Ideology in Modern Society*. Minneapolis: University of Minnesota Press, 1988.

Atlas do Império do Brasil comprehendo as respectivas divisões administrativas, ecclesiasticas, eleitoraes e judiciarias dedicado a sua magestade o Imperador O Senhor D. Pedro II, destinado à instrucção pública no Imperio com especialidade a dos alumnos do Imperial Collegio de Pedro II organisado por Cândido Mendes de Almeida. Rio de Janeiro: Instituto Philomathica, 1868.

Azevedo, Celia Maria Marinho de. *Onda negra medo branco. O Negro no imaginario das elites século XIX*. Rio de Janeiro: Paz e Terra, 1987.

Azevedo, Fernando de. *As Ciencias no Brasil*. 2 vols. São Paulo: Edições Melhoramentos, 1956.

Baer, Warner. *The Brazilian Economy: Its Growth and Development*. Columbus, OH: Grid Publishing, 1979.

Banco Nacional. *Exposição apresentada à Assembléa Geral de Accionistas em 28 de Julho de 1879 peolos seus directores*. Rio de Janeiro: Typographia da "Gazeta de Noticias," 1879

Barickman, B. J. "Persistence and Decline : Slave Labor and Sugar Production in the Bahian Recôncavo, 1850-1888." *Journal of Latin American Studies* 28. 3 (Oct. 1996): 581-633.

Barman, Roderick J. "The Brazilian Peasantry Reexamined: The Implications of the Quebra-Quilo Revolt, 1874-1875." *HAHR* 57. 3 (Aug., 1977): 401-24.

_____. *Brazil: the Forging of a Nation, 1798-1852*. Stanford: Stanford University Press, 1988.

_____ and Jean Barman. "The Role of the Law Graduate in the Political Elite of Imperial Brazil." *Journal of Inter-American Studies and World Affairs* 18. 4 (Nov. 1976): 423-50.

_____."The Prosopography of the Brazilian Empire." *Latin American Research Review* 13. 2 (1978): 78-97.

Barretto, Rozendo Moniz. *Exposição Nacional de 1875. Notas e obervações*. Rio de Janeiro: 1875.

Barros, Roque Spencer Maciel de. *A ilustração brasileira e a idéia de universidade*. Preface by Antonio Paim. São Paulo: Convívio, Editora Universidade de São Paulo, 1986.

Beiguelman, Paula. *A formação do povo no complexo cafeeiro: aspectos políticos*. São Paulo: Livraria Pineira, 1968.

Bethell, Leslie and José Murilo de Carvalho. "Brazil from Independence to the middle of the nineteenth century." In *The Cambridge History of Latin America*, ed. Leslie Bethell. Cambridge, UK: Cambridge University Press, 1985. 3: 679-746.

Blake, Augusto Victorino Alves Sacramento. *Diccionario bibliographico brazileiro*. 7 vols. Rio de Janeiro: Typographia Nacional, 1883-1902.

Borges, Dain. *The Family in Bahia, Brasil, 1870-1945*. Stanford: Stanford University Press, 1992.

Bourdieu, Pierre. *Outline of a Theory of Practice*. Trans. Richard Nice. Cambridge, UK: Cambridge University Press, 1977.

Branco, José Moreira Brandão Castello. *Moreira Brandão*. Reprint from Instituto Histórico e Geográfico Brasileira, *Revista*, 242 (Jan.-Mar. 1959). Rio de Janeiro, 1959.

Brasiliense (de Almeida e Melo), Americo. *Os programas dos partidos e o Segundo Império*. Brasília and Rio de Janeiro: Senado Federal; Fundação Casa de Rui Barbosa-MEC, 1979.

Brazil. Ministerio da Educação e Cultura. *Organizações e programas ministeriais*. Org. Jorge João Dodsworth, Baron of Javri. Brasília: Ministerio da Educação e Cultura, Instituto Nacional do Livro, 1979.

_____. Ministerio da Fazenda, *Ministros da Fazenda, 1822-1972*. Rio de Janeiro, 1977.

Bruno, Ernani Silva, ed. *O sertão, o boi e a sêca, Maranhão, Piauí, Ceará e Rio Grande do Norte*. 2nd ed. São Paulo: Editôra Cultrix, 1959.

_____. *História do Brasil, geral e regional*. Vol. 2, *Nordeste*. São Paulo: Editora Cultrix, 1967.

Buescu, Mircea. "Regional Inequalities in Brazil during the second half of the Nineteenth Century." In *Disparities in Economic Development Since the Industrial Revolution*, ed. Paul Bairoch and Maurice Levy-Leboyer. New York: St. Martin's, 1981: 349-58.

Burns, E. Bradford. *A History of Brazil*. 3rd ed. New York: Columbia University Press, 1993.

Bushnell, David and Neil J. Macaulay. *The Emergence of Latin America in the Nineteenth Century*. New York: Oxford University Press, 1988.

Callado, Antônio. *Os industriais da sêca e os "Galileus" de Pernambuco. Aspectos da luta pela reforma agrária no Brasil*. Rio de Janeiro: Editôra Civilizaçao Brasileira, 1960.

Calmón, Pedro. *História do Brazil, Vol. 5, O Império e a ordem liberal, século XIX-conclusão*. Rio de Janeiro: Livraria José Olympio Editora, 1959.

Carli, Gileno dé. *Séculos de sêcas*. Recife: np., 1984.

Carreira, Liberato de Castro. *História financeira e orçamentária do Império do Brasil*. 2nd ed., 2 vols. Rio de Janeiro: Senado Federal, Fundacao Casa de Rui Barbosa-MEC, 1980.

Carvalho, José Murilo de. *A construção da ordem. A elite política imperial*. Contribuições em ciencias sociais, 8. Rio de Janeiro: Editora Campus, Ltda., 1980.

_____. "Political Elites and State Building: The Case of Nineteenth-Century Brazil." *Comparative Studies in Society and History* 24. 3 (July 1982): 378-99.

_____. *Teatro de sombras: A política imperial*. São Paulo:Vértice, Editora Revista dos Tribunais, 1988.

Cascudo, Luís da Câmara. *História da cidade do Natal*. Natal: Prefeitura do Municipio do Natal, 1947.

_____. *Historia do Rio Grande do Norte*. Rio de Janeiro: Ministerio de Educação e Cultura, Serviço de Documentação, 1955.

_____. *O Livro das velhas figuras: pesquisas e lembranças na história do Rio Grande do Norte*. 7 vols. Natal: Instituto Histórico e Geográfico do Rio Grande do Norte, 1974.

_____. *Governo do Rio Grande do Norte*. 2 vols. Natal: Livraria Cosmopolitana, 1989.

_____. *Mossoró e Areia Branca*. Coleção Mossoroense, Series B, no. 1083, 1991.

Castro, Hebe Maria Mattos de. "Beyond Masters and Slaves: Subsistence Agriculture as a Survival Strategy in Brazil during the second half of the Nineteenth Century." *HAHR* 68. 3 (1988): 461-89.

Chalhoub, Sidney. *Trabalho, lar e botequim: o cotidiano dos trabalhadores no Rio de Janeiro da Belle Epoque*. São Paulo: Brasiliense, 1986.

_____. "The Politics of Disease Control: Yellow Fever and Race in Nineteenth Century Rio de Janeiro." *Journal of Latin American Studies* 25. 3 (Oct. 1993): 441-64.

Chandler, Billy Jaynes. *The Feitosas and the Sertão das Inhamuns*. Gainesville: University of Florida Press, 1972.

_____. *The Bandit King. Lampião of Brazil*. College Station: Texas A & M Press, 1978.

Chartier, Roger. *Cultural History. Between Practices and Representations*. Trans. Lydia G. Cochrane. Ithaca: Cornell University Press, 1988.

_____. *On the Edge of the Cliff. History, Language, and Practices*. Trans. Lydia G. Cochrane. Baltimore and London: The Johns Hopkins University Press, 1997.

Chorover, Stephan L. *From Genesis to Genocide. The Meaning of Human Nature and the Power of Behavior Control*. Cambridge, MA: MIT Press, 1979.

Coelho, Jorge. *As secas do Nordeste e a indústria das secas*. Petrópolis: Vozes, 1985.

Collichio, Therezinha Alves Ferreira. *Miranda Azevedo e o darwinismo no Brasil*. Belo Horizonte: Editora Itatiaia, 1988.

Colson, Roger Frank. "The Destruction of a Revolution. Polity, Economy, and Society in Brazil, 1870-1891." Ph. D. diss., Princeton University, 1979.

Congresso Agrícola. *Colleção de documentos*. Rio de Janeiro, 1878.

Conrad, Robert. *The Destruction of Brazilian Slavery 1850-1888*. Berkeley: University of California Press, 1972.

Costa, Emília Viotti da. *The Brazilian Empire: Myths and Histories*. Chicago: University of Chicago Press, 1985.

_____. "Brazil: The Age of Reform, 1870-1889." In *The Cambridge History of Latin America*, ed. Leslie Bethell. Cambridge, UK: Cambridge University Press, 1985. 5: 725-77.

Costa, João Craveiro. *O Visconde de Sinimbu; Sua vida e sua atuação na política nacional (1840-1889)*. São Paulo: Companhia Editora Nacional, 1937.

Costa, João Cruz. *A History of Ideas in Brazil. The Development of Philosophy in Brazil and the Evolution of National History*. Trans. Suzette Macedo. Berkeley and Los Angeles: University of California Press, 1964.

Cunniff, Roger L. "The Great Drought: Northeast Brazil, 1877-1880." Ph.D. diss., University of Texas, Austin, 1970.

_____. "The Birth of the Drought Industry: Imperial and Provincial Response to the Great Drought in Brazil's Northeast, 1877-1880." *Revista de Ciencias Sociais* 6:1-2 (1975): 65-82.

Dean, Warren. *The Industrialization of São Paulo 1880-1945*. Austin and London: University of Texas Press, 1969.

_____. *Rio Claro: A Brazilian Plantation System, 1820-1920*. Stanford: Stanford University Press, 1976.

Drescher, Seymour. "Brazilian Abolition in Comparative Perspective," *HAHR* 68. 3 (Aug. 1988): 429-60.

Duncan, Julian Smith. *Public and Private Operation of Railways in Brazil*. New York: Columbia University Press, 1932.

Eakin, Marshall C. "Race and Identity: Silvio Romero, Science, and Social Thought in late 19th Century Brazil." *Luso-Brazilian Review* 22. 2 (Winter, 1985): 151-74.

Eisenberg, Peter L. *The Sugar Industry in Pernambuco: Modernization Without Change, 1840-1910*. Berkeley: University of California Press, 1974.

_____. "A mentalidade dos fazendeiros no Congresso Agrícola de 1878." In *Modos de produção e realidade brasileira*, comp. José Roberto do Amaral Lapa. Petrópolis: Editora Voces, 1980): 167-94.

Felipe, José Lacerda. *Mossoró: Um espaço em questão*. Coleção Mossoroense, 141. Mossoró, RN: 1980.

_____. *Elementos de geografia do Rio Grande do Norte*. Natal, RN: Editora Universitária, 1986.

Ferri, Mário Guimarães and Shozo Motoyama, comp. *História das ciencias no Brasil*. São Paulo: E. P. U.-Editora Pedagógica e Universitária Ltda., 1979.

Filho, João Medeiros and Itamar de Souza. *Os Degredados Filhos da Seca. Uma análise sócio-política das secas do Nordeste*. Petrópolis: Editora Vozes, 1983.

Filho, Lycurgo de Castro Santos. "A Medicina no Brasil." In *História das ciencias no Brasil*, comp. Mário Guimarães Ferri and Shozo Motoyama. São Paulo: E. P. U.-Editora Pedagógica e Universitária Ltda.: 1979 191-218.

Fleiuss, Max. *Historia administrativa do Brasil*. 2nd. ed. São Paulo: Companhia. Melhoramentos, 1922.

Flory, Thomas. *Judge and Jury in Imperial Brazil, 1808-1871. Social Control and Political Stability in the New State*. Latin American Monographs 53. Austin: University of Texas Press, 1981.

Foucault, Michel. *Politics Philosophy Culture. Interviews and other writings, 1977-1984*. Trans. Alan Sheridan and others. Ed. and intro.by Lawrence D. Kritzman. New York and London: Routledge, 1988.

Franco, Afonso Arinos de Melo. *The Chamber of Deputies of Brazil: Historical Synthesis*. Brasília: Câmara dos Deputados, 1977.

Freire, Adelino Antonio de Luna. "Côlonia Socorro." *Revista do Instituto Arqueológico e Geográfico Pernambucano* 49 (1896): 31-78.

Freise, Friedrich W. "The Drought Region of Northeastern Brazil." *The Geographical Review* 28 (1938): 363-78.

Gabaglia, Giacomo Raja. *Ensaios sobre alguns melhoramentos tendentes a prosperidade da provincia do Ceará*. Rio de Janeiro: Typographia Nacional, 1877.

Galvão, Miguel Arcanjo. *Relação dos cidadãos que tomaram parte no governo do Brasil no período de março de 1808 a 15 de novembro de 1889*. 2nd ed. Rio de Janeiro: Arquivo Nacional, 1969.

Garner, Lydia Magalhães Nunes. "In Pursuit of Order: A Study in Brazilian Centralization. The Section of Empire of the Council of State 1842-1889." Ph.D. diss., The Johns Hopkins University, 1987.

Gebara, Ademar. *O mercado de trabalho livre no Brasil (1871-1888)*. São Paulo: Editora Brasiliense, 1986.

Gibbs, Jack P. *Norms, Deviance and Social Control: Conceptual Matters*. New York: Elsevier, 1981.

Goff, Jacques Le. *Time, Work, and Culture in the Middle Ages*. Trans. Arthur Goldhammer. Chicago: University of Chicago Press, 1980.

Graham, Richard. "Brazil from the Middle of the Nineteenth Century to the Paraguayan War." In *The Cambridge History of Latin America*, ed. Leslie Bethell. Cambridge, UK:Cambridge University Press, 1985. Vol. III: 747-794.

_____. *Patronage and Politics in Nineteenth-Century Brazil*. Stanford: Stanford University, 1990

Graham, Sandra Lauderdale. "The Vintem Riot and Political Culture: Rio de Janeiro, 1880." *HAHR* 60. 3 (Aug. 1980): 431-49.

Greenfield, Gerald Michael. "The Great Drought and Elite Discourse in Imperial Brazil." *HAHR* 72. 3 (Aug. 1992): 375-400.

Guerra, Paulo de Brito, *A Civilização da Seca. O nordeste é uma história mal contada*. Fortaleza: Ministério do Interior, Departamento de Obras Contra as Secas, 1981.

Guerra, Phelipe and Theophilo Guerra. *Seccas contra a secca*. 3rd. ed. Coleção Mossoroense, 24, 1980.

Guimarães, Fábio de Macedo Soares. *Divisão regional do Brasil*. Rio de Janeiro: Instituto Brasileiro de Geografia e Estatística, 1942.

Hahner, June E. *Poverty and Politics. The Urban Poor in Brazil, 1870-1920*. Albuquerque: University of New Mexico Press, 1986.

Hall, Anthony L. *Drought and Irrigation in North-East Brazil*. London: Cambridge University Press, 1978.

Haring, C. H. *Empire in Brazil, A New World Experiment With Monarchy*. New York: W.W. Norton & Company, 1958.

Harootunian, H. D. *Things Seen and Unseen: Discourse and Ideology in Tokugawa Nativism*. Chicago: University of Chicago Press, 1988.

Hasenrath, Stephen. *Climate Dynamics of the Tropics*. Dordrecht: Kulwer Academic Publishers, 1991.

Hartt, Fred. *Geology and Physical Geography of Brazil*. Boston: Fields, Osgood & Co., 1870.

Headrick, Daniel R. *The Tools of Empire, Technology and European Imperialism in the Nineteenth-Century*. New York: Oxford University Press, 1981.

Hoffnagel, Marc Jay. "From Monarchy to Republic in Northeast Brazil: The Case of Pernambuco, 1868-1895." Ph.D. diss., Indiana University, 1975.

Huggins, Martha Knisely. *From Slavery to Vagrancy in Brazil, Crime and Social Control in the Third World*. New Brunswick, NJ: Rutgers University Press, 1985.

Kennedy, Diane. "The Perils of the Midday Sun: Climate Anxieties in in the Colonial Tropics." In *Imperialism and the Natural World*, ed. John W. Mackenzie. Manchester: Manchester University Press, 1990: 118-43.

Kiple, Kenneth F. "The Nutritional Link with Slave Infant and Child Mortality in Brazil." *HAHR* 69. 4 (Nov. 1989): 677-90.

Koster, Henry. *Travels in Brazil*. Ed., intro. by C. Harvey Gardiner. Carbondale and Edwardsville, IL: Southern Illinois University Press, 1966.

Kowarick, Lucio. *Trabalho e vadiagem. A origem do trabalho livre no Brasil*. São Paulo: Editora Brasiliense, 1987.

Landim, Teoberto. *Sêca, a estação do inferno: uma análise dos romances que tematizam a sêca na perspectiva do narrador*. Fortaleza: Universidade Federal de Ceará, Casa de José Alencar, 1992.

Leão, Filho, J. de Sousa. *O Barão de Vila Bela, apontamentos histórico/genealógicos*. Rio de Janeiro, 1968.

Leff, Nathaniel H. *Underdevelopment and Development in Brazil, 2, Reassessing the Obstacles to Economic Development*. London: George Allen & Unwin, 1982.

Leite, Beatriz Westin de Cerqueira. *O Senado nos finais do Império (1870-1889)*. Brasília: Senado Federal & Editora Universidade Brasília, 1978.

Levine, Robert M. *Pernambuco in the Brazilian Federation, 1889-1937*. Stanford: Stanford University Press, 1978.

_____. *Vale of Tears. Revisiting the Canudos Massacre in Northeastern Brazil, 1893-1897*. Berkeley: University of California Press, 1992.

Lewin, Linda. "Oral Tradition and Elite Myth: The Legend of Antônio Silvino in Brazilian Popular Culture." *Journal of Latin American Lore* 5.2 (1979): 157-204.

_____. *Politics and Parentela in Paraíba. A Case Study of Family-Based Oligarchy in Brazil*. Princeton: Princeton University Press, 1987.

Lima, Oliveira. *O Império brasileiro (1821-1889)*. Coleção Reconquista do Brasil. Belo Horizonte: Editora Itiatiaia, 1989.

Linhares, Maria Yedda, et al. *História geral do Brasil*. Rio Comprido, RJ: Editora Campus, 1990.

Lobo, Eulalia Maria Lahmeyer. *História político-administrativo da agricultura Brasileira 1808-1889*. np., nd. [betw. 1977 and 1982].

Lyra, Augusto Tavares de. *Historia do Rio Grande do Norte*. Rio de Janeiro: Typographia Leuzinger, 1921.

_____. *Os ministros de estado da independência à república*. Rio de Janeiro: Imprensa Nacional, 1949.

Macedo, Antonio Marco de. *Observações sobre as seccas do Ceará e os meios de augmentar o volume das aguas nas correntes do Cariry*. Rio de Janeiro: Typographia Nacional, 1878.

Magalhães, José. "Previsões Folclóricos das Sêcas e dos Invernos no Nordeste Brasileiro." *Revista do Instituto do Ceará*, 1952: 253-68.

Martins, Wilson. *História da intêligencia brasileira*, 3. São Paulo: Cultrix, Editora da Universidade de São Paulo, 1977.

Matta, Roberto da. *Carnivals, Rogues, and Heroes—An Interpretation of the Brazilian Dilemma*. Trans. John Druty. Notre Dame, IN: University of Notre Dame Press, 1991.

Medeiros, Viriato de. *Ponderações sôbre a memoria do dr. André Rebouças, A secca nas provincias do Norte*. Rio de Janeiro:Typographia Acadêmica, 1877.

Melo, Evaldo Cabral de. *O norte agrário e o Império, 1877-1889*. Rio de Janeiro: Editora Nova Fronteira, 1984.

Menezes, Adolfo Bezerra. *Breves considerações sôbre as seccas do norte*. Rio de Janeiro: Guimarão, 1977.

Menezes, Djacir. *O outro Nordeste, ensaio sobre a evolução social e política do Nordeste da "civilização do couro" e suas implicações históricas nos problemas gerais*. 2nd ed., rev. and enlarged. Rio de Janeiro: Editora Artenova, 1970.

Meznar, Joan E. "Deference and Dependence: The World of Small Farmers in a Northeastern Brazilian Community, 1850-1900." Ph.D. diss., The University of Texas at Austin, 1983.

_____. "Orphans and the Transition from Slave to Free Labor in Northeast Brazil: the Case of Campina Grande, 1850-1888. *Journal of Social History* 27. 3 (Spring 1994): 499-516.

Milet, Henrique A. *Auxilio à lavoura*. Recife: Typographia do Jornal do Recife, 1876.

Monteiro, Hamilton de Mattos. *Crise agrária e luta de classes (O Nordeste brasileiro entre 1850 e 1889*. Brasília: Horizonte Editora Limitada, 1980.

_____. *Nordeste insurgente (1850-1890)*. São Paulo: Brasiliense, 1981.

Montengro, Abelardo F. *História dos partidos políticos cearenses*. Fortaleza: author's ed., 1965.

Motoyama, Shozo. "A Física no Brasil." In *História das Ciencias no Brasil*, coord. Mário Guimarães Ferri and Shozo Motoyama. São Paulo: E. P. U.-Editora Pedagógica e Universitária Ltda., 1979: 61-92.

Nabuco, Joaquim. *Um estadista do imperio, Nabuco de Araujo*. Complete works of Joaquim Nabuco, vols. 3-6. São Paulo: Instituto Progresso Editorial, 1949.

Nachman, Robert G. "Positivism, Modernization, and the Middle Class in Brazil." *HAHR* 57. 1 (Feb. 1977): 1-23.

Needell, Jeffrey. *A Tropical Belle-Epoque. Elite Culture and Society in turn-of-the-century Rio de Janeiro*. New York: Cambridge University Press, 1987.

Neto, Leonardo Leite. *Catálogo biográfico dos Senadores brasileiro de 1826 a 1896*. 4 vols. Brasília: Senado Federal, Centro Gráfico, 1986.

Nonato [da Silva], Raimundo. *Figuras e tradições do nordeste*. Rio de Janeiro: Pongetti, 1958.

Oliveira, André Frota. *A Estrada de Ferro de Sobral*. Fortaleza, 1994.

Oszlak, Oscar. "The Historical Formation of the State in Latin America: Some Theoretical and Methodological Guidelines for its Study." *Latin American Research Review* 16. 2 (1981): 3-32.

Paim, Antonio. "Trajetória da Filosofia no Brasil." In *História das Ciencias no Brasil*, coord. Mário Guimarães Ferri and Shozo Motoyama. São Paulo: E. P. U.-Editora Pedagógica e Universitária Ltda., 1979: 9-34.

Paiva, Maria Arair Pinto. *A elite política do Ceará provincial*. Rio de Janeiro: Tempo Brasileiro, 1979.

Pang, Eul-Soo. "Modernization and Slavocracy in Nineteenth-Century Brazil." *Journal of Interdisciplinary History* 9. 4 (Spring, 1979): 667-88.

_____ and Ron L. Seckinger. "The Mandarins of Imperial Brazil." *Comparative Studies in Society and History*, 14, no.2 (March 1972): 215-44.

Parker, D. S. *The Idea of the Middle Class White Collar Workers and Peruvian Society, 1900-1950*. University Park: Penn State University Press, 1998.

Peard, Julyan G. "Tropical Disorders and the Forging of a Brazilian Medical Identity, 1860-1890. *HAHR* 77. 1 (Feb. 1977): 1-44.

Pereira, Lafayette Rodrigues. *Cartas ao irmão*. Ed. João Camilo de Oliveira Torres. Brasiliana 342. São Paulo: Companhia Editora Nacional, 1968.

Perruci, Gadiel. *A república das usinas. Um estudo de história social e econômica do nordeste, 1889-1930*. Rio de Janeiro, Paz e Terra, 1977.

_____. *Trabalhos do Congresso Agrícola do Recife, outubro de 1878*. Recife: Fundação Estadual de Planejamento Agrícola de Pernambuco, 1978.

Pinto, Edmundo da Luz. *Principais estadistas do segundo reinado*. Rio de Janeiro: Livraria José Olympio, 1938.

Pombo, José Francisco da Rocha. *Historia do Estado do Rio Grande do Norte*. Edição comemorativa do centenario da independencia do Brasil (1822-1922). Rio de Janeiro: Editores Anuario do Brasil, 1922.

Potter, Jonathan and Margaret Wetherell. *Discourse and Social Psychology: Beyond Attitudes and Behavior*. London and Newbury Park, CA: Sage, 1987.

Queiroz, Rachel de. *The Three Marias*. Trans. Fred P. Ellison. Austin: University of Texas Press, 1963.

_____. *O quinze*. São Paulo: Siciliano, 1993.

Rebouças, André. *A secca nas provincias do norte. Propaganda no Jornal do Commercio, no Instituto Polytechnico, na Associação Brazileira de Acclimação e na Sociedade Auxiliadora da Industria Nacional*. Rio de Janeiro: Typ. de G. Leuzinger & Filhos, 1877.

Rego, Antonio José de Souza. *Relatorio da 2a Exposição Nacional de 1866, publicado em virtude de ordem do ministro e secretario de estado dos negocios da agricultura, commercio e obras públicas*. Rio de Janeiro: Typographia Nacional, 1866.

Ridings, Eugene. *Business Interest Groups in Nineteenth Century Brazil*. New York: Cambridge University Press, 1994.

Robinson, Harry. *Latin America. A Geographical Survey*. Rev. ed. New York: Praeger, 1967.

Rodrigues, José Honório, org. *Atas do Conselho de Estado*. Obra comemorativa do Sesquicentenário da Instituição Parlamentar, vol. X, Terceiro Conselho de Estado, 1875-1880. Brasília: Senado Federal, 1973.

_____ *O Conselho de Estado: O quinto poder?* Brasília: Senado Federal, 1978.

Rohan, Henrique de Beaurepaire. *Relatório final da Commissão Geral do Imperio apresentado ao Ministerio da Agricultura, Commércio e Obras Públicas pelo Marechal do Campo Henrique de Beaurepaire Rohan*. Rio de Janeiro: Typographia Nacional, 1878.

Samarin, William J. *The Black Man's Burden, African Colonial Labor on the Congo and Ubangi Rivers, 1880-1900*. Boulder, CO: Westview Press, 1989.

Santos, José Americo dos. *Secca no Norte do Brazil, Março de 1878*. Rio de Janeiro: Typographia e lithographia de Machado & Companhia, 1883.

Schepper-Hughes, Nancy. *Death Without Weeping: The Violence of Everyday Life in Brazil*. Berkeley: University of California Press, 1992.

Schwarcz, Lilia Moritz. *O espetáculo das raças: cientistas, instituições e questão racial no Brasil, 1870-1930*. São Paulo: Companhia das Letras, 1993.

Schwartzman, Simon. *Formação da comunidade científica no Brasil*. São Paulo: Editora Nacional, Rio de Janeiro: FINEP-Financiadora de Estudos e Projetos, 1979.

_____. *A Space for Science, The Development of the Scientific Community in Brazil*. University Park, PA: The Pennsylvania State University, 1991.

Schwarz, Roberto. *Misplaced Ideas. Essays on Brazilian Culture*. Ed., intro.by John Gledson. London: Verso, 1992.

Silva, Eduardo. *Prince of the People. The Life and Times of a Brazilian Free Man of Colour*. Trans. Moyra Ashford. London: Verso, 1993.

Skidmore, Thomas E. "Racial Ideas and Social Policy in Brazil, 1870-1940." In *The Idea of Race in Latin America, 1870-1940*, ed. Richard Graham. Austin: University of Texas Press, 1990.

Soares, Antonio. *Dicionário histórico e geográfico do Rio Grande do Norte*, vol. 1 A-E. Coleção Mossoroense, 417, Reprint of 1930 edition. Natal: Imprensa Oficial, 1930.

Souza, Eloy de. *O Cavalrio das sêcas*. Natal: Imprensa Oficial, 1938.

Stepan, Nancy Leys. *Beginnings of Brazilian Science. Oswaldo Cruz, Medical Research and Policy, 1890-1920*. New York: Science History Publications, 1976.

_____. *The Idea of Race in Science: Great Britain 1860-1960*. London: The Macmillan Press and Archon Books, 1982."

_____. *The Hour of Eugenics," Race, Gender and Nation in Latin America*. Ithaca and London: Cornell University Press, 1991.

Studart, Guilherme. *Dicionario bio-bibliographico cearense*. 3 vols. Fortaleza, 1910-15.

Sweigart, Joseph E. *Coffee Factorage and the Emergence of a Brazilian Capital Market, 1850-1888*. New York: Garland Press, 1987.

Taunay, Afonso de Escragnolle. *O Senado do Império*. ed. ilustrada. São Paulo: Livraria Martins, 1941.

_____. *A Câmara dos Deputados sob o Império*. São Paulo: Imprensa Oficial do Estado, 1950.

Theophilo, Rodolpho. *História da secca do Ceará (1877 a 1880)*. Fortaleza: Typographia do Libertador, 1883.

Trabalhos do Congresso Agrícola do Recife em outubro de 1878 comprehendendo os documentos relativos aos factos que o precederam. Recife, 1879.

Vargas, Milton. "A Tecnologia no Brasil." In *História das Ciencias no Brasil*, comp. Mário Guimarães Ferri and Shozo Motoyama. São Paulo: E. P. U.-Editora Pedagógica e Universitária Ltda., 1979: 331-373.

Vasconcellos, Barão de and Barão Smith de Vasconcellos. *Archivo nobiliárchico brasileiro*. Lausane, Switzerland: Imprimerie La Concorde, 1918.

Vaugn-Williams, Phillip. *Brasil. A Concise Thematic Geography*. London: Dell & Hyman, Ltd., 1986.

Viana, Oliveira. *O ocaso do Império*. 4th ed. Preface by Walter Costa Porto. Recife: Fundação Joaquim Nabuco, Editora Massangana, 1990.

Wasserman, Renata R. Mautner. *Exotic Nations. Literature and Cultural Identity in the United States and Brazil, 1830-1930*. Ithaca and London: Cornell University Press, 1994.

Webb, Kempton E. *The Changing Face of Northeast Brazil*. New York: Columbia University Press, 1974.

INDEX

www.ingramcontent.com/pod-product-compliance
Lightning Source LLC
Chambersburg PA
CBHW061755260326
41914CB00006B/1116